"Ma
muc
the
—G

"En
not
Low

"Fev
look
bool
Siler
mat
Irres
a me
enli
Chr

"[A

into great detail about the intellectual and business roots of Monopoly."
—John Gapper, *Financial Times*

"This past November, a New Hampshire woman was charged with
domestic violence for slapping her boyfriend during a game [of
Monopoly]. The British royal family, Prince Andrew said in 2008, isn't
permitted to   ll of these

people, and my own family, and anyone else who has threatened to eviscerate a loved one over their income-tax accounting, should be required to read Mary Pilon's enthralling new history of the long, pitched battle over the origins of the game." —*Slate*

"Pilon takes us on a jaunt through turn-of-the-century America, where we learn about such far-flung things as the origins of the price tag, the founding of Atlantic City, and the fact that one of the most coveted addresses in the game was home to some of the earliest gay bars in America. This is a must read for anyone who loves the game, and really, who doesn't?" —**Erik Larson**

"The true—and downright bizarre—origin story of one of the most popular games ever made . . . A brisk read, and the readability is considerably heightened throughout by the author's sense of outrage . . . Fascinating." —*The Daily Beast*

"That history is interesting even if you don't love the game . . . *The Monopolists* is a quick, enjoyable read that takes less time than a game of Monopoly." —*Star Tribune* (**Minneapolis–St. Paul**)

"What enormous fun this book is! Clever, engaging, finely crafted, and endlessly surprising—and revealing in passing much about the ghastliness of American corporate greed. Much like the game itself, indeed." —**Simon Winchester, author of** *The Professor and the Madman*

"A deep dive into industrial and pop culture apocrypha . . . Riveting . . . The book is superlative journalism." —*Paste*

"Smart and revealing . . . Pilon's refreshingly direct prose and ample storytelling skills make for a breezy, enlightening inquiry into the plight of an under-appreciated innovator." —*The Rumpus*

"Mary Pilon's page-turning narrative unravels the innocent beginnings, the corporate shenanigans, and the big lie at the center of this iconic boxed board game." —Stefan Fatsis, author of *Word Freak*

"[A] dive into the *real* Monopoly." —*Flavorwire,* "10 Must-Read Books for February"

"Thanks to Mary Pilon's meticulous reporting and mellifluous prose, we now know the real story of the corporate greed and relentless cover-up that scars Monopoly, one of the most beloved and successful board games of all time. Finally, the truth is out." —William D. Cohan, author of *The Last Tycoons*

"Pilon's research is deep, and it makes for a solid caper about corporate greed." —*Bloomberg*

"Excellent . . . Mary Pilon revisits the sordid story of Monopoly . . . in glorious detail." —*Mental Floss*

"With more twists and turns than an Agatha Christie mystery, reporter Pilon reveals the tumultuous history of Monopoly . . . More entertaining than the game itself." —*Publishers Weekly* (starred review)

The
MONOPOLISTS

The

MONOPOLISTS

Obsession, Fury, and the Scandal Behind the
World's Favorite Board Game

MARY PILON

B L O O M S B U R Y

NEW YORK · LONDON · OXFORD · NEW DELHI · SYDNEY

Bloomsbury USA
An imprint of Bloomsbury Publishing Plc

1385 Broadway   50 Bedford Square
New York   London
NY 10018   WC1B 3DP
USA   UK

www.bloomsbury.com

BLOOMSBURY and the Diana logo are trademarks of Bloomsbury Publishing Plc

First published 2015
This paperback edition published 2016

ISBN: HB: 978-1-60819-963-1
            PB: 978-1-60819-965-5
            Trade PB: 978-1-62040-838-4
            ePub: 978-1-62040-571-0

LIBRARY OF CONGRESS CATALOGING-IN-PUBLICATION DATA

Pilon, Mary.
The monopolists: obsession, fury, and the scandal behind the world's favorite board game / Mary Pilon.
pages cm
Includes bibliographical references and index.
ISBN: HB: 978-1-60819-963-1
            PB: 978-1-60819-965-5
            Trade PB: 978-1-62040-838-4
            ePub: 978-1-62040-571-0

1. Monopoly (Game)—History I. Title.
GV1469.M65P55 2014
794—dc23
2013047463

2 4 6 8 10 9 7 5 3 1

Typeset by RefineCatch Ltd, Bungay, Suffolk

Printed and bound in USA by Berryville Graphics Inc., Berryville, Virginia

To find out more about our authors and books visit www.bloomsbury.com. Here you will find extracts,
author interviews, details of forthcoming events and the option to sign up for our newsletters.

Bloomsbury books may be purchased for business or promotional use. For information on bulk
purchases please contact Macmillan Corporate and Premium Sales Department at specialmarkets@
macmillan.com.

For Mom and Uncle Larry

The last player left in the game wins.
—1935 MONOPOLY BOARD GAME RULES

CONTENTS

CHAPTER 1

THE PROFESSOR
AND THE
TRUST-BUSTING
GAME

"The courtiers were shown the board, and after a day and a night in deep thought one of them, Buzurjmihr, solved the mystery and was richly rewarded by his delighted sovereign."

—KARNAMAK-I-ARTAKH SHATR-I-PAPAKAN, ABOUT 600 A.D.

ONE DAY DURING the depths of the Great Depression, an unemployed salesman named Charles Darrow retreated to his basement. He had no money, no prospects, and a wife and children he was desperately trying to support.

Sitting in his dank basement, Darrow suddenly had an inspiration. Pulling out a piece of oilcloth, he began to draw a board game featuring Atlantic City streets and properties. If he couldn't support his family, he could at least entertain *them, with a game that would bring back memories of the better days they'd spent vacationing together on the New Jersey shore.*

Working quickly, Darrow finished his game and introduced it to his family. Immediately, they became addicted. They loved buying the pieces of the game board and miniature houses with the paper money he'd created and moving their tokens around the board to the sound of the roll of the dice.

Darrow decided to try to market his game. He sent his invention to game giants Parker Brothers and Milton Bradley. Both turned it down. But Darrow persevered, and largely through word of mouth the game began to sell. Parker Brothers, now on the verge of economic collapse, reconsidered and bought Darrow's "monopoly game." It became a thunderous success and rescued both Parker Brothers and Darrow from destruction.

In the mid-1930s and for decades after, Parker Brothers tucked this compelling tale of the game's creation into every Monopoly box it sold.

There was only one problem: The story wasn't exactly true.

•

RALPH ANSPACH, PROFESSOR of economics at San Francisco State University, slammed his car door shut. Finally he was home. It had been another excruciating commute from his classroom in San Francisco to where he lived with his family in Berkeley.

He stomped up the steps of his ramshackle yet oddly majestic Victorian house, mumbling under his breath. The rush hour traffic between San Francisco and Berkeley had always been bad, but now he and the other commuters had to contend with mile-long stretches of cars backed up at exits, in search of gas. It was 1973, and a national oil crisis had begun. The Organization of the Petroleum Exporting Countries (OPEC), led by its Arab members, had jacked up the prices of world oil, putting an end to decades of cheap energy. U.S. government price controls had gone into effect, along with rationing systems. On certain days, gas sales were limited to those with license plates ending in odd numbers; on other days, to those with plates ending in even numbers. Ralph kicked at the floorboard. This is what happens when a monopoly has control, he thought.

A disheveled-looking man in his mid-forties, Ralph had piercing blue eyes and stood about five feet nine inches tall. The son of a Jewish banker and a homemaker, he had been born in 1926 in the free German ministate of Danzig, under Polish administrative governance but also under the shadow of Adolf Hitler's rising Nazi state. Growing up, Ralph had become accustomed to anti-Semitic slogans, taunts from children, and dodging into alleyways to avoid potential conflict. Fortunately, though, he and his family had left Danzig in 1938 to settle in New York City, where Ralph attended school, worked odd jobs to help his family make ends meet, and became a U.S. citizen. After graduating from high school, he served in the U.S. Army and was stationed in the Philippines during World War II.

In 1948, Ralph took part in the Arab-Israeli War. He traveled to the region under the guise of doing farmwork, but in actuality took up arms for the Israelis—ignoring the fact that the United States, under a neutrality act, had forbidden its citizens from participating. Ralph was not one to sit passively by while others acted.

Pulling open his front door, Ralph called out a hello to his wife, Ruth, and his two sons—Mark, age twelve, and William, age seven. He was looking forward to eating a simple dinner with his family and perhaps playing a board game with them afterward.

Ralph had met Ruth, the daughter of famed economist Leo Rogin, when they were both students at Berkeley. She had been studying for her undergraduate degree, and he had been a Ph.D. hopeful. Ruth was petite, smart, and as interested in social and political causes as he was. Together, the two had marched against the Vietnam War and with Women for Peace. Ruth was one of the founders of the organization's Berkeley chapter and had overseen countless meetings and phone trees. Years later, in 1988, Ralph would learn that he was among those whose political involvement at that time had come to the attention of the Federal Bureau of Investigation, which had begun examining, among other things, his "loyalty" and monitoring his whereabouts.

That evening after dinner, Ralph's sons suggested playing Monopoly and eagerly pulled the familiar long white box out of the closet. As smart and feisty as their parents, the boys were more politically aware than most children their age and were precocious Monopoly players. They loved everything about the game—its iconic Atlantic City properties, its tiny homes, its play money, its idiosyncratic tokens. The object of the game was to bankrupt all opponents and be the last person standing by acquiring real estate and charging rent. As players made their way around the board, they acquired or negotiated trades for properties. Then, they tried to get all of a like color grouping and build houses and hotels on their monopolies to jack up the rent, thus clearing out the coffers of their rivals.

As the boys set up the board and counted out the money, Ralph recalled playing his first game of Monopoly in Czechoslovakia in 1937. His big brother Gerry had summoned him to the game, which at that time he had understood to have only been around for a few years. Monopoly had given Ralph one of his first glimpses of America—then still a far-off land that lived only in atlases and on globes, light-years removed from grim Europe.

An evening filled with much laughter, shouting, and cutthroat deal-making ensued. Happily, Ralph, Ruth, Mark, and William maneuvered their metal trinkets around the board, past run-down Baltic Avenue, busy St. Charles Place, and elite Boardwalk. They passed Go, they collected two hundred dollars, they went straight to Jail, they drew Chance and Community Chest cards. William, the younger of the two Anspach boys, won the game.

Little did Ralph know that this particular evening, as ordinary as it was, was about to change his life.

•

THE NEXT MORNING, as Ruth prepared breakfast, Ralph grumbled over the headlines in the *San Francisco Chronicle*—more bad news about the oil crisis. With his boys beside him, absorbing his every word, he began a diatribe against the OPEC oil cartel and the evils of monopolies. Price wars were good, he ranted, because they brought down prices, but when one company or organization gained a monopoly over a product, consumers suffered.

Getting warmed up, Ralph then railed against the economic culture that had fostered the current oil crisis—it was a far cry from the anti-monopoly climate that had existed in the United States in the late 1800s and early 1900s, he said. Back then, "trust-busting," or the breaking up of large monopolies and trusts, had been part of the national political discourse, and strong anti-monopoly laws had been put into effect. The laws had come in the wake of John D. Rockefeller's and Andrew Carnegie's strongholds on the oil and steel industries, respectively, which had raised prices sky-high and, critics said, destroyed many small businessmen and seriously undermined America's standard of living.

Suddenly, William interrupted his father. He had just won a game of Monopoly the night before, he reminded him. It had been a lot of fun.

So how could monopolies be so bad? Had he done something wrong by winning the game?

Ralph pondered his son's query. Impressed, he admitted that he had a good point. The board game rewarded something in play that hurt people in reality. Making money wasn't a crime, but he felt that monopolizing a product or industry and crushing one's opponents was. Ralph continued to think about what his son had said during his long morning commute to San Francisco.

•

AT SAN FRANCISCO STATE, Ralph was well-known among the students for his wrinkled corduroy jackets with leather patches at their elbows, his hair that looked "as if it was combed with a fork," his regular presence at political protests, and his large Economics 101 lecture classes. His office was an ocean of papers, his handwriting a cryptic scrawl.

The seventies were in full throttle: Drugs were flowing, free love was abounding, and tensions were running high between the more radical students at the university and the starchier members of the school's administration. In one recent incident, a graduate student had ditched his customary suit and tie and come to class in all-out drag—fishnets, a wide-brimmed hat, a shoulder-exposing dress, and a fur coat—to get people to reevaluate their ways of thinking, he said.

It was into this kaleidoscope that Ralph was trying to inject his views on Adam Smith, the man widely recognized as the George Washington of economics. In a graduate seminar, Ralph taught Smith's 1759 work *The Theory of Moral Sentiments*, in which Smith argues that people are motivated by self-interest, but also like to do well by others if the circumstances are right. One example that Ralph offered: In a family or other small group, altruism prevails, but the farther away a person gets from an individual, the less altruistic he or she behaves toward them. It was in *Moral Sentiments* that Smith introduced his famous "invisible hand" metaphor to describe self-regulating behavior. Ralph's students also learned about how self-interested companies like to squash their competition by fixing prices to gain control of an industry in order to increase profits. Ralph's punch line: Competitive capitalism is the best economic system in the world, but it is constantly being undermined by greedy monopolists. Since Adam Smith had also argued against monopolists, his theories couldn't have been more relevant to what was happening in the 1970s, at least as far as Ralph was concerned.

When his seminar met on the morning of his son's query regarding Monopoly, his mind kept drifting back to the game. Was there any way he could use it to illustrate his anti-monopoly argument, despite the game's emphasis on stomping out competition? Or, better yet, was there another, more philosophically pleasing version of the game that he could use? Over the next few days, he called a few toy stores to find out but came up empty-handed.

Shortly thereafter, while discussing Adam Smith in one of his classes, Ralph mentioned that much to his dismay, one of the world's most popular board games gave people a warm and fuzzy feeling toward the word "monopoly" because it reminded them of having played the game in their childhood. A better capitalist board game, Ralph said, would be one in which players competed against each other to produce better-quality, lower-priced goods while government regulated or abolished monopolies. In short, the game would teach the opposite of what the Parker Brothers game taught.

Then it hit him. He could create an anti-monopoly game of his own.

•

WITH THE HELP of his sons, Ralph soon set about doing just that. Mark drew the cards, and Ralph created the play money by copying the Japanese occupation currency he had acquired in the 1940s. Around the perimeter of the game board he drew spaces that represented metal, steel, oil, tire, and railroad companies. The object of the game was to break the conglomerates apart, and each player was a "trustbuster." Players earned points both by breaking up monopolies and by doing other good deeds. The winner was the one with the highest score.

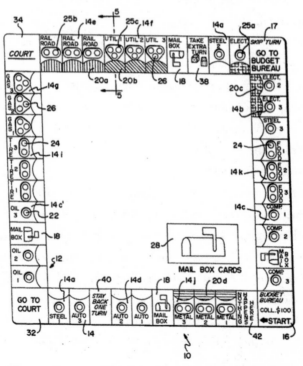

A drawing of economist Ralph Anspach's trust-busting Anti-Monopoly game.
(United States Patent and Trademark Office)

When a player landed on a space on the Anti-Monopoly board, she or he could serve the monopoly with an indictment. The more indictments served, the more points earned. Players purchased indictment chips and brought cases against companies with spoofed corporate names: Egson Oil, Fort Auto, and Nazareth Steel. The game also featured mailbox cards, which were miniature letters sent from the antitrust division of the Justice Department. Instead of having a banker, as in Monopoly, the game had a budget director.

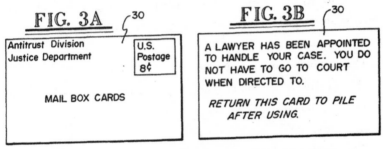

Drawings of cards from Ralph Anspach's Anti-Monopoly. The object of the game was to terminate "the monopolistic practices of plural company combinations."
(United States Patent and Trademark Office)

Ever the professor, Ralph couldn't refrain from including some of his economic beliefs in the game's rule book: "Monopolism is good for the monopolies. It is bad for the great majority of businesses, and even worse for the economy as a whole" was but one example. His was probably also the only board game rule book to invoke the Sherman Antitrust Act of 1890 (a landmark act that outlawed certain anti-competition activities and allowed the government to investigate trusts), the Federal Trade Commission Act of 1914 (which established the Federal Trade Commission and allowed the government to issue "cease and desist" orders to halt monopolistic trade), and the Clayton Antitrust Act of 1914 (an expansion of the Sherman Act).

At first, Ralph called his creation Bust-the-Trust—the Anti-Monopoly Game. But friends and family who played the game found the name confusing. The term "trust-busting" had been popularized by Theodore Roosevelt in the 1890s, but by the 1970s, most people didn't know what it meant.

To find a name that would be more widely understood, Ralph decided to do some market research in one of his classes at San Francisco State.

"How many of you know what antitrust is?" he asked his class of thirty students, most of them juniors and seniors who were not majoring in economics.

Three students raised their hands.

"How many of you understand, or have some idea of, what 'anti-monopoly' would mean?" he asked.

Eighteen people raised their hands.

That settled it: Ralph would call his game Anti-Monopoly. But before publicly doing so, he checked in with two trademark lawyers. Both told him the same thing: According to previous ruling, a product name starting with the prefix "anti" was not easily confusable with something that was its opposite. This did not guarantee that Ralph would not be sued, but he reasoned that legal precedent was on his side.

Now Ralph needed to find a company to produce the game—not an easy task given how overtly political and academic it was. He didn't bother submitting it to Parker Brothers, as he thought they weren't likely to support Monopoly's antithesis. Instead, he fired off his pitch to a variety of small and midsize game companies.

Rejection after rejection arrived in the mail.

Ralph then turned to Simons Inventions, a company that paired game inventors with buyers. Ralph paid Simons a thousand dollars up front, only to have his game pitched to almost the exact same list of companies he had already tried. His one thousand dollars vanished into thin air.

With little hope of a major backer, Ralph felt that he had no choice. He decided to try to manufacture the game on his own.

Throughout the summer and fall of 1973, headlines about OPEC and the worsening oil crisis continued to be plastered across the pages of the *San Francisco Chronicle*, and there was talk of further gas rationing, carpooling, and the dimming of Christmas lights. The speed limit in parts of California was reduced from 70 to 65 miles per hour, and then to 50 miles per hour. Airlines eliminated and consolidated flights and reduced cruising speeds. Consumers began to prefer small cars over gas-guzzlers, a sharp reversal from earlier patterns of behavior. The San Francisco Ferry Building went dark for the first time since World War II.

The crisis and OPEC's part in it helped Ralph find like-minded partners for his Anti-Monopoly effort. He wrote to and became friends with another entrepreneur and inventor of games, the brassy, big-haired Arlene Martin. A successful marketer of games in the Bay Area, Martin took up the Anti-Monopoly cause and agreed to help market the game. Through her, Ralph met her business partner, Jay Thornton, who also vowed his support. Ralph liked Thornton's southern drawl and working-class background as a painter. Gene Donner, a reporter turned public relations man, also joined the early Anti-Monopoly team.

To jump-start the game, Ralph needed about five thousand dollars. To raise it, he taught summer school, and he compensated Thornton, Martin, and Donner with shares in Anti-Monopoly Inc. Little by little, Anti-Monopoly was starting to resemble a company.

Finally, in the fall of 1973, Ralph found a printer named Al De Nola, who agreed to print two thousand Anti-Monopoly game boards and boxes for five thousand dollars. Next, relying chiefly on credit cards,

Ralph purchased dice and cone-shaped snap ties (a type of clip used in construction) to serve as playing pieces. Several of the first two thousand games that rolled off the press were covered in spots, due to a printing error, but Ralph wasn't concerned. Rather, he saw the spotted games as potentially highly desirable first editions and spent hours autographing them. Surprisingly, his hyping of these "special" games would prove to be effective, as some store owners would tell Ralph that customers were coming in asking to buy the game's first edition.

Through a family friend, Ralph and his sons succeeded in getting an Anti-Monopoly promotional flyer placed on a bulletin board in the offices of the Federal Trade Commission in Washington, D.C. The Anspachs thought the move would help generate publicity. Instead, it eventually aroused the interest of a postal inspector, who was concerned that the company was not delivering the goods it advertised. An inspector arrived at the Anspachs' home and audited the Anti-Monopoly books. The Anspachs were cleared.

Anti-Monopoly hit the market around the time that news about Watergate broke. In the ensuing weeks, details about the scandal, followed by denials from the Richard Nixon White House, unfolded day by day. Meanwhile, OPEC announced a plan to cut oil production by 25 percent. Ralph thought all the bad news boded well for sales of his antiestablishment pastime.

He sent an early Anti-Monopoly game to famed consumer advocate Ralph Nader, saying that Nader epitomized "what the game is all about." In Anti-Monopoly, attorneys similar to Nader were cast as heroes battling against corporate America. Ralph never heard back from the tall, lanky lawyer, but he did later learn that Patty Hearst, the newspaper heiress kidnapped by the Symbionese Liberation Army, had given her father, Randolph Hearst, a copy of the game as a joke.

As part of its rollout, the Anti-Monopoly team fired off a blast of advertisements in the mail, introducing the new game at a suggested retail price of $7.95. Under Donner's guidance, Ralph also purchased ads in the *San Francisco Chronicle* and the *Berkeley Gazette*.

In October, the first order for Anti-Monopoly arrived, from the library at Slippery Rock State College in Pennsylvania. Ralph and his family and colleagues were elated. Someone was actually buying the game. Their business was taking off.

Just as Ralph and Ruth had once coordinated political rallies, meetings, and phone trees, they now coordinated the selling of Anti-Monopoly. Ruth's skills as a secretary for Women for Peace were put to good use, and Donner drew up a press release with the headline PROFESSOR AGAINST THE MONOPOLISTS: A "DAVID AND GOLIATH" STORY. "It'll make me very happy to know I'm reaching a lot of people far beyond the classroom with my message," Ralph said. "And if it makes any money, well, teachers have always been able to use a little extra."

Ralph, Ruth, and the rest of the Anti-Monopoly team worked out of the Anspach home, the aging madam sitting on a fault line between a stable part of the Berkeley Hills and land that was sliding toward San Francisco Bay at the rate of about an inch per year. The house was built on an incline, and just outside its windows hulked cranes and related construction equipment that served as constant reminders of Ralph's determination to get the house back on its foundation. The interior was constantly under construction. Power tools and slabs of drywall were part of the family's daily existence, as was a rotating cast of hippie construction workers.

Ralph had been able to purchase the house at a discount because it was condemned due to its position on a fault line. Ralph had figured that the family wouldn't live in the home long enough to run the risk of its sliding away. But here it was, years later, and instead of residing in the quaint Bay Area manor he had originally envisioned, he and his family were still living in the lopsided house befitting a twisted children's fairy tale.

Ralph's sons loved seeing their home turned into Anti-Monopoly's headquarters. When a toy store called to place an order, Mark and William eagerly picked up the phone to ask, "How many?" Ralph and the two boys walked up and down the hilly streets of the Bay Area, personally delivering stacks of Anti-Monopoly games to local stores.

A negative story about the game appeared in the *San Francisco Chronicle*. "I can't help thinking this game would be much improved if it didn't constantly remind the player of its classic predecessor," the *Chronicle* reporter wrote. "It's a little like living in your first husband's house with a second husband." Ralph was at first dismayed by the story, but he soon learned the truth of the adage that any press is good press—Anti-Monopoly sales went up dramatically. Ten days after Anti-Monopoly went on the market, all two thousand copies of its initial production run had been sold.

By December, it was becoming clear that the company's printing scheme was not sustainable by De Nola's factory, which was designed to produce corrugated boxes, as orders for tens of thousands more copies of Anti-Monopoly poured in. The game had gone national and had garnered press nationally, both in large magazines and a plethora of local papers.

Inventors of other games began contacting the family, seeking advice on how to repeat their success. Ralph announced plans to present the game to Senator Philip Hart, a Democrat from Michigan who was heading the U.S. Senate's Antitrust and Monopoly Subcommittee.

Ralph also applied for a patent. The lawyer he consulted warned him that first-time patent applications were often rejected because first-level examiners liked to take a conservative stance to "cover their flanks." On his lawyer's advice, Ralph wrote to game distributors to emphasize that Anti-Monopoly was produced by Anti-Monopoly Inc., which was not associated with Parker Brothers.

On June 25, 1974, Ralph's application was turned down. The name was deemed "likely to cause confusion, or to cause mistake, or to deceive," the letter from the U.S. Department of Commerce's Patent Office read. Trademarks—which protect words, logos, and taglines associated with a good—are used to distinguish one good from another, to let consumers know where a product comes from. A trademark does not entitle someone to prevent others from making the same product, but it does prohibit others from marketing a product with a confusingly similar words, logos, or taglines.

Ralph didn't think much about this rejection. After all, his lawyer had warned him about first-time trademark applications.

•

IN FEBRUARY OF that year, an unassuming envelope had arrived at the Anspach home. Inside was a letter from a law firm printed on intimidating letterhead. Although Ralph had brushed off the patent application rejection, to him, this felt like a direct threat.

Mr. Ralph Anspach
February 13, 1974
1060 Keith Avenue
Berkely {sic}, California

Dear Mr. Anspach:

As attorneys for Parker Brothers of Salem, Massachusetts, owners of the registered trademark MONOPOLY, we are writing to you regarding the promotion and sale of game equipment under the trademark ANTI-MONOPOLY.

We understand that you have claimed never to have been requested by Parker Brothers or General Mills to cease and desist from advertising and offering for sale game equipment under the name ANTI-MONOPOLY.

We enclose a copy of our letter to The Computer Industry Association dated November 14, 1973 regarding this matter. We have never heard from The Computer Industry Association but assumed that a copy of our letter had been forwarded to you, if, in fact, you are not associated with The Computer Industry Association.

You will note from the enclosure that in our opinion your use of the term ANTI-MONOPOLY on game equipment infringes on our client's trademark rights. We further wish to advise you that your use of MONOPOLY in promotional and advertising materials adds to the damaging effect of this infringement.

It would appear from material we have seen, and, specifically Mr. George Lazarus' article of February 11, 1974, that this protest may be ignored. However, for the record, we request that you give us your assurance that the term ANTI-MONOPOLY will be discontinued as the name of your game equipment which would appear to be more properly TRUST-BUSTING or ANTI-TRUST as Mr. Lazarus proposes.

> *Yours very truly,*
> *Oliver P. Howes, Jr.*

ENCLOSED WITH THE letter was a copy of a 1974 column by *Chicago Tribune* columnist George Lazarus, headlined, PARKER BROS.—JEALOUS OF

ITS MONOPOLY? The earlier letter that Howes referred to had indeed been sent to the Computer Industry Association, a group that had been promoting and selling Anti-Monopoly. But the letter had been addressed to the association, not him.

Ralph viewed the Howes letter as a "put the fear of God in you" note, and it also frightened his wife. While Ruth considered herself political and willing to take on causes, her fervor for the game did not match Ralph's. Howes wrote on behalf of General Mills, the cereal king and Betty Crocker steward that had purchased Parker Brothers in 1968. Parker Brothers president Robert Barton, in consultation with his son, Randolph, had agreed to sell in order to diversify the family's financial portfolio, and General Mills aspired to be a massive consumer conglomerate, part of an industry-wide trend toward mergers. Seen in a positive light, the thinking was that such acquisitions gave General Mills multiple avenues to reach consumers and allowed the company to pool resources and leverage different assets of its empire. Seen otherwise, they were creating a Frankencompany, a hodgepodge of businesses that shared little more than an earnings report.

Regardless, Ralph was not interested in changing the name of his game. He felt that just as Monopoly used common language to convey to consumers what the game was about, Anti-Monopoly had the same right. He had two choices: Either he could stop producing Anti-Monopoly, or he could challenge Parker Brothers for the right to market his game under its current title.

CHAPTER 2

A WOMAN INVENTS

*"I'm thankful that I was taught how to think
and not what to think."*
—LIZZIE MAGIE

To ELIZABETH MAGIE, known to her friends as Lizzie, the problems of the new century were so vast, the income inequalities so massive, and the monopolists so mighty that it seemed impossible that an unknown woman working as a stenographer stood a chance at easing society's ills with something as trivial as a board game. But she had to try.

Night after night, after her work at her Washington, D.C., office was done, Lizzie sat in her home, drawing and redrawing, thinking and rethinking. It was the early 1900s, and she wanted her board game to reflect her progressive political views—that was the whole point of it—which centered on the economic theories of Henry George. A charismatic nineteenth-century politician and economist who had passed away just a few years before, George had been a proponent of the "land value tax," also known as the "single tax." His main tenet was that individuals should own 100 percent of what they made or created, but that everything found in nature, particularly land, should belong to everyone. Land was not meant to be seized, bought, sold, traded, or parceled into city blocks where people were forced to pay exorbitant rents. Since, however, some people did own land, they should pay a tax for that privilege. All other goods should remain strictly untaxed.

The Landlord's Game was a teaching tool inspired by Henry George, a popular politician, economist, and author of the 1879 *Progress and Poverty*. (Library of Congress)

George's message had resonated deeply with many Americans in the late 1800s, when poverty and squalor were on full display in the country's urban centers. Poor immigrants and natives alike were packed tightly together in noxious slums, where they slaved long hours in dirty, dangerous factories, earning little more than a pittance. The single-taxers believed that if all taxes were eradicated except for the one on property, and the poor and the working class were able to keep more of their hard-earned dollars, poverty levels would quickly diminish. A single tax would also boost production, as workers would be happier and healthier, and force business owners to improve working conditions.

George "is neither a 'Communist,' nor a free-lover, nor even an infidel, so far as can be seen," an 1881 *New York Times* article stated. "But he recognizes the social disease that makes itself felt in tramps, railway riots, and the criminal classes of great cities, and is the only man who has not merely put down clearly in black and white what are the causes of the disease, but offered a cure."

During the 1880s, his manifesto *Progress and Poverty* was rumored to have sold more copies than any book except the Bible. He spoke regularly before sold-out halls, and his face was plastered everywhere—on banners, newspapers, and even cigar boxes. The list of people who were later influenced by his philosophy included Winston Churchill, Frank Lloyd Wright, and Leo Tolstoy.

George was an ardent anti-monopolist, and many of his followers formed anti-monopoly political parties. "Chattel slavery is dead," he once told an evening crowd at the Brooklyn Academy of Music. "But labor slavery lives. That kind of slavery is increasing and social opinion is beginning to rise against it."

The anti-monopoly parties also served as staging areas for the women's rights movement. At the time, the battle for women's suffrage was already decades old, having been started by middle-class white women in Seneca Falls, New York, some forty years earlier. But it felt to many as though little progress had been made. Women still did not have the right to vote, and their accomplishments were still being routinely dismissed by most men—a problem that Lizzie would personally face throughout her life. Outspoken female activists were often stigmatized, sometimes in the name of enforcing obscenity laws.

When George made a bid for mayor of New York City in 1886, he advocated not only the single tax but also equal pay for women, more stringent building inspections, and putting an end to police interference in peaceful demonstrations. His platform appealed to many voters, but he lost to a Tammany Hall candidate (though ahead of a young Republican named Theodore Roosevelt).

The Georgists, as George's followers were known, faced formidable ideological opposition in the form of industrial titans such as John D. Rockefeller, one of the richest men in history, thanks to his Standard Oil Trust. Through secret agreements and shell companies that appeared independent but were in fact operated by Standard Oil, the trust had wiped out its competition and by the late 1800s, the company controlled nearly 90 percent of America's refined oil flows. Critics such as George noted that capitalism was good at creating wealth, but it could be lousy at distributing it.

When Henry George died in 1897, many of his followers feared that without their magnetic leader, the ideals he espoused would be lost forever and the monopolists would take control for good. It was up to Georgists such as Lizzie to keep his message alive. She felt that the economic fate of the country depended on it.

•

A DISTINCTIVE-LOOKING WOMAN in her thirties, with curly dark locks and bangs that framed her face, Lizzie had inherited the bushy eyebrows of her father. The descendant of Scottish immigrants, she had pale skin, a strong jawline, and a strong work ethic. As she aged, she took to wearing her long, wavy hair in a bun, which accentuated her finely etched features.

In the early 1900s, Lizzie was unmarried, unusual for a woman of her age at the time. Even more unusual, however, was the fact that she was the head of her household. Completely on her own, she had saved up for and bought her home, along with several acres of property.

She lived in Prince George County, a Washington, D.C., neighborhood where the residents on her block included a dairyman, a peddler who identified himself as a "huckster," a sailor, a carpenter, and a musician. Lizzie shared her house with a male actor who paid rent and a black female servant.

At the turn of the century, Washington was finally beginning to take shape out of the swamps upon which it had been built. To one side was the White House, facing the Washington Monument, and to another was the U.S. Capitol, overlooking a thicket of small homes and office buildings built along the city's neatly organized grid system. The shouts of food-cart salesmen and bicyclists could barely be heard over the clanging of streetcars. Petty thieves thrived in the Center Market, and burlesque theaters welcomed thousands through their doors. Horses pulled wooden carts down wide, bumpy roads, leaving manure behind—a putrid backdrop for the political arguments that had become commonplace in the young republic's national capital.

Lizzie's political views had been influenced, albeit indirectly, by Abraham Lincoln. In 1858, before she was born, Lizzie's father, James

Magie, accompanied Lincoln and Joseph Medill, the thirty-five-year-old publisher of the *Chicago Tribune*, as the lanky lawyer traveled around Illinois debating politics with Stephen Douglas.

In earlier years, Lizzie's father had worked as a printer in Newark, New Jersey, and as a city editor at the Brooklyn *Daily Advertiser*. He had lost a wife and an infant daughter, leaving him to raise his surviving son, Charles, on his own. But by the time he met Lincoln, he was living in Illinois with his second wife, Mary, née Ritchie, from New Brunswick, New Jersey, and working as the editor of the *Oquawka Plaindealer*.

Young, bright, and ambitious, James was itching to see political change come to the country, and he believed that Lincoln was the man to bring about that change. James used the pages of his newspapers to drum up support for abolition, as well as gaining a reputation for being an arousing stump speaker. Lincoln was elected president of the United States in November 1860. In 1861, James moved to Macomb, Illinois, where he assumed editorial control of the *Macomb Journal*, eventually becoming its sole owner. The Southern states seceded in the spring of that year.

James enlisted in the Union army and in the summer of 1862 began to recruit other men in Illinois for the Northern cause. He was a private and refused promotion throughout the war, even though many called him "Sergeant." At the front, James channeled his impassioned prose into his regular letters home to his wife in Illinois. "I scarcely know where to begin or how to tell you of the scenes, the strife, and the excitements which we have passed through in the last five days," he began one note dated January 1, 1863.

Less than a week after General Robert E. Lee's surrender at Appomattox Court House, Abraham Lincoln was assassinated and Andrew Johnson became president. His administration appointed James postmaster of Macomb, but James resigned after less than a year because he felt that Johnson had betrayed his own political beliefs and promises. Selling his interest in the *Macomb Journal*, James moved his family to Canton, where he purchased a half interest in the *Canton Register*. In 1866, Elizabeth, soon known as Lizzie, was born, to be joined a few years later by her sister, Alta. The family was solidly middle-class, with James continuing to work as a newspaperman and Mary tending to the home and children.

As the nation rebuilt itself on top of the rubble of the Civil War, the second Industrial Revolution was under way, with technology, even more than politics, bringing about great change. The electric lamp and the telephone were invented in James's time, to eventually transform daily life for his daughter's generation. Cheaper steel meant more bridges, skyscrapers, and railroad tracks. Vulcanized rubber created a tire industry and new ways of thinking about transit. The telegram made those physically afar feel nearer.

James began teaching his intellectual values to his children when they were still very young. Hoping that they would carry on his fight for equality, he told them about his early days as a politically motivated editor and about his friend Abraham Lincoln. From a young age, Lizzie had exposure to newsrooms. She also watched and listened during the years when her father clerked in the Illinois legislature and ran for office on an anti-monopoly ticket—an election that he lost.

The steam age gave way to the motor age, built on the backs of workers who did not necessarily share in the bounty, and creating massive corporations. In Illinois, Lizzie saw this play out every day: wealthy kingpins strolling down the streets alongside child laborers clad in tattered clothing, titan landowners living lives defined by carriages and high fashion alongside ordinary farmers struggling to survive. A national debate arose: Should government bust up the large corporations that were forming, or not?

When Lizzie was thirteen, her family suffered significant financial losses, probably due to the Panic of 1873, which had started six years earlier and was still having repercussions. It was triggered by several causes, including a fall in silver prices, railroad speculation, a trade deficit, property losses, and general economic malaise tied to the Franco-Prussian War. Lizzie had to leave school to help support her family, a fact that she lamented long into her adulthood.

She attended a convention of stenographers with her father and soon found work in that field. At the time, stenography was a growing profession, one that had opened up to women as the Civil War removed many men from the workforce. The typewriter was gaining commercial popularity, leaving many to ponder a strange new world, one in which typists sat at desks, hands fixed to keys, memorizing seemingly illogical arrangements of letters on the new QWERTY keyboards.

Lizzie's father also shared with his daughter a copy of Henry George's bestselling 1879 tome, *Progress and Poverty*. The early seeds of what would later evolve into one of the most popular modern board games of all time had been planted.

•

AROUND 1890, THE MAGIES moved to Washington, D.C., where James found work in government service and helped found a church. Lizzie was his constant companion, and as time passed, the political and physical similarities between father and daughter deepened.

"I have often been called a 'chip off the old block,'" Lizzie said of her relationship with her father, "which I consider quite a compliment, for I am proud of my father for being the kind of an 'old block' that he is."

Like James Magie, Lizzie traveled in highly political circles. She served as the secretary of the Woman's Single Tax Club of Washington and counted Henry George Jr., the like-minded son of her single tax idol, as one of her friends. The younger George worked as a reporter in Brooklyn and eventually served as a U.S. representative from New York.

Lizzie found work as a stenographer and typist for the chief clerk of the Dead Letter Office, the receptacle for the nation's undeliverable mail. Sometimes letters found their way to the office because of lousy penmanship. Other times there was no address at all. Prank letters arrived, senders unknown.

The Dead Letter clerks, many of them women, were responsible for sorting lost envelopes and parcels, and for disposing of the unclaimed mail, either by destroying it or by auctioning off its contents. The clerks also tallied up any enclosed money and handed the funds over to the U.S. Treasury. Only workers in the Dead Letter Office had the authority to open the mail, and some became lay detectives. Through their work, stories emerged of mothers reunited with lost sons and employees at last collecting long-missing paychecks.

The Dead Letter Office had begun hiring women in the 1860s during the Civil War. And after the war, the office continued to employ women, believing them to be more honest and "faithful in the performance of their duties than the men." Most women who worked there were intentionally tucked away—obscure secret keepers amid the nation's growing flow of correspondence.

"Equal pay for equal work" was beginning to be discussed as a concept in America after the Civil War, but it wasn't remotely close to being enforced. Women like Lizzie usually earned a fraction of what their male counterparts earned. An 1869 article in the *New York Times* argued that women should not make "the mistake of demanding equal payment with men" because "so long as their labor is *cheaper* than that of men, there will be a powerful reason for employing it."

In the evening after work, Lizzie pursued literary ambitions, writing poetry and short stories, and, as a player in Washington's nascent theater scene, performed on the stage, where she earned praise for her comedic roles. Though small-framed and only in her twenties, she had a presence—the audience at the Masonic Hall exploded with laughter at her comical rendition of a simpering old maid. She also sometimes took on male roles. "She wants to fly," James said of his daughter, "but hasn't got the wings."

One sweltering Washington summer, Lizzie wrote a dozen poems, ranging from "Genius Imprisoned," in which she described a grim scene of modern industrial life—"a dark and dingy place" where a "plain old office clock / Ticks out the tedious time" to an "imprisoned poet soul"— to "Self," in which she pondered the relationship of the individual to others. "All, all are selfish / There is not one who does not live himself to please," she wrote. Yet in such egoism, she went on, could be found generosity: "The happiest are those who are to others kindest / And who cause most happiness to all / The great are those who make the world / The better by their deeds."

The themes of pain, romance, nature, and unfairness were constants in her work. In the fall of 1892, she bound her poems into a book, *My Betrothed*, and printed 500 copies, the most she could afford. The title poem told the story of a man's love for Roberta, a woman ten years his junior whom he had known since birth and loved "with burning soul and body / With impetuous desire."

Unusual for a nineteenth-century woman, Lizzie also dabbled in engineering. She invented a gadget that allowed paper to pass through typewriter rollers with more ease. The invention also allowed typewriter users to place more type on a given page and made it possible for documents of different sizes to be placed into the machine.

On January 3, 1893, Lizzie went to the U.S. Patent Office to lay legal claim to her invention. As a woman, she would have been a standout in that office at any age, but at twenty-six, she was a phenomenon. Beside her and there to serve as her witness was her father, himself no stranger to the patent process, having applied for and won a few through the years (including one for a permutation, or combination, lock).

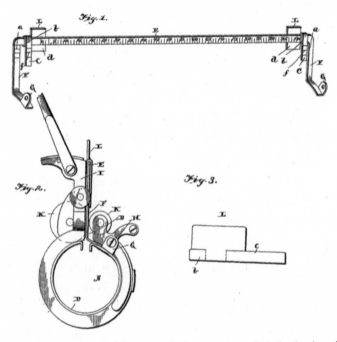

In 1893, Lizzie Magie applied for a patent for her typewriter gadget. The daughter of a known newspaperman and a writer and stenographer herself, she was among the handful of women inventors of her time. (United States Patent and Trademark Office)

James Magie's witnessing of his daughter's patent application, which was ultimately approved, was to be one of his final acts. Less than two weeks later, he fell ill amid the January cold and died while visiting his son, Charles, in Brooklyn. Lizzie was inconsolable.

•

TWO YEARS AFTER the death of her father, Lizzie published a short story titled "For the Benefit of the Poor" in the January 1895 issue of *Frank Leslie's Popular Monthly*, one of the more prominent and popular journals of her time, counting Henry James among its contributors. The story told of an impoverished boy struggling to support himself and his invalid mother by selling bonbons in a theater. Nearly a century before the term the "Matthew effect" would be commonly used to describe the phenomenon in which the rich get richer and the poor get poorer, Lizzie included the pertinent passage from the Gospel of Matthew in her story: "For unto everyone that hath shall be given, and he shall have abundance; but from him that hath not shall be taken away even that which he hath."

About two years later, Lizzie's story "The Theft of a Brain: The Story of a Hypnotized Novelist and a Cruel Deed" was published in *Godey's*, a women's magazine based in Philadelphia. An important platform for men and women thinkers, *Godey's* had published authors such as Frances Hodgson Burnett, Washington Irving, and Edgar Allan Poe.

"The Theft of a Brain" was about an aspiring novelist named Laura Lynn, who said to a friend that if she could write something that everybody read, she would be "perfectly happy." Laura was talented and passionate, and her real difficulty was a lack of confidence. She sought out a professor, who hypnotized her into writing. Under hypnosis, she wrote a story titled "Privileged Criminals," about a woman who was convicted of a crime she hadn't committed. When Laura woke up, the professor told her that she had become a successful writer who was selling her short stories for five hundred dollars each. Laura was elated. She continued to write short stories for some time and then wrote a novel. But when she tried to publish the novel, she found that a plagiarized copy already existed and had become a bestseller. The plagiarist was none other than the hypnotist professor.

"I stole the brains of other undeveloped geniuses," he confessed.

The plotline that Lizzie had created would soon hold eerie parallels to her own life.

•

THOUGH THE POPULARITY of Henry George's theories was ebbing with attendance at meetings and lectures dwindling and Georgist political goals stalling in statehouses and at the polls, Lizzie Magie still believed in them and taught classes about the single tax theory in the evenings after work. But she wasn't reaching enough people. She needed a new medium—something more interactive and creative.

At the turn of the twentieth century, board games were becoming increasingly commonplace in middle-class homes. In addition, more and more inventors were discovering that the games were not just a pastime but also a means of communication. Lizzie took out her pen and paper.

She began speaking in public about a new concept of hers, which she called the Landlord's Game. "It is a practical demonstration of the present system of land-grabbing with all its usual outcomes and consequences," she wrote in a 1902 issue of the *Single Tax Review*. "It might well have been called the 'Game of Life,' as it contains all the elements of success and failure in the real world, and the object is the same as the human race in general seem[s] to have, i.e., the accumulation of wealth."

For Lizzie to try to put her ideas out in public so brazenly was something of a risk at that time. Most women didn't do such things. It would be nearly two decades before women gained the right to vote, and while innovations such as the typewriter and the telephone had afforded new professional opportunities for women, common thought still held that they had little to contribute to the world of ideas. As one newspaper would put it in 1912, women may have greater longevity than men because "they don't use their brains as much as men."

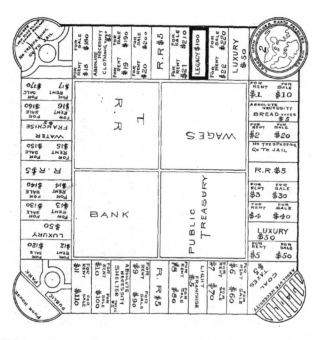

In 1904, Lizzie Magie patented her Landlord's Game, the forerunner to what millions of game players would later know as Monopoly. Among other things, her patent features the phrase Go to Jail, railroad spaces, and a Public Park space that predates Free Parking.

(United States Patent and Trademark Office)

Lizzie's game featured play money and deeds and properties that could be bought and sold. Players borrowed money, either from the bank or from each other, and they had to pay taxes.

Like Pachisi, later known as Parcheesi, a game from the Indian subcontinent that many Americans were already familiar with, Lizzie's game featured a path that allowed players to circle the board—in contrast to the linear-path design used by many games at the time. In one corner were the Poor House and the Public Park, and across the board was the Jail. Another corner contained an image of the globe and an homage to Henry George: "Labor upon Mother Earth Produces Wages." Also included on the board were three words that have endured for more than a century after Lizzie scrawled them there: GO TO JAIL.

Lizzie drew nine rectangular spaces along the edges of the board between each set of corners. A railroad was in the center of each nine-space grouping, with spaces for rent or sale on either side. Absolute Necessity rectangles offered goods like bread and shelter, and Franchise spaces offered services such as water and light. When players landed on the Luxury space, they paid fifty dollars to the public treasury to receive a luxury ticket, which yielded sixty dollars at the end of the game.

As gamers made their way around the board, they performed labor and earned wages. Every time players passed the Mother Earth space, they were "supposed to have performed so much labor upon Mother Earth" that they received one hundred dollars in wages. Players who ran out of money were sent to the Poor House.

Players who trespassed on land were sent to Jail, and there the unfortunate individuals had to linger until serving out their time or paying a fifty-dollar fine. Serving out their time meant waiting until they threw a double. "The rallying and chaffing of the others when one player finds himself an inmate of the jail, and the expressions of mock sympathy and condolence when one is obliged to betake himself to the poor house, make a large part of the fun and merriment of the game," Lizzie said.

After going around the board a predetermined number of times, players retired, but still remained in the game until the last player had completed his or her final round. The person with the most wealth at the end of the game won.

Lizzie even created rules for when there weren't any rules: "Should any emergency arise which is not covered by the rules of the game," she wrote, "the players must settle the matter between themselves; but if any player absolutely refuses to obey the rules as above set forth he must go to jail."

From its inception, the Landlord's Game aimed to seize on the natural human instinct to compete. And, somewhat surprisingly, Lizzie created two sets of rules: an anti-monopolist set in which all were rewarded when wealth was created, and a monopolist set in which the goal was to create monopolies and crush opponents. Her vision was an embrace of dualism and contained a contradiction within itself, a tension trying to be resolved between opposing philosophies. However, and of course unbeknownst to Lizzie at the time, it was monopolist rules that would later capture the public's imagination.

On some level, Lizzie understood that the game provided a context— it was just a game, after all—in which players could lash out at friends and family in a way that they probably couldn't in daily life. She understood the power of drama and the potency of assuming roles outside of one's everyday identity. Games like hers provided a respite from the often-dreary conditions of daily life.

The Landlord's Game was a sophisticated way to get players interested in the single tax theory. The goal was to obtain as much land and wealth as possible, but the means of attaining them were Georgist—even when playing by the monopolist set of rules. When players landed on an "absolute necessity" space, such as bread, coal, or shelter, the player had to pay five dollars into the Public Treasury. "This represents indirect taxation," Lizzie said. Each time a player went around the board, noted by the "Mother Earth" space, the player received one hundred dollars for having "performed so much labor upon mother earth," Lizzie wrote, concurrent with the Georgist view that people should own value that they created on their own. While other games of the time espoused moral instruction and/or entertainment, Lizzie's game embodied her unrelenting hope that if more people learned about George's theories, they would become proponents of them and the world would be better for it.

Lizzie believed that children as young as nine or ten years old could play the Landlord's Game. "They like to handle the make-believe money, deeds, etc.," she said. "And the little landlords take a general delight in demanding the payment of their rent. They learn that the quickest way to accumulate wealth and gain power is to get all the land they can in the best localities and hold on to it. Let the children once see clearly the gross injustice of our present land system and when they grow up, if they are allowed to develop naturally, the evil will soon be remedied."

After years of tinkering, writing, and pondering her new creation, Lizzie entered the U.S. Patent Office for the second time on March 23, 1903, to secure her legal claim to the Landlord's Game. She quit her one-hundred-dollars-a-month job at the Dead Letter Office and went to work at a private firm. Soon thereafter, she opened an office of her own.

In one of history's coincidences, Lizzie filed her claim on the same day that Orville and Wilbur Wright filed theirs for their "flying machine." Lizzie's application made its way through the agency's paperwork web more quickly than the Wrights', and on January 5, 1904, her patent was approved. At the time, less than one percent of all patents issued in the United States went to women.

At least two years later, Lizzie published the game through the Economic Game Company, a New York–based firm that counted Lizzie as a part owner. The company produced a version of the game that was similar to what Lizzie had patented, but with signature single-taxer flair she had made a few changes. The game now included new spaces such as Oil Fields, Timberlands, Coal Mines, and Farmlands—the type of goods that George and his followers felt should not be monopolized, as they were natural resources.

Her experimenting done, Lizzie faced what befalls all creators when their work is sent out into the world: the agony of waiting to see how it will be received.

CHAPTER 3

A UTOPIA CALLED ARDEN

"You are welcome hither . . ."
—Greeting placard in Arden, Delaware

IN THE EARLY 1900s, an unusual community was developing in New Castle County, Delaware. Known as the Village of Arden, it was a progressive utopian society based on the single tax principle, with a devotion to arts, crafts, and theater. It had a town meeting form of government, and much of its land was forest and greens, which were not taxed. Technically, the land in Arden was communal property owned by the village and could not be bought or sold. Instead, the land had a renewable ninety-nine-year lease, and the "land lease" fee was not increased because of improvements.

Arden residents were among the first to play the Landlord's Game. Years later, no one could remember exactly who had introduced the game to the village, but it was quickly embraced by the quirky community.

Arden had been founded in 1900 by a stern-faced, thin-lipped sculptor named Frank Stephens and a bearded Quaker architect named William Price, both from Pennsylvania. Stephens, Price, and a number of other activists had traveled around Delaware in 1895, hoping to raise political support for the single tax movement.

About five years later, with financing from soap magnate Joseph Fels, Stephens and Price returned to purchase a farm in New Castle County around which to design a single tax town. Connected to Philadelphia by the nearby Baltimore & Ohio Railroad, Arden was at first a summer resort, where people went to vacation simply, in tents and rustic dwellings. But as Stephens and Price spread the word about their village among their many well-educated, progressive friends and contacts, it soon blossomed into a year-round community.

Arden's design was heavily influenced by Price, a prominent architect in the Arts and Crafts movement. Though Price would later become most famous for the extravagant hotels he designed in Atlantic City, his dwellings in Arden were modest Craftsman homes—quaint cottages nestled in the forest. Residents would later embellish them with caterpillar-like extensions and rooms perched on top.

Ardenites delighted in the simplicity of their village's design and function. Large trees shaded the roads, and from one side of town came the soothing gurgle of a sparkling-clean stream. Nearby was a lush lake that made for an ideal swimming hole, where skinny-dipping and, it was rumored, free love thrived. Near the town green stood a craft shop where metalware and stitched goods were made and sold, a barn theater, and an outdoor theater where Stephens regularly staged Shakespeare productions. The town also had its own print shop and weaving studio.

Arden's young people were allowed an unusual amount of freedom for the time, horseback riding and hiking through the surrounding woods as they pleased. Families gathered at Arden's ice cream parlor for refreshments and sipped water from the village's six water pumps. The town also organized field days, which often included sprinting events for women, sack races for men, and pie-eating contests for everyone. In 1909, the women of Arden formed their own baseball team, which sometimes competed against its male counterpart.

Everything about Arden's operation was communal, with regular meetings held to discuss the distribution of the general community fund. How much money should go to the library? How much to roads? Women and even children were allowed to vote at the meetings.

Famed author and socialist Upton Sinclair was among the revolutionaries who made their way to Arden—in his case, in 1910, after his own utopia in New Jersey had burned down, then been disbanded. Sinclair's Arden home, nicknamed the Jungalow, had a large front porch overlooking the town green.

It is very possible that Lizzie Magie, as an activist in the single tax community, visited Arden in its early years, although there are no records to prove this. Lizzie attended some of the same conferences that Stephens attended, and embraced the ideals that Arden espoused.

Arden was both a residential town and a political destination. The community hosted conferences on women's suffrage (Georgists would later put forward Carrie Chapman Catt as a presidential candidate) and attracted many northeastern intellectuals looking for a fresh-air retreat during the summer. Similar single tax communities were also established in Fairhope, Alabama, and Andorra, a microstate in southwestern Europe. All were fueled by the dollars of Joseph Fels.

Fels's dollars were instrumental in keeping Arden afloat, feeding debate among scholars about whether or not a single tax community could prosper without the help of a benefactor like him. The child of

German Jewish parents, Fels was a social reformer and philanthropist who used his wealth as a Philadelphia-based soap manufacturer to promote the single tax movement and various land reforms. His most successful product was Fels-Naptha soap, which was later manufactured by Dial. Fels harbored hopes for the establishment of a Jewish homeland founded on single tax principles but felt that it was up to him to first finance smaller single tax communities to prove that the concept could work.

As games and sports flourished among the assemblage of communists, anarchists, socialists, and single-taxers living in Arden, they came to the attention of scornful local law officials. "Gaming on the Sabbath" was forbidden, and Upton Sinclair and Scott Nearing, a professor at the University of Pennsylvania's Wharton School of Finance and Commerce (as it was then called), were among those arrested in 1911 for playing baseball and tennis on a Sunday. A long-standing enemy of Arden had reported the group. The athletes spent the night in jail, but the charges were eventually dropped.

Poet Harry Kemp came to Arden to stay with Sinclair and his wife during the period when Upton was working on his book *Love's Pilgrimage*. "Folk of every shade of radical opinion," wrote Kemp, "[came to Arden to] escape the galling mockeries of civilization and win back again to pastoral simplicity." In one of Arden's more scandalous moments, Kemp later ran off with Sinclair's wife.

Lizzie Magie also reached out to Sinclair, by sending him some of her writings on Georgism and politics. Her work didn't make it into Sinclair's 1915 collection *The Cry for Justice: An Anthology of the Literature of Social Protest*, which included selections from his own book *The Jungle* and from Henry George's *Progress and Poverty*, but she was acknowledged in his preface.

Given the ideological bent of most of the rebels at Arden, it was hardly surprising that they enjoyed playing the Landlord's Game. Even those who might not have been particularly interested in the single tax theory would have been strongly opposed to the harsh consequences of monopolies taking over in the new, chaotic modern age.

The Arden players made their own board games out of wood, cloth, and crayon, taking pride in the fact that they were not playing with commercially manufactured materials. They often improvised as they went along, and their large wooden Landlord's-based boards included spaces such as Wayback, Lonely Lane, the Farm, Speculation, Boomtown, and Goat Alley. The Jail was still located in one corner, but the Public Park of Lizzie's board was now Central Park Free. Some boards also featured a space for the Bowery and one for George Street—a nod to the single-taxers' philosophical idol. There was a Gee Whiz R.R., a Go to Jail spot, and a Lord Blueblood's Estate. One whole row was devoted to expensive, mostly New York properties: Wall Street, Fifth Avenue, Broadway, and Madison Square. The Mother Earth space conjured up environmental concerns.

Some of the property spaces on the earliest Landlord's boards played in Arden and elsewhere in the early 1900s were grouped not by color but by small numbers written on the perimeter of the board. Eventually, though, players replaced the numbers with colors.

Sinclair and Nearing were among those who took their handmade versions of the Landlord's Game from Arden to other locales in the Northeast, spreading the anti-monopoly game to an unknown number of players. Nearing introduced the game to his students and colleagues at Wharton as early as 1910 and played it on and off for nearly a decade. His brother, Guy, who also lived in Arden, helped spread the game as well. None of the handmade games had written rules, or if they did, they didn't survive.

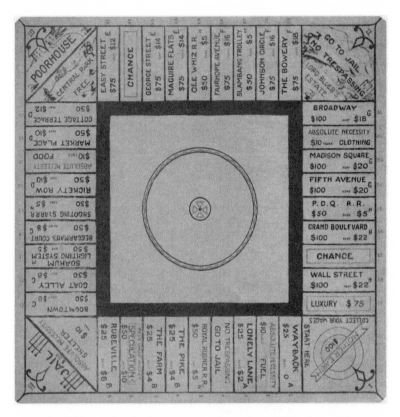

A Landlord's Game believed to have been played as early as 1904 in Arden, Delaware, a popular single tax enclave. (Tom Forsyth and Ron Jarrell)

The Nearings were also among those who started calling the Landlord's Game "monopoly" or the "monopoly game"—shorthand for what they felt was the game's core message. "Arden was a single tax community—hence anti-Monopoly," Nearing wrote many years later. "The game was used to show the anti-social nature of Monopoly." Of the two different rule sets that Lizzie had described in her rule book, Nearing most likely played and taught the monopolistic, rather than the anti-monopolistic, set.

In 1915, the University of Pennsylvania refused to renew Nearing's contract to teach. His involvement with the anti-child-labor movement and his radical teachings had become too much for the university's board, loaded with financiers. His ouster sparked one of the biggest controversies over academic freedom in U.S. history, and progressives rallied around the Nearing cause for decades to come.

Nearing never knew who had invented the original monopoly game, and his ignorance was an early but significant sign that Lizzie Magie's name had become detached from the product she had created.

CHAPTER 4

GEORGE PARKER
AND THE CARDBOARD
EMPIRE

*"A game . . . is like role playing. It's drama. It takes you out of
the situation you're living in and puts you in a new one. A
game applies, therefore, more to the libido than the superego. It's
a fantasy, not a teaching machine."*

—MARVIN GLASS

BY THE SUMMER of 1883, George Parker was a charismatic, driven
sixteen-year-old who had earned the reputation for being a ferocious
player of games. He and his brothers, along with their friends in Salem,
Massachusetts, spent endless hours after school and on the weekends
playing dominoes, chess, checkers, Moksha Patam (an ancient Indian
game later modified to become Chutes and Ladders), and other games
from the Far East that had made their way to America through the
help of seamen like George's father. After the Civil War, industrialism

expanded leisure time and diversion, meaning that games continued to evolve and improve as Americans' lives did.

During the second half of the nineteenth century, Salem was one of the world's premier seafaring towns. George Parker grew up surrounded by people, buildings, and ships that all reflected the water and the sky—a palate of blues, grays, and whites. For over a century, young men had departed from Salem's docks for multimonth voyages to Europe, India, Zanzibar, and Japan. The Far East locales were all but unknown to most Americans at the time, but to the Salemites these places were oddly familiar, as they had heard multiple stories about them in pubs and around dinner tables, the world seemingly shrinking with every epic voyage. Gifts from afar, such as spices, teas, fashionable clothing, and board games, were all brought home to Salem, early tidbits of globalization and the cross-pollination of ideas between continents.

The ocean had captured the imagination of George's father, George Augustus Parker, who worked as a captain in the shipping industry for much of his career. In 1852, at age thirty-two, Parker married twenty-year-old Sarah Hegemen. The union produced Edward in 1855, Charles in 1860, and George in 1866.

George Jr. enjoyed a relatively privileged and idyllic childhood. By the 1870s, the United States was emerging as a great economic power, and the post–Civil War industrial Northeast was booming. Boston-area factories were at the head of industrial innovation, the dollar was gaining international clout as a currency, and the United States was a backwater colony no longer. The third-largest country in the world by population, it controlled a quarter of the world's domestic product.

With the rise of international commerce and shipping, the Parker family became wealthy. George Sr. shifted his business from shipping to real estate, only to lose much of his fortune in the Panic of 1873 and its aftermath, then referred to by many as the Great Depression. Shortly thereafter, George Sr. became violently ill with kidney disease and died, in 1877. Sarah Parker was left to raise three boys, including ten-year-old George, largely on her own.

The three Parker boys looked like carbon copies of each other, with George as the smallest imprint: pale skin, brown hair with a slight wave on top, stern eyes, unimposing nose, and thin lips often pursed in a polite, almost starchy manner. Puberty made George leaner, with a longer neck and a slightly more upturned nose, but the soft features of his boyhood refused to vanish even as adulthood beckoned. His earnest appearance belied a cutthroat streak, though, perhaps born of necessity, given his status as the youngest sibling.

Despite his growing up among people of the sea, shipping didn't appeal to George. He wanted to become a newspaper reporter or a purveyor of board games. Games had the same ability to reach audiences as newspapers did, maybe even more, he thought. Newspapers provided instant gratification, but board games provided community and intimacy. People played them for hours and formed fond associations with them whereas newspapers were eventually discarded and inherently replaceable. Board games were intimate keepsakes.

●

IN CONTRAST TO the games from the Far East, most American board games of the 1800s were designed to teach moral or intellectual lessons—a quality that had helped them gain societal and parental approval in the straitlaced new country. Among the first widely selling board games in the United States were Mansion of Happiness, an "instructive moral and entertaining amusement" that had been around since the early 1800s; Anagrams, a tile-based word game developed by a Salem schoolteacher in the 1850s; and Authors, a card game depicting famous nineteenth-century authors like Louisa May Alcott, Charles Dickens, and Nathaniel Hawthorne, devised by a teacher whose students had helped with the design.

George Parker found all that teaching boring.

He and his friends wanted to play something different, something more exotic, something that was perhaps even a bit rebellious, the younger generation pushing up against the older one. "They felt that they had enough preaching in church and instruction in school," a Parker Brothers corporate history later recounted. Even as a sixteen-year-old, George felt that there was a flaw in the thinking of most American game inventors. They thought more about education than they thought about entertainment, and they didn't seem to realize that the country was changing. Thanks in part to technological advances, adults had more leisure time, and fewer children were working than ever before. Everyone had more time to play games, and when they did, they wanted to have fun.

The young Parker also had an avid interest in business—as did many Americans of his time. The U.S. economy was booming and bold, new capitalists were making fortunes overnight. Giant mergers—in steel, railroads, manufacturing—had become more common, and a new generation of power brokers was joining the top echelons of society. Quaker Joseph Wharton had established his Wharton School at the University of Pennsylvania in 1881, and other elite, academic business institutions were emerging. In addition, the power of promotion was beginning to be recognized. When devising his light bulb, Thomas Edison built on the work of several inventors before him. Nonetheless, through promotional efforts and creating an integrated system for his lights, Edison had established himself as the face of the invention, a legacy that endures today.

It was against this backdrop that sixteen-year-old George and his friends discovered and modified a card game revolving around simulated financial transactions, eventually renaming it Banking. George added a "borrowing" rule to the game, and it was this crucial change, according to Parker lore, that would hook fans. Players could now borrow money and try to repay the loan at a 10 percent interest rate, thereby vicariously living the real-life highs of investors dancing the tightrope between risk and reward. The game reflected a national pattern: Despite being only a century old, the American financial system had already experienced several booms and busts.

By adding the element of speculation to Banking—making it oddly reminiscent of gambling and all but allowing the practice of usury—George had made the game a lot more fun. If one couldn't be the richest man in Salem, or even the most powerful boy among one's brothers, one could at least beat them at Banking. In its universe, it was possible to become rich by crushing your siblings and friends. In fact, it was sometimes necessary to do so.

At first George played the game only among his cohorts. But then one day, a friend suggested that he turn the game into a real-life experiment in entrepreneurship. Since the boys enjoyed playing the game so much, his friend reasoned, there was a good chance that it could be marketed and sold to others for a profit.

George listened. He was only sixteen years old and still in high school, but with his father dead, his mother was relying on him and his two brothers to be self-sufficient. Should his fervor for Banking prove to be contagious and he was able to be the one selling the games he stood to profit significantly. That summer, George, his two brothers, Edward and Charles, and their friends played the game over and over, trying to perfect it.

In developing Banking, George tapped into a collective ambition, which in its best light resembled driven entrepreneurship; in its worst, downright greed. The game was about the desire to get rich quick, but also about people being able to live out a fantasy. If people liked to play rich, they might also like to play detective, world traveler, or star author, he reasoned.

George submitted Banking to two Boston book publishers. Both turned him down. Undeterred, he used fifty dollars he had earned selling fruit grown on his family's land to publish the game himself. Five hundred copies of Banking hit the market just before Christmas of 1883.

Needing time to develop his small business, George asked for and was granted a three-week leave of absence from high school. He then traveled throughout New England selling his game, to clear a profit of one hundred dollars. Before graduating from high school, George published two more games, Baker's Dozen and Famous Men, the latter designed by one of his teachers.

In spite of his success with games, George was drawn to journalism. After high school, he worked as a junior reporter at a Boston newspaper and tried to juggle his reporting duties with his games business. His interest in games was little more than a hobby, he thought. He lacked an office, a printing press, and employees, and the future of the game industry was unclear. The newspaper industry, on the other hand, was flourishing.

But juggling the two businesses proved to be too much. George became ill with a severe case of bronchitis, and his doctor advised him to choose between the two careers, because his serious illness proved that he could not do both. George chose games.

•

MILTON BRADLEY, THE MAN who would later become George Parker's chief competitor, had gotten his start decades earlier. Born in Vienna, Maine, in 1836, into a family that had endured epic suffering since arriving in New England two centuries earlier, Bradley was already past his failing career as a printer and into game invention when George was born.

Bradley's early years had been marked by poverty. By the time he was ten years old, his family was broke, thanks to his father's botched investment in a process to turn potato crops into starch. Bradley started college, but due to lack of funds was forced to drop out and live in his parents' home, working as a draftsman and a lithographer.

A tall man with sharp shoulders, Bradley parted his hair to the right and kept it as smooth as his beard was scraggly. His sage face was cast in pale skin with deeply set eyes and a long nose.

In 1860, Bradley created his first game, the Checkered Game of Life, claiming it to be the first "game with a purpose"—one that "taught a lesson of success through integrity and right living." The game was derived in part from a body of ancient Asian games, and its goal was a "Happy Old Age" . . . of fifty. Perhaps reflecting the dark times from which it had been created, the board had an Intemperance space that led to Poverty, a Government Contract space that led to Wealth, and a Gambling space that led to Ruin. A square labeled Suicide had an image of a man hanging from a tree, and other squares were labeled Perseverance, School, Ambition, Idleness, and Fat Office. Since purists still associated dice with gambling, the Checkered Game of Life used a spinner to determine how many spaces a player moved on his or her turn.

In 1860, Parker Brothers rival Milton Bradley created his first game, the Checkered Game of Life, claiming it to be the first "game with a purpose"—one that "taught a lesson of success through integrity and right living." (The Strong)

Bradley's game was a success, selling more than forty thousand copies in its first year, an astronomical feat at the time that proved there could be a mass market for board games. He was among the first to realize that it wasn't enough to make an entertaining product—one also had to market it, as disposable middle-class income was slim to nonexistent.

But Bradley was much more focused on education than the teenage George Parker would be. One day in the late 1860s, his fortune in board games already made, he attended a lecture on the "kindergarten movement," which had begun in Germany based on the teachings of Friedrich Fröbel. After the lecture, Bradley became one of its key advocates in the United States, and he is credited with publishing one of the country's first books on kindergarten. And while that contribution may have been a more profound one in the long-term for the United States, his name would become far more intertwined with his games legacy.

•

GEORGE PARKER understood that it wasn't enough to peddle Banking and a handful of other games if he wanted to build a lasting business. Buyers and players demanded variety—and rivals such as Milton Bradley were consistently producing new titles. He needed to expand his inventory with new and exciting games not just to grow his company but to survive.

In 1885, the first George S. Parker Company catalog was published, featuring several other games along with George's originals. In 1886, George published the Dickens Game, "a new social entertainment" with characters from the famous author's novels. Around that same time, in an attempt to appear more mature, George began wearing an elegant tailored suit every day—a habit that he was to continue for the rest of his life.

Next, George bought up the rights to other games from local game publishers and rebranded them as Parker titles. This allowed him to promote himself as a prolific game inventor without having to go through the time-consuming process of researching what the public wanted, inventing and testing new games, and finding out how much people would be willing to pay for them. Unlike the authors of books or composers of music, the creators of the board games were generally not mentioned in the games' promotion or even acknowledged at all. In a testament to the rapid growth of George's company, he was even able to buy out the company that owned the rights to the popular Mansion of Happiness as a Parker game, the upstart buying out its predecessor. He was still in his twenties.

By the late 1800s, George had amassed a catalog of more than 125 items, the bulk of which came from outside firms. His shift away from education-focused, morally charged board games was all but complete. One Parker title, the Strange Game of Forbidden Fruit, promised players "no instruction but quantities of fun." A rapturous public bought and played the Parker games. Ever more affordable and widely available, games had tapped a collective desire.

George opened up a small storefront in Salem from which to sell his wares. Original Parker games filled only some of the shelves, and games acquired from other companies filled up the rest. Also in the store were children's toys, which at that time were reflections of daily adult life— miniature farm plows, rakes and mowers, toy coal carts equipped with mules and drivers, and small steamships and locomotives.

The demands of the company grew until George could no longer handle its operations by himself. He enlisted the help of his older brother Charles, who joined the company in 1888. Previously, Charles had worked as a partner in a coal and oil firm, where he had demonstrated his prowess in finance and management. With his long, somber face, Charles had a reputation for being more organized than his younger brother, as well as savvier about managing money and people. With the addition of Charles, the George S. Parker Company became Parker Brothers Inc.

Partially as a result of the efforts of the two brothers, shoppers found an abundance of games to choose from. In the five years since introducing Banking, the company sold Game of War, Innocence Abroad, Crossing the Ocean, and the Railroad Game, among others. Through the Parker games, players could act as characters in the political, cultural, and social arenas that they read about in the newspapers or heard about through word of mouth. A player could be a soldier, sailor, railroad magnate, financier—or whoever else he or she pleased.

•

A COMMON PROBLEM in this era was the stealing of ideas. "Very often I hit on a good thing," an unnamed toy and game manufacturer told the *New York Times* in 1895. "And a good thing is worth a good deal of money. The other manufacturers are on the lookout for something that will pay well, and we keep our designs under cover as long as possible. Anything new, if good, will be copied quickly."

Concerns also existed over whether the games craze was only a fad—or a new fixture in the American landscape. All signs seemed to be pointing toward the latter scenario. "We may divide the whole struggle of the human race into two chapters," James Garfield said, before being elected president. "First, the fight to get leisure; and then the second fight of civilization—what shall we do with our leisure when we get it." Activists argued that playtime improved a child's development and began constructing playgrounds in urban slums that allowed children to climb and swing under police supervision. Once considered slovenly and slothful in the face of hard work, play was now considered a sign of economic success and a personal right.

Game makers wanted to be perceived not just as businessmen but as innovators. In 1893, Milton Bradley and Parker Brothers won acclaim at the Chicago World's Fair for their "huge, well-arranged" exhibit of toy soldiers and games, displayed not far from what was then branded as the Edison lamp. Through George Parker and Milton Bradley, games had become an important part of the entertainment business.

In the late 1880s and early 1890s, a tiddlywinks craze swept across Europe. Played by popping circular disks into a pot, the game was a simple one that undoubtedly had ancient predecessors. It was resonating wildly among European children and adults alike, and George sought out the rights to its trademark in the United States. He wanted to ensure total control of the game in his market, and in the 1890s he got his way. More than a dozen different sets of tiddlywinks joined the Parker Brothers catalog, with the company reaping handsome profits.

The joy didn't last long. Parker Brothers' trademark on tiddlywinks was challenged when competing firms like Milton Bradley made their own flavors of the game. Tiddlywinks was eventually deemed to be in the public domain, meaning that other companies could market their own versions of it. Parker Brothers soon had competition, and its tiddly-winks profits dropped precipitously, as did interest in the game. It was a lesson to George, and one that highlighted a commonplace problem for game makers: their inability to grab hold of trends already popular in the public domain. It was extremely profitable to have exclusivity over the newest, hottest game, but it was difficult to obtain, maintain, and justify the sole control of a bestselling phenomenon.

Although he was consumed by business, George did find time to fall in love. He courted twenty-one-year-old Grace Mann, and in 1896 they married, to settle not far from where George had grown up. A year after their wedding, their first son, Bradstreet, was born. Three years later, their second son, Richard, was born, and in 1907, Grace gave birth to a daughter, Sally.

George's siblings also married and started families. Charles and his wife had two children who died as infants and a daughter, Mary, who survived. The family's oldest brother, Edward, and his wife had a son, Foster. Edward left his work as a newspaper editor to join the company in 1898, and now all three Parker brothers were engaged in the family game business full-time.

Parker Brothers had become one of America's premier toy and game companies, but many felt that George, when left to his own devices, was not the best of managers. George paid his critics little mind, though. With hundreds of game titles now published, he was just starting to build his empire of wood and cardboard.

•

As THE NINETEENTH century tipped into the twentieth, the assembly line of ladies painting Parker Brothers game sets and puzzles by hand had faded into the past. Lithography and other innovations in mass printing meant that the production of games became cheaper and simpler.

More games produced with lower labor costs meant higher profits for George and his extended family, who began to enjoy the high social status that came with their new wealth. Their company was now one of Salem's most significant and celebrated employers. Living in elegant homes tucked away on shaded streets, the Parker women wore only the most fashionable silk dresses of the time. They were elected to community boards, and their names appeared frequently in the Boston-area society columns.

The Parkers and their social set were precisely the sort of people who were interested in a new highbrow fad called Ping-Pong, a kind of miniature tennis, played on a table with small paddles and a petite celluloid ball. Ping-Pong had taken hold in Victorian England, and even though it was being played in the United States, Parker lore claimed that George Parker encountered it during a visit to London in 1902 and immediately saw its potential in the United States. While some in the United States were already playing the game, it was clear to George that whoever controlled ping-pong's exclusive trademark there as it grew in popularity stood to profit enormously. Later that same year, a Parker Brothers version of the game hit the U.S. market, along with advertisements featuring long-skirted, bun-wearing women pinging and ponging, the name supposedly coming from the noise made when playing. Parker Brothers also began to sponsor Ping-Pong tournaments, with players fighting to win the Parker Cup, in an effort to cement ties between the company and the Ping-Pong brand.

What started as buzz soon turned into an all-out phenomenon, complete with the publication of Ping-Pong poetry and Ping-Pong tournaments held among brokers on Wall Street. That women could play "almost if not quite as well as men" was "among the principal reasons of its popularity," the *Philadelphia Inquirer* proclaimed. Manufacturers of Ping-Pong sets couldn't always meet the demand and sometimes fell behind on their orders. A champion player asked Parker Brothers for permission to print the official Ping-Pong guidebook. It appeared that George Parker's strategy was working, at least initially.

Perhaps out of fear of having a repeat of the tiddlywinks situation, George pushed stories in the press to remind people that the term "Ping-Pong" was owned by Parker Brothers. But as some people began using the terms "Ping-Pong" and "table tennis" interchangeably, the distinction between the two terms became murky. The company's ability to sell the game exclusively was being threatened.

Much to George's dismay, the Table Tennis Association was formed, to compete directly with Parker Brothers' Ping-Pong Association. Because of Parker Brothers' claim to Ping-Pong's rights, no player could belong to both organizations, thus creating two national titles: one in table tennis and one in Ping-Pong. Eventually, in 1933, the United States Table Tennis Association was formed.

George lost exclusive rights to the game and was reminded yet again of how difficult it was to maintain the ownership of a concept. Technically speaking, Ping-Pong was a trademarked brand of table tennis equipment. However, table tennis was the name for the actual sport. It's hard to say just how much money Parker Brothers lost after control of the game slipped out of its grasp, meaning it now produced the game alongside a fleet of competitors. But over the course of the last century, whatever one chooses to call the pastime, it has become a classic in the West, a craze in Asia, and an Olympic sport. The loss of profits was surely maddening to George Parker and his brothers, and to their descendants.

•

PERSONAL LOSSES HIT the Parker family hard as well. In the fall of 1915, the eldest brother, Edward, the company's treasurer and executive for seventeen years, died at his home in Salem at age sixty. Charles and George were both aging too, and George began to think about the implications of passing the reins of the family business to a younger generation.

Edward, George, and Charles Parker, circa 1914. (Philip Orbanes)

George's oldest son, Bradstreet, was not interested in discovering the next Ping-Pong or tiddlywinks, or in being part of New England high society. Instead, he fled Harvard to try to become a pilot. When George heard about what his son had done, he traveled to bring Bradstreet home, calling him a "lost cause." Bradstreet fled again, this time taking a leave from Harvard to enlist in the navy. But he didn't make it to the battlefront of World War I. Bradstreet fell ill in the great 1918 flu pandemic as it swept through New England and died in the hospital with his parents at his side. He was twenty-one years old.

Devastated by the loss, George put the succession question aside for a while as the family grieved and the board game business continued to soar. Electric lighting was becoming common in American homes, meaning that games could now be played more safely and enjoyably, and for longer hours, than had been possible during the gas lamp era, a reinvention of the daily routines.

With Bradstreet's untimely death, Richard, George's middle child, became Parker Brothers' heir apparent. Unlike Bradstreet, Richard was an obedient son and a sterling student. He was exactly the kind of successor whom George could rely on to take the firm into a brave new decade with an economy that was promising to roar. Cars were on roads, the Standard Oil Trust had been broken up, World War I was over, and women were voting.

Richard had inherited his father's pale complexion and delicate features. His was a Northeast pedigree: He'd graduated president of his class at a top prep school and had been accepted into Harvard's class of 1922. At the university, he joined several organizations, including the *Lampoon*.

In the summer of 1921, Richard journeyed to Europe with his parents and sister, Sally—one of the family's many Atlantic voyages. When the rest of the Parker family sailed back to the United States, Richard stayed behind with some of his Harvard classmates to see more of Europe. He traveled with his friends to Strasbourg, France, and his friends proceeded on to Germany. But Richard had forgotten his passport. He decided to take a quick flight back to Paris to retrieve it and join his friends in Germany the next day.

With jovial spirits, on September 8, Richard and four others boarded an express airliner. But the plane crashed upon landing, killing Richard and everyone else on board. He was twenty-one years old, the same age as his brother Bradstreet when he died.

Halfway across the Atlantic, George received a telegram with the tragic news. In only three years, he and his wife had gone from having two sons to having none. As soon as George reached New York, he boarded a boat bound back to France to retrieve his son's body, making funeral arrangements from sea. Richard was buried with his Harvard classmates acting as pallbearers.

CHAPTER 5

NEW LIFE FOR THE LANDLORD'S GAME

"Every girl yearns for entertainment."
—LIZZIE MAGIE

LIZZIE MAGIE MOVED to Chicago in 1906, just two years after patenting the Landlord's Game—now becoming increasingly known as the "monopoly game." One of many young, professional women who were drawn to the vibrant city at the time, she lived in a flat at 307 Chicago Avenue in an era when the stinking stockyards and diseased meatpacking factories of the city were becoming nationally notorious. Thirteen years before, Chicago had hosted the glittering World's Fair, with its large Ferris wheel offering panoramic views of the city's growing skyline, increasingly lit by electricity. Cars would gradually replace horses on the town's wide promenades, and large smokestacks belched with productivity. In the decades after the Great Fire, Chicago's population had ballooned, fueled by an influx of immigrants eager to be a part of the metropolis that was challenging New York City's supremacy.

Finding it difficult to support herself on the ten dollars a week she was earning as a stenographer, Lizzie staged an audacious stunt that made national headlines. Purchasing an advertisement, she offered herself for sale as a "young woman American slave" to the highest bidder. The ad read:

> *Intelligent, educated, refined; true; honest, just, poetical, philosophical; broad-minded and big-souled, and womanly above all things. Brunette, large gray-green eyes, full passionate lips, splendid teeth, not beautiful, but very attractive, features full of character and strength, yet truly feminine; height 5 feet 3 inches; well proportioned, graceful.*

Lizzie also said that she had "rare and versatile dramatic ability; a born entertainer; strong bohemian characteristics, can appreciate a good story at the same time she is deeply and truly religious—not pious." She said that she didn't go to church, but obeyed the laws of God. She was a "crackerjack typewriter, but typewriting is hell." She didn't mention her age: forty.

The ad quickly became the subject of news stories and gossip columns in newspapers around the country. The goal of the stunt, Lizzie told reporters, was to make a statement about the dismal position of women.

"Money only has a relative value," Lizzie said. "Once $10 might have been opulence. I do not know, but $10 in a city like Chicago or New York can buy only the bare necessities of life. If we could be reduced to the character of a machine, having only to be oiled and kept in working order, $10 perhaps would be sufficient for the purpose. We are not machines. Girls have minds, desires, hopes and ambition. They see on every side women enjoying pretty clothing, comfortable homes, refined entertainment, and other luxuries. These they want also . . . But they cannot have them.

"In a short time, I hope a very short time, men and women will discover that they are poor because Carnegie and Rockefeller, maybe, have more than they know what to do with. My people believe that the only way to help working girls is to get rich and give something to the poor. That is just the way not to do it. Working girls want only what they produce. If they get that they will have all they need. They can have silk underwear then."

Lizzie described the salary that she earned for the work she performed as "slavery of one kind or another." She also said that men were blind to the plight of the victims that the capitalist system created.

Despite the fact that Lizzie was forty years old at the time that she took out the advertisement, she was described by one reporter as "the girl with the gray-green eyes" and by another as "the girl of a thousand moods." A *Washington Post* reporter wrote that she was "always strange and frank."

"I'm thankful that I was taught how to think and not what to think," Lizzie said. "I'm thankful that I've got good eyesight and better brainsight than most people have by a darn sight . . . I am thankful for what we have left of free speech."

Lizzie's mother, Mary, described her daughter as "a woman of high ideals. Some may think she is crazy, but she isn't. I really believe she published the notice in Chicago purely for self-advertising purposes . . . Elizabeth has always been what one might call eccentric. But she numbered her friends by the hundreds and they swear by her. I think she is a genius, but I can't say I fancy being the mother of a genius."

Many likened Lizzie to Mary MacLane, a writer who was openly bisexual and so the subject of never-ending gossip. A pop culture legend of her time, MacLane was both hailed and scorned for her provocative views on sexuality and politics. She published an autobiography, *The Story of Mary MacLane*, in 1902, when she was twenty-one years old, laying out in plain language the need for women to liberate themselves from the mores of the Victorian era. "I am not good," MacLane wrote in *I Await the Devil's Coming*. "I am not virtuous. I am not sympathetic. I am not generous. I am merely and above all a creature of intense passionate feeling. I feel—everything. It is my genius. It burns me like fire." Lizzie was among the many young women readers who were moved by MacLane's words. "People may think Mary McLane [*sic*] is crazy," Lizzie told her mother. "They will be saying the same thing about me some day."

Lizzie found herself besieged by a flood of responses. One man offered her $100,000. Another, a trip to Europe. A crank proposed paying her $150 dollars "to pose as a freak in a dime museum." She looked upon these offers with contempt and pity.

One of the most attractive offers came from an elderly couple living on a twelve-acre farm in Wisconsin. They offered to provide her with free room and board, noting that they had a piano and a good library. "If you come you may read and write and do whatever you feel like doing," the elderly man wrote. "You can say damn once in a while."

Lizzie had placed her ad in part because she was in search of a benefactor, a financial angel who could provide her with the time and means she needed to develop and promote several games she was working on. "I wish to be constructive," she said, "not a mere mechanical tool for transmitting a man's spoken thoughts to letter paper." She wanted an "opportunity to develop the best that is in me," and therefore found the offer from the elderly couple in Wisconsin to be the most meaningful of those she received. On their envelope she wrote: "the highest bid."

One of the most flattering responses came from none other than Upton Sinclair, who immediately understood the meaning of Lizzie's advertisement. He sent her a check for an unknown sum and invited her to meet him in New York, explaining that he might give her a writing assignment. Lizzie promptly traveled to the city and met Sinclair, finding him to be "one of the most fascinating men I ever knew."

Lizzie's "slave stunt" story endured, living on in the papers years after she took out her ad, and while she did not regret her action, she did feel that she had been greatly misunderstood. She felt dazed by the furor that her advertisement had unleashed.

One fall night, as she was going through some of the replies, she began to cry, tearing them into bits and scattering them over the floor. Some of the letters were incredibly angry, including one from a clergyman in New York who called her stunt "offensive and a disgrace against morality." Others were intensely personal, including a note from a married man asking for Lizzie's photograph. "I offered to sell myself to the highest bidder for the purpose of meeting some person who could place me where I belong in the ranks of the world's workers," she said to a reporter. "What had my appearance to do with that?"

"Most people missed the point in my advertisement for bids," she added. "They thought it a freak, but, on the other hand, a multitude understood and I may now have an opportunity to be heard."

If Lizzie's goal had been to gain an audience for her ideas, she succeeded. But the marriage offers did not appeal to her, and in the fall of 1906 she took a job as a newspaper reporter. Some members of her family in Washington, D.C., who "at one time rather scornfully criticized Elizabeth's action" were "now loud in their praise of her shrewdness," one paper reported.

Putting the mental anguish of her slave stunt behind her, Lizzie began working on a book. It was to "reveal the shadowy side of human nature," she told the *Washington Post* during a visit from Chicago with her brother in Bethesda, Maryland. "Picture the fickleness of mankind and portray the insincerity of the soul. From a psychological standpoint it will probably be unique," she said of her book.

Lizzie told the reporter that she lamented the widespread plagiarism of her day and the fact that her generation had no Shakespeare, Dumas, Dickens, or Goethe. "Why?" she said. "Because there is an obvious lack of originality." She described marriage as "a germ" and likened it to "a disease." "What is love? Nobody knows," she said. Marriage was not for her, she added, unless she could see her spouse only once every three days. She didn't want anyone to interfere with her ability to go off into her den and spend hours plodding through books as she pleased. "Personally, I love solitude, and were I married I could not enjoy this luxury."

A copy of Lizzie Magie's Landlord's Game, 1906. (Tom Forsyth)

Another image of Lizzie Magie's 1906 Landlord's Game. (Tom Forsyth)

Lizzie kept on the feminist warpath, sometimes delivering lectures in what the press at the time called "woman's graphic language." As her father had felt slavery to be the defining issue of his time, so Lizzie felt women's equality to be for her generation. More states were granting women the right to vote (including Illinois in 1913), but women were still bound by corsets and had virtually no voice in the political system.

In 1909, Lizzie authored a paper titled "A Graphic Description of Hell by One Who Is Actually in It." In the piece, she described the embarrassments and hardships she had gone through "because she is self-sustaining." What she experienced from the public at large, she wrote, was in sharp contrast to the reactions of the pro-suffrage Georgist community that usually surrounded her.

She went on, "It is hell to have a superior education and to have to work for and obey the command of ignorance.

"To have a sensitive and refined nature and have to be forever brushing up against pigs.

"To have an ear for fine music and have to be tortured by street organs.

"To know that you can do some things better than other people and never have an opportunity to prove it."

•

THE ECONOMIC GAME Company was continuing to publish the Landlord's Game, and its popularity was spreading—mostly to pockets of intellectuals along the eastern seaboard. Its reach had become multigenerational. Some children who had watched their parents play, or even joined in, were making their own copies of the game, perhaps unaware that it was being commercially published. The game was still being taught and played in Arden as well.

Lizzie invented a new game. Called Mock Trial, it was played with cards and its theme was justice. Humorous in tone, Mock Trial played off Lizzie's experience as an actress and a writer. Players took on various roles and engaged in charades. In 1910, Lizzie sent her new game idea off to Parker Brothers—now an acclaimed toy company—in the hopes that George Parker would publish it. To her great delight, he did.

Also in 1910, Lizzie ended decades of speculation about her sexual status as a fiery, feminist, single woman when, on October 27, in Chicago, she married Albert Phillips, who, at fifty-four years old, was ten years Lizzie's senior. The union was an unusual one—a woman in her forties embarking on a first marriage, and a man marrying an outspoken feminist who had publicly expressed her loathing of marriage as an institution.

A businessman who had been married before, Phillips was not immune to scandal. In 1889, he had been taken to court over a publication he oversaw called *Climax*. The publication was "devoted to the interests of a matrimonial bureau," included photos of curvaceous women with sultry faces and exposed arms and knees, and Phillips was charged with using the mails for "fraudulent purposes by means of misleading and bogus advertisements."

In 1913, Lizzie's profile as a game maker rose when a Scottish version of the Landlord's Game was published under the name Brer Fox and Rabbit. The game featured liberal British statesman David Lloyd George, a follower of Henry George and a fellow advocate for land tax reform, as its main character. The game's cover portrayed a forest scene, with a rabbit peeking out from behind a door on a tree labeled Land as a fox with a man's head looked on. The board had a more streamlined design than the Landlord's board, and its center was divided into two sections, the Public Treasury and the Bank. One corner of the board was a square split in two and labeled Chance and Poorhouse.

Essentially, the rules of Brer mimicked the rules of Landlord's. One difference was that in Brer, a player who became bankrupt could go to the nearest Natural Opportunity space, "where land is free, without payment of rent, and where he can earn wages to pay his debts." Then, on his next throw, the player received one hundred pounds in wages. If that one hundred pounds was enough to pay off his creditors, he could move on. If it wasn't enough, he had to remain on the spot until he collected enough funds. This rule meant that Brer had the potential to go on for a very long time.

•

LIZZIE'S UNUSUAL MARRIAGE was apparently a happy one, and her change in marital status did little to stifle her theatrical bug. She continued to perform monologues and enjoyed playing pranks on her husband and others. "Her realistic interpretation of boy characters is something that's something," the Boston Sunday Post noted years after one of her performances.

Nor did Lizzie's marital status hamper her quest to have her games published and her single tax message heard. But a few years later, the latter was facing a new and challenging barrier: a fear of communism. Common land ownership, one of the main tenants of Georgism, was being viewed as a form of collectivism and therefore un-American (even though the United Stats had allied with Russia in World War I). Yet Georgism was not socialism: Karl Marx himself had spoken out against Georgism, calling its founder "utterly backward" in what Marx described as George's attempt "to save capitalist domination and indeed to establish it afresh on an even wider basis than its present one." But as the Bolshevik Revolution touched off the 1919–1921 Red Scare in America, leading to the mass arrests of radicals of many stripes, the distinction between socialism and Georgism became muddled in the public's mind.

The single tax community had also lost the support of its main financial backer, Joseph Fels. In 1914, the soap magnate and supporter of Arden had passed away, and with the family's finances stretched thin, his widow had refashioned his foundation to be more focused on a Zionist mission. The single tax theory, which had electrified a generation of intellectuals, was starting to fade into extinction.

•

ON APRIL 28, 1923, Lizzie, now in her fifties and known professionally as E. M. Phillips, filed to update her Landlord's Game patent. She used the opportunity to revise some of the game's features.

Though the core of the game remained the same, Lizzie added Chicago-based spaces to the board, including Lake Shore Drive and the Loop. She also added small numbers on the outside perimeter, denoting separate property groupings, and included more references to the single tax culture. There was now a George Street, a Fels Avenue, and a Slambang trolley, the latter so named because George had been opposed to the trolley monopolies of his day.

At some point, Lizzie and Albert left Chicago to move to the Washington, D.C., area. Lizzie had left newspapers for work in menial secretarial jobs. She still had her spark and passion for the single tax theory, but from where she was sitting, no one appeared to be listening.

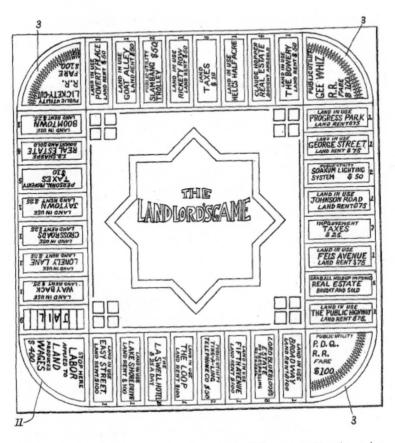

In 1924, Lizzie Magie, now married and credited as E. M. Phillips, renewed her claim to her Landlord's Game, originally conceived as a single tax teaching tool. (United States Patent and Trademark Office)

Little did she know, variations of the Landlord's Game were continuing to spread throughout the Northeast and had become popular at several universities. At least one member of Fiorello La Guardia's staff played the monopoly game in the early to mid-1920s, together with Ernest Angell, an attorney who later became the chairman of the board of the American Civil Liberties Union. Though now less directly tied to

Georgism, Lizzie's brainchild was still a darling among left-wingers of the day.

Thanks to Scott Nearing, the game was still being played at the University of Pennsylvania's Wharton School, and at Columbia University in New York City, Rexford Tugwell was teaching the game to his students.

Born in Sinclairville, New York, in 1891, the handsome Tugwell was an agricultural economist whose early work was influenced by progressives like Nearing and Upton Sinclair. Tugwell had begun his studies at Wharton under Nearing, but it was at Columbia that he completed his doctorate and developed his economic ideas, many of which centered on creating agricultural opportunities for the blighted rural areas of America after World War I. The U.S. government, Tugwell reasoned, played a crucial role in handling the issues of supply and demand for agricultural goods and therefore controlled—and could improve—the welfare of farm dwellers.

Tugwell spread the game at Columbia in the early to mid–1920s, just as Nearing had spread the game at Wharton around 1910. In 1932, Tugwell received an invitation to join president-elect Franklin Roosevelt's Brain Trust (a term coined for his circle of close advisers), and may have toted his Landlord's board with him, to just a few miles away from Lizzie's home.

Tugwell's monopoly game teachings lived on with his students and followers, among them George Mitchell, who had taught at Columbia under Tugwell and later became a significant figure in the antitrust movement. Mitchell introduced the game to his soon-to-be wife, Alice. The Mitchells' version of the game didn't have play money, and instead of tokens the players used miscellaneous pieces of jewelry to mark their places on the board. The couple played the game constantly while living in New York City and taught it to many friends, some visiting from out of town. Alice made more copies of the game for George's brothers and sisters and for his sister-in-law in Chapel Hill, North Carolina. All were drawn and painted by hand and were exactly alike. And so the game spread, with its rules tweaked here and there and its spaces customized.

The Mitchells then moved to Washington so that George could work with Tugwell on developing the New Deal. They took their monopoly game with them and played it at least two dozen times while in the capital.

Alice's handmade boards—like the boards made at Arden, the Wharton School, Columbia, and elsewhere—did not typically come with written rules. Whether Lizzie received any credit for these early copies of her game is not clear, but it seems unlikely.

•

NOW GOING BY her married name, Elizabeth M. Phillips, Lizzie took to the podium at the 1931 Henry George Congress in Baltimore. Over twenty years had passed since her slave stunt had brought her more attention than any of her games, stage roles, or poetry ever had. Women now had considerably more independence. They wore makeup, and their short hair hung loose. World War I had given some women a taste of the work force. They could finally vote.

The Georgists had not made much progress in advancing the single tax movement since the death of its charismatic leader in the late 1890s, but Lizzie and her fellow conference-goers were undeterred. In fact, they were energized. The stock market crash of 1929 had underscored the downside of capitalism. Lizzie and the other speakers at the conference offered up orations with titles such as "Unemployment, a Challenge to Democracy" and read aloud from Henry George's *Progress and Poverty*, his words seeming as fresh to them in 1931 as when they'd first heard them decades earlier. The convention chairman updated attendees on his efforts to change some of Maryland's tax policies, and an explanation of the Landlord's Game was offered to "those interested."

Nearly thirty years after Lizzie had created her game, she was still trying to breathe life into the late thinker's ideas. But both her role as the inventor of the game and the game's central Georgist message were about to be further obscured.

CHAPTER 6

FRAT BOYS AND QUAKERS CHANGE THE GAME

"I wasn't out to make a whole lot of money."
—BROOKE LERCH

THE LANDLORD'S GAME may have begun as a political and educational tool, but by the late 1920s it had become a sensation in the fraternity scene at the then-all-male Williams College, an elite institution of elegant brick and stone buildings nestled in the Berkshires, in New England. Daniel Layman, a member of Delta Kappa Epsilon, one of the oldest fraternities in the world, counting Theodore Roosevelt among its members, had stumbled across a homemade variant of the game in 1927 and, along with his friends Ferdinand and Louis Thun, introduced it to his fraternity brothers, who immediately became addicted.

The Thun brothers, who would become two of the game's greatest enthusiasts at Williams, had played a version of what they referred to as the "monopoly game" before, and since Layman was unsure of the rules and there were no written instructions, they taught him how to play. The trio then taught some twenty-five to fifty other young men, with Layman drawing handmade boards and passing them out among his friends—including Pete Daggett, a childhood friend from Indianapolis who would later introduce the game to the Midwest. The college players always referred to their new pastime as the "monopoly game"—they were unaware that the Landlord's Game existed.

In June 1929, Layman graduated from Williams. The following September, he entered Harvard Business School. But that October, the stock market crashed and Layman returned to his home in Indianapolis, never to finish his studies in Cambridge.

After being unemployed for about a year, Layman found a job at an advertising agency. But he hadn't forgotten the fascination that he and his fraternity brothers had had with the monopoly game, and in 1931 he began to produce his own version of it, hoping to sell it on a mass scale. The board he designed measured thirty inches square, and the property names he used varied somewhat from those printed on the boards he'd played on in college—he changed Grand Boulevard to La Salle Street, for example. His game also used poker chips, printed money, and miniature houses. The idea of using houses had been introduced to him by his college friends the Thuns, who had returned from a trip to the Ukraine with sets of little houses and churches. When they played, they made each church represent five houses and called it an "apartment," even though it had a steeple.

Dubbing his game Finance, Layman sold it with the help of a friend through a company called Electronic Laboratories Inc. The company's primary business was manufacturing batteries, but it also had some printing capabilities. Layman knew that he hadn't invented Finance, but he did claim to have written its rules. These he handed off to a printer in Indianapolis, which produced a batch of rule books. Layman tucked one into every set of the game he released.

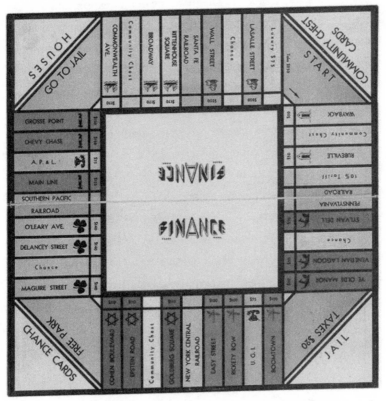

Years before Parker Brothers published Monopoly in 1935, Dan Layman had sold his game Finance to other game companies. Parker Brothers later acquired these rights. (Tom Forsyth)

Layman chose to name his game Finance largely because some attorney friends advised him against using the word "monopoly." That name was already in informal use for a game being played in Indiana, Pennsylvania, and Massachusetts, they said, and therefore could not be patented or marketed. It was also Layman's understanding at the time that all he needed to do to obtain a copyright for his game was to have it sold over the state line—an easy enough task.

The jargon could trip up even the savviest of inventors.

Copyrights are intended to safeguard the unique expressions of ideas and are registered at the U.S. Copyright Office, a department within the Library of Congress. They protect creators of works such as literature, films, and musicals and generally last the lifetime of an author plus seventy years. Patents, issued by the U.S. Patent and Trademark Office, grant inventors exclusive property rights to their ideas and products as well, but they are not issued for products already in use and last for a more limited period of time. Whereas trademarks—protecting words, logos, and taglines—are also registered at the U.S. Patent and Trademark Office and can last indefinitely, as long as they are in active use and are renewed every ten years.

The initial sales of Finance were strong, and in 1932, Layman's unemployed friend Brooke Lerch began to sell the games for him. "I wasn't out to make a whole lot of money," Lerch later said. "I was trying to do something during the Depression."

For half a year, Lerch peddled Finance in and around Reading, Pennsylvania. Word of mouth fueled sales, with potential buyers calling him directly. Lerch also tried to sell Finance to Wanamaker's in Philadelphia. One of the first department stores of its kind in the country, Wanamaker's boasted a grand central court, high opulent ceilings, and a decor more befitting a museum than a general store of the type that most Philadelphians were accustomed to. John Wanamaker was credited with having popularized the price tag—a Quaker concept that had originally taken hold in England. Both the Quakers and Wanamaker believed that haggling over prices with self-interested storekeepers did not lead to equal shopping opportunities, so fixed prices made everyone equal in the eyes of God. Other Wanamaker innovations included an in-store restaurant and the practice of giving customers refunds for returned purchases.

Lerch showed up for his meeting with the Wanamaker's buyer carrying a green faux-leather board painted with the names of properties, including the Reading Railroad (the "Royal Route to the Sea," linking Philadelphia and Atlantic City) and the Pennsylvania Railroad (linking New York and Atlantic City, and known for its buffet car). The game included Chance cards, which could change a player's fortune with a single draw; Property cards, which listed property costs and rents; and miniature houses.

To demonstrate Finance's viability, Lerch played the game with the Wanamaker's buyer. But the man didn't bite. The game took too long to play, he said. Lerch then took Finance to buyers at other stores, but they questioned the game's appeal to children. Only a few years later, in 1934 or 1935, and through the help of a good friend, Lerch would be able to place a few copies of Finance in a store's toy department.

Desperately needing money, Layman sold his interest in Finance to Lerch for two hundred dollars.

That was the only money I ever got out of it, he later said. "That was a small fortune to me." Tucking his Finance board away, he moved on. But not before teaching the game to some Quaker friends, who would modify it and change its course in the most unlikely way.

•

IN THE 1850S, a New Jersey physician named Jonathan Pitney envisioned a place for city dwellers to go to escape the dank and exhausting conditions of urban life—a health resort by the sea, a place reachable by rail. Shortly thereafter, Atlantic City was born, and its first few hundred visitors arrived. In 1870, the first section of the soon-to-be-famous Boardwalk—the first of its kind in the country—went up, and in 1875, the Atlantic City Gas and Water Company was formed, helping to turn Atlantic City into a playground for adults. At that time, water and electricity were not yet widespread public goods, and the technology seemed relatively novel and decadent. Hotels popped up like gleaming castles in the sand, along with more ordinary boardinghouses, which were the true backbone of the city, as they catered to the thousands of middle-class tourists who started pouring in, many arriving by rail from Philadelphia.

Among those who arrived—and then took up residence—in Atlantic City were a group of Quakers, who hoped to establish a healthy, fresh-air community, complete with modest accommodations and prayer lodges. Others who decided to settle in the new resort town came from New York City; Newark and Trenton, New Jersey; and other northeastern cities, with the wealthier among them building impress-ive-looking homes on States Avenue. African Americans from the South arrived and stayed as well, hoping to find better economic and social opportunities in the North. But Atlantic City was no bastion of civil rights: Blacks were welcome to work at the hotels and restaurants, but they could not sleep in the hotels' beds or eat at the restaurants' tables.

One of Atlantic City's most famous landmarks, the Steel Pier, went up at the turn of the century. An unrivaled entertainment venue located on the Boardwalk, it hosted opera, theater, movies, concerts headlined by the likes of John Philip Sousa, and, later, high-diving horses and boxing cats. The Boardwalk was a mecca for marketers, who knew that they could reach millions of middle-class urbanites from all over the

Northeast in one place. Ketchup maker Heinz sponsored a popular pier where tourists could get free pickled snacks. The Boardwalk was also home to a large rotating wheel designed by William Somers in 1892. A year later, George Ferris would design a similar wheel for the Chicago World's Fair, and it would be his name, not Somers's, that would be attached to the wheel for centuries to come.

In 1920, Prohibition began and Atlantic City exploded with booze and vice. Bootleggers ruled roads paved with pork barrel, as questionable officials proffered payouts and threats. One could acquire alcohol in Philadelphia or New York City, but typically it could be found only in hidden, out-of-the-way speakeasies—not out in the open like in Atlantic City. Booze, gambling, sex—it was all there and all easily accessible, on the Boardwalk and in the hotels. Law enforcement looked the other way and sometimes even partook.

Prohibition cleaved Atlantic City in two. On one side were the masters of vice and those who tolerated that vice because of the wealth pouring into the town. On the other side were the reformists, including the Quakers, who wanted Atlantic City to be a clean, middle-class getaway, not a sordid playground. They tried to avoid the clamor of the city's proudly flaunted debauchery, but that was hard to do—their own neighbors were often among the city's darker characters.

By the mid-1920s, Atlantic City had more than twelve hundred boardinghouses and hotels, accommodating nearly four hundred thousand guests. Ninety-nine trains came in and out of the city daily in the summer, sixty-five in the winter. The resort was also home to three airports, four newspapers, and twenty-one theaters. It was the city that had been built by corruption and excess, a collection of immigrants trying to live in prosperity along the shore, of tailcoats and torn shirts with little in between.

Atlantic City's rise was a reflection of America at the time, a country experiencing mass immigration that was both remaking society and fueling a desire among a growing class of nouveaux riches to say, "I've made it." Being seen on the Boardwalk, booking a room in a palatial hotel, or indulging in an illicit drink or two or three at one of the resort's high-class entertainment joints was a way of doing that.

Enoch "Nucky" Johnson, a bald, heavyset man with thick black glasses and checkerboard teeth, spearheaded an effort to construct the Atlantic City Convention Hall in order to bring in large events and year-round visitors. Opening in 1929, the hall began hosting the Miss Atlantic City Competition, greyhound races, and occasional indoor football games. Its facade was made of cut limestone adorned with an overload of stone sea horses, porpoises, shells, and crustaceans. Johnson himself held court in a penthouse atop the Ritz-Carlton, which offered panoramic views of the Boardwalk and the seemingly infinite waters beyond. Other, more occasional guests at the Ritz included Calvin Coolidge, Herbert Hoover, Al Capone, and Lucky Luciano. Johnson's reputation only ballooned with his work in gambling, prostitution, and bootlegging, all of which helped him build and maintain power over the Boardwalk.

Hotels were the undisputed kings of Atlantic City, with their owners engaged in a race to create the best and grandest accommodations ever seen. On Indiana Avenue reigned the magnificent Brighton Hotel, and on Park Place and the Boardwalk shone the Marlborough-Blenheim Hotel, the first "fireproof" building in town, its construction of reinforced concrete supervised by Thomas Edison and designed by Quaker William Price, the same man who had designed the modest cottages of utopian Arden.

Ironically, some of the city's most famous and elegant hotels were owned by simplicity-loving Quakers and single-taxers like Price. On

North Carolina Avenue was the Quaker-owned Chalfonte-Haddon Hall, which served no alcohol and was known for its elegant teas, available in posh dining rooms set with white porcelain and silver teapots. On Virginia Avenue was the Quaker-owned Morton Hotel, and nearby was the Quaker-owned Glaslyn Chatham. The St. Charles Hotel on St. Charles Place was a favorite venue among single-taxers for their regular meetings, thanks to its large porch, rocking chairs, and bay windows overlooking the sea.

One of the largest and most magnificent hotels in town was the Hotel Traymore, described by one newspaper reporter of the day as the "Taj Mahal of Atlantic City." The Traymore had also been designed by Price. Boasting fourteen stories, six hundred rooms, a palatial patio, and a ballroom that could accommodate four thousand, it claimed to be the first large hotel in the country to include a private bathroom in every guest unit. Its dining room offered six kinds of champagne, along with brandies and whiskeys, all served in glasses etched with frosted seashells—the same motif used in the hotel's decadent lobby. Guests flocked to its popular outdoor deck, and at night the building glowed like a ship on the water ready to set sail.

A bald man with a well-trimmed snow-white beard and wire-frame spectacles, Price had obtained his earliest architectural commissions through his connections to the Quaker church. A pioneer in the Arts and Crafts movement, he scorned elegance in his personal life—he felt more at home in Arden than he did in Atlantic City—but built hotels that rivaled the palaces of European royalty. He and other Quakers like him may have originally envisioned Atlantic City as an alcohol- and dance-free fresh-air resort, but as the profits associated with decadence soared, so too did their involvement in creating that lushness.

Among the many institutions funded by the wealthy Quaker Atlantic City hoteliers was the Atlantic City Friends School, where pretty Ruth

Hoskins, a recent college graduate, went to work as a teacher in 1929, just before the stock market crash. Hoskins brought with her a board game that she had learned in Indianapolis the winter before from her friends Pete and James Daggett. The Daggett brothers had called the game "monopoly," and they showed Hoskins how to make her own handmade board, complete with residential properties, railroads, and utilities. All the board's property names referenced midwestern and northeastern locales—among them Grosse Pointe (Michigan) and the Bowery (New York City). The board had Jail and Go to Jail spaces, and players received two hundred dollars every time they passed Go.

Ruth introduced the game to other Quakers in Atlantic City, including Cyril and Ruth Harvey, who also taught at the Atlantic City Friends School. The Harveys' six-year-old daughter, Dorothy Alice, better known as Dottie, was a student at the school, and the family lived not far from the famed Boardwalk. Many years later, Dottie would remember hearing her parents and their friends constantly playing the game and couldn't remember a time when talk of the game wasn't bandied about.

Ruth Harvey created copies of the game for her friends on a long sheet of oilcloth that covered the entire dining room table. Using a small paintbrush, she drew tick lines to separate the boards' properties. Sometimes it took her days to create a board—painting, waiting for the paint to dry, repainting, waiting. It was often sloppy work, especially since Dottie had a habit of plopping her hand down onto the middle of a board to see if it was dry. Later, Dottie referred to the memory of watching her mother make the board as "the most astounding image of my life."

Dottie often went with her mother to buy supplies for the game, such as paper for making play money, at a little store owned by a Jewish family on Atlantic Avenue. Sometimes, when they ran out of paper for making the Community Chest and Chance cards, they improvised by using Old Maid cards on which they typed instructions such as "Go by GO and take 200 dollars." Community chests started appearing before World War I, when businessmen formed volunteer-based organizations to pool donations from around their communities, perhaps inspiring the spaces on the board that sometimes offered players good fortune. At some point, a corner space on the board that had previously been a community park turned into Free Parking. Atlantic City hotels had started using that phrase in their marketing materials, as more and more travelers were now arriving by car rather than by rail.

Jesse Raiford, a real estate agent and a friend of the Harveys, assisted Ruth by making little wooden boxes to use as the game's houses. Jesse then experimented with using color sequences on the board, finally deciding to divide the properties into groups of three. Closely familiar with Atlantic City property values, he also affixed prices to the game board. Dottie was more interested in the tokens that players pulled out of their pockets to play the game—a tie clip, a penny, an earring.

Soon, the Harveys' card table seemed to be permanently set up for game nights, with dozens of players rotating in and out. Most were fellow Quakers, old college or boarding school friends, or unmarried women teachers. Often, the games lasted until late into the night, as the players bought properties that increased in price as they moved around the board and picked up Community Chest and Chance cards. The Harveys also loaned out their board to many of the hotels in town, including the Chalfonte-Haddon, the Marlborough-Blenheim, and the Traymore.

The streets on the board mirrored the Quaker social network. The Harveys themselves lived on Pennsylvania Avenue, while their friends

The monopoly game flourished among the Quakers of Atlantic City, who regularly hosted monopoly nights. (Becky Hoskins/Anspach archives)

the Joneses lived on Park Place, an expensive part of town, and the Copes lived on Virginia Avenue, at the Quaker-owned Morton Hotel. Ventnor Avenue was where the Harveys had lived when Dottie was younger, and the Boardwalk was where they often went for a stroll.

Better-off neighborhoods like Margate and Ventnor had high walls and neighborhood covenants that made clear that African American families were not welcome, even though they made up as much as a fifth of the city's overall population. Most blacks were relegated to working service jobs, but there was a thriving black business community and a network of entertainment venues on Kentucky Avenue—or "Ky. at the curb," as locals called it—within earshot of the segregated beaches along the Boardwalk. Kentucky Avenue had a movie theater and vibrant clubs, including Club Harlem, which often catered to white guests. On Illinois Avenue stood the Paradise Club, where the Count Basie Orchestra played, and at one end of Indiana Avenue was a black beach—until the owners of the nearby Claridge Hotel complained. Chinese restaurants and kosher eateries and shops thrived on Oriental Avenue and Pacific Avenue, the latter also home to the Post Office Building, where FBI agents would call witnesses in their attempt to take down Nucky Johnson.

The Harveys employed a black maid, Clara Watson, whom they adored. Clara lived in one of the poorer African American neighborhoods, on Baltic Avenue, right near Mediterranean Avenue, where an economy separate from that of the grand hotels existed. Poor white residents and prostitutes also lived nearby. The placement of these poorer properties on the monopoly board reflected the harsh reality of the city—a reality that was not acknowledged in the tourist brochures or perky postcards.

The Atlantic City streets often acted as fences, segmenting the town's population by race, religion, ethnicity, economic status, and, in some places, sexual preference. New York Avenue gained a reputation for male prostitution and was home to some of the earliest gay bars in the country. Prostitution of all kinds was prevalent in Atlantic City, with black and white men and women selling their wares to a wide swath of customers.

Much of the resort's round-the-clock activity came to a halt with the stock market crash in 1929. Some families, including the Harveys, began renting out spare rooms to impoverished friends and neighbors, while others who were down on their luck found refuge in steeply discounted surplus hotel rooms, a trend which made its way onto the boards of the Atlantic City monopoly game.

Four years later, in 1933, Prohibition was repealed, and it was hard to tell which was worse for the formerly high-flying town: the Depression or the return of legalized booze. Vacationers who used to come for the weekend now came only for a day or not at all. Most of the major hotels were running deficits, and ten of the fourteen local banks buckled. Atlantic City had lost its competitive edge, and the lucrative schemes set up by Nucky Johnson and his ilk were unraveling.

To make ends meet, Cyril Harvey began working as a physical education teacher by day and a life insurance salesman by night. But the Harveys' monopoly nights, usually held on the weekends, continued, with the players talking, laughing, hollering, and arguing as always as they played the game.

Sometimes, their arguments were about whether or not to allow the auctioning off of properties, a feature Lizzie Magie had included in her 1924 Landlord's Game patent. In the real world, most Quakers did not care for the noise associated with auctions or that they created the potential for sellers to lie to and mistreat consumers. Thus, many around the Harveys' table who held silence to be a tenant of their faith were against allowing auctioneering to be part of the game.

Most Quakers considered monopoly to be a game for adults, but sometimes children joined in, usually playing with their parents as a team. And when they did, auctioneering became even more unpopular. Auctions were complicated, and most children didn't have the skills or interest to conduct them.

Slowly, the auctioneering option of Lizzie Magie's game began to lose emphasis among the Atlantic City players. Just as a modified version of the Landlord's Game had spread in Arden years earlier, so now a modified version of the monopoly game spread among the Quakers.

Other changes to the game began developing as well. "We were in a hotel town," Cyril Harvey later said—so the players started adding hotels to the game. Next came a space devoted to an electric company and another space devoted to the trolley—the vehicle that shuttled the resort's pleasure seekers to and fro. "We wanted a real game," Cyril said. "A game that fit our situation, was the whole idea of it."

The Harveys and their friends didn't bother writing down the game's rules. They knew how to play; they didn't need written instructions. The roll of the dice was a matter of chance, but how a player reacted to that roll, along with his or her deal-making skills, determined who won the game. This very deal-making aspect of the game, however, as well as its use of still morally-suspect dice, made some players nervous about playing monopoly. One time when Ruth Harvey's mother came to visit, the Harveys hid their monopoly board. Another time, they lied about playing monopoly, saying that they had been playing another, more wholesome game.

•

IN SEPTEMBER 1932, the newlywed Philadelphians Ruth and Eugene Raiford came to pay a visit to Eugene's brother, Jesse Raiford, the Atlantic City realtor who had helped affix prices to Ruth Harvey's game board's properties. Eager to socialize and meet Jesse's friends, they were invited to the Harvey house to play a game of monopoly. Returning to Philadelphia shortly thereafter, they took a copy of the game with them. "Come to our house," Ruth Raiford began telling her in-laws and friends. "We're going to teach you how to play monopoly. We're having a monopoly party."

Among the Raifords' friends were Charles and Olive Todd. The two couples were neighbors at the Emlen Arms apartment complex, which was managed by Charles. An astute businessman, he was defying the odds by increasing the profitability of the complex year after year despite the Depression.

The Raifords and the Todds often played bridge together, and one night, tired of that, the Raifords taught the Todds the new real estate game that they had learned in Atlantic City. Being in real estate himself, Charles loved it.

One day soon after, while strolling down the streets of Philadelphia, Charles Todd ran into Esther Jones, a childhood friend from West Grove, Pennsylvania. The two had gone to a Quaker school together, but had lost contact. Esther was now married to a man named Charles Darrow, and they lived only a couple of blocks away from the Todds. The two old friends made plans to dine together with their spouses.

At dinner, the couples conversed about their families, about how they had handled the boom and the bust, and about the neighborhood. As they cleared their plates, Charles Todd mentioned to the Darrows that the next time they got together, he and his wife would teach them how to play the monopoly game.

I've never even heard of it, Esther said.

They set a date.

CHAPTER 7

CHARLES DARROW'S SECRET

"How many men are there who fairly earn a million dollars?"
—HENRY GEORGE

ONE NIGHT, THE Darrows and the Todds sat around Charles Todd's monopoly board, enthusiastically rolling the dice, buying up properties, and moving their tokens around. For a few hours, the anxieties of the Great Depression were forgotten as the players immersed themselves in a make-believe world. The Todds were pleased that the Darrows liked the game so much—especially Esther, whom Charles Todd remembered from their school days as being hard to please.

The board they were playing on had small colored triangles distinguishing the different property groups, included all of the Atlantic City property names that the Raifords had imported from the Harveys, and featured Go, Free Parking, Community Chest, and Chance spaces, all derivatives of concepts that Lizzie Magie had sketched onto her board thirty years earlier.

However, when Todd had made his copy of the board, using the Raifords' board as his guide, he had inadvertently made a spelling error. Instead of writing "Marven Gardens," the name of the Atlantic City housing development in Margate and Ventnor, he had written "Marvin Gardens," substituting an "i" for an "e." That one-letter slip was to become one of the most repeated spelling errors in history.

The Darrows were so taken with the game that Charles Todd made them a monopoly set of their own and began teaching them some of the more advanced rules.

Over time, Darrow's questions about the game became more complicated, so the Todds invited the Raifords over to join them more often, as they knew the game better. They all played monopoly together many times, with the Darrows often hosting the game at their home. "Just the six of us," Ruth Raiford recalled later, adding that although the Todds had already taught the Darrows the game, "they wanted to be sure they were doing it right."

One day, despite all of Darrow's exposure to the game, he asked Charles Todd for a written copy of the rules. Todd was slightly perplexed, as he had never written up rules for monopoly. Nor did it appear that written rules existed elsewhere. Why do you want them? Todd asked Darrow. Darrow replied that he'd like to have them to help him teach others the game.

As a favor to his old school friend Esther, Todd did as Darrow had requested and wrote down the rules. He then asked the Raifords to review them for accuracy and had his secretary create several carbon copies. He gave two or three copies to the Darrows and a copy to the Raifords and kept the rest for himself.

In all likelihood, the Todds, like many friends of the Darrows, did not fully realize how difficult life had become for the Darrows at that time. Charles Darrow was unemployed and had no prospects. He had done some course work at the University of Pennsylvania and had served in the military during World War I, but he had no college degree. Little of the life that he was trying to establish for his family was working out, and he had to rely on Esther's income from working at a weaving studio to make ends meet. The couple had two sons—preschool-age William and an infant, Richard, called Dickie—and as much joy as the boys brought into their lives, they were also two more mouths to feed.

The son of a civil engineer, Charles had a round face and a big smile and wore wire-frame glasses. Born in Maryland but raised mostly in Pennsylvania, he had grown up as an only child and was at heart a working-class man. In contrast, Esther was a Pennsylvanian with fetching looks whose name had often been mentioned in the local newspaper's society columns. Her father had worked in the roofing business, her mother had tended to the children, and their household, like many of the time, had employed an Irish chambermaid. Some members of Esther's family were Quakers, which is what had led her to attend a Friends school.

Charles and Esther had thought they were on track to repeat the successes of their parents. The two had a home in Germantown, a neighborhood in northwest Philadelphia lined with colonial buildings and comforting foliage. But then came the Depression. A salesman in a country that was no longer buying, Charles lost his job.

•

IN JANUARY 1932, Philadelphia's mayor proclaimed, "There is no starvation in Philadelphia"—a gross misstatement. Soup kitchen lines were stretching endlessly down city blocks, and sprawling shantytowns were taking over the parks. Some three hundred thousand Philadelphians were looking for work, and at times, as many as a third of the city's heads of household were spending their days aimlessly perched on porches or wandering the streets. Thousands of landlords had lost their properties, and repossessed houses were being resold by the sheriff's office at the rate of thirteen hundred per month.

"There is a good deal of 'squatting,'" Lorena Hickok, a chief investigator for the Federal Emergency Relief Administration, wrote in August 1933. "In smaller communities as well as in Philadelphia, in abandoned houses, so bad that no one who could raise a cent to pay rent would ever live in them. The condition of some of these places is frightful."

Some Philadelphians established a Community Chest campaign to raise money for the needy, but the funds were soon depleted. Similar campaigns took place all across the country in the early 1930s, but as the Depression grew deeper, even the wealthiest donors lost their ability to be philanthropists. Private dollars could no longer be counted on to help the poor, and the birth of the modern American welfare system was under way, with policy wonks, local and federal leaders, and social workers debating the merits of handing out government aid to families like the Darrows who were down on their luck.

•

ONE DAY, THE Darrows' youngest son, Dickie, developed a fever, a sore throat, and a rash that gave his normally soft skin a sandpapery feel. The Darrows were very worried, but eventually Dickie's fever went away and he began to recover. His parents breathed a sigh of relief—until noticing that something was desperately wrong. Dickie wasn't playing with other children, and he was moving more slowly than he had before. Even the most basic child's play seemed beyond him.

They took him in for evaluation and received tragic news. Dickie had probably been a victim of scarlet fever. In the 1930s, the disease was poorly understood and was often left untreated, even though the fever could lead to long-term brain damage. Some doctors at the time marveled that many of those who were stricken had survived at all.

At that time, families with mentally disabled children, who were sometimes shunned in their communities, had few resources to help them. Teachers of the mentally impaired were few and far between, and life expectancies for the afflicted were low. Conditions in many institutions were akin to those in prisons, with patients locked to their beds, half starved, and sometimes made the subjects of primitive medical experimentations.

The Darrows did hear of one caring facility in New Jersey that might be able to help their son. Called the Training School at Vineland, it was revolutionary for its time in its humane treatment of the mentally impaired. Situated on a leafy campus where most residents lived full-time, the school taught basic educational, vocational, and agricultural skills, while emphasizing self-sufficiency. Vineland had space for Dickie, but its cost was prohibitively high for the Darrows.

Charles and Esther wanted to keep Dickie at home and include him in their everyday lives, but the effort was proving to be too much for them. Once when the children were playing by a lake, Dickie began walking into deeper water, unaware that he could drown—another child grabbed him just in time. Little by little, the Darrows were beginning to face the painful fact that they weren't equipped to handle the rigorous demands of Dickie's impairments. Yet they didn't know where to turn.

In only a few short years, the quiet middle-class suburban life that the Darrows had previously enjoyed had been destroyed, and their future appeared far more daunting than they had ever imagined. Although the couple had each other and some good friends, Charles had lost a job in a business that showed no sign of coming back soon, Dickie was becoming more and more dangerous to himself and others, and the family was completely broke.

•

IT WAS DURING this dark period in their lives that Esther and Charles befriended Franklin and Blanche Alexander, who lived a few blocks away from them with their two young daughters. Alexander was a political cartoonist (working under the name F. O. Alexander) who had just taken a new job in Philadelphia. His career was flourishing—the public was seeking diversion now more than ever. Franklin and Charles got along immediately. Both men loved fishing and sharing stories and banter over an occasional drink. The two families quickly became friends.

Esther explained to Blanche that because of his illness, Dickie was suffering from permanent brain damage. The public schools would do little to accommodate him, and for the rest of his life, the Darrows were destined to navigate the complicated world that surrounded the mentally impaired. It was one more rooted in eugenics and sterilization than humane treatment.

One day Darrow asked Alexander if he would do him a favor. He had just played a new game with some friends, he said, and wanted to give marketing it a whirl. But before doing so, he needed to jazz up its design a bit. Could Alexander help him?

A prolific working artist, Alexander had studied at the prestigious School of the Art Institute of Chicago and Northwestern University. He was best known for his work on *Hairbreadth Hairy*, a popular series focused on a boy hero trying to rescue a girl from a recurring villain. A World War I veteran, he had also written *Finney of the Force* and *The Featherheads*. Later in his career, he would take an overt antiwar stance.

Sometimes with drinks in hand, sometimes by a card table, sometimes on the Alexanders' porch, and sometimes in the cartoonist's third-floor studio, Darrow and Alexander played the monopoly game, with Alexander slowly adding illustrations to the board. Darrow had made a round oilcloth copy of the board from the Todds' version, and the Darrows and the Alexanders played a few rounds on the newly illustrated board together.

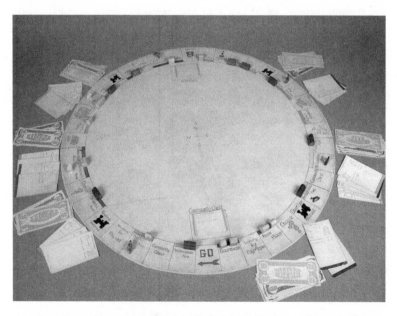

An early round Darrow monopoly board, which legend had it was designed to fit a dining room table. (The Strong)

Alexander didn't expect to make any money from his drawings. In fact, feeling that he was making only a trivial contribution to the game, he didn't even sign his name to his work, making it difficult to discern years later his contributions from those of another overlooked graphic designer.

Darrow began to market the monopoly game, complete with the written rules he had received from Charles Todd and the "Marvin Gardens" misspelling. With little money to finance his operation, he started on a small scale, feeling that even if he wasn't successful, he had nothing to lose.

While he was publishing the game on his own, Darrow did not register the word "monopoly" as a trademark on his game's written rules, and his boxes simply read MONOPOLY, without an R or TM after the word, meaning that he had neither registered a claim to the name nor was he in the process of trying to obtain one. He didn't immediately apply for a patent, either. But the board itself did have a Darrow copyright line printed on it—COPYRIGHT 1933 CHAS B. DARROW—perhaps to lay claim to the artwork and design. Decades later, however, it's unclear what specific claims Darrow did or did not make, because sometime after 1933, the critical, original documents related to his claim disappeared from the U.S. Copyright Office.

Wanamaker's, the Philadelphia-based department store that had rejected Finance years earlier, agreed to publish Darrow's monopoly game and included it in its holiday catalog.

It's unclear whether the early Mr. Monopoly was Alexander's creation, but the original character, which is stylized and drawn in thick black lines, bears a strong resemblance to his cartoon work. Inside the game were more illustrated figures, including a scolding police officer and a criminal sulking behind bars in the Jail space. The Go to Jail and railroad property cards were virtually identical to the cards found inside Monopoly games today, but the Chance and Community Chest cards were still devoid of illustration. Property cards were printed on assorted colors of paper, and paper money—including a five-hundred-dollar bill—was provided.

The new art and elegant packaging of Darrow's game elevated it to something approaching a work of art—a game people would want to bring into their homes, present to their friends, and play for hours. Early copies of the Landlord's Game had also had bright colors, elegance, and an ambitious design, but the Darrow monopoly board was delightfully charming and sleek. It also lacked many of the Landlord Game's direct references and iconography related to Henry George. Many of the symbols in Darrow's version of the game—the Chance question mark, railroads, collecting money when passing Go—could easily be read as positive takes on capitalism rather than as the critiques that Lizzie Magie had intended thirty years earlier, a fantasy interpretation of a financial system that had drawn such cynicism.

Darrow hired a Pennsylvania-based printer to accommodate the growing demand for the game. But like Daniel Layman and Lizzie Magie before him, he aspired to finding a mass publisher and submitted the monopoly board with its new artwork to Milton Bradley and Parker Brothers.

On May 31, 1934, a letter with elegant Milton Bradley letterhead arrived at the Darrow home at 40 Westview Street.

> *Dear Sir:*
> *After giving your directions of the game of MONOPOLY, which you sent our Mr. DeMeyer some time ago, our very careful review and consideration, we do not feel we would be interested in adding this item to our line.*

*We are returning your directions herewith, but thank you for
bringing the matter to our attention.*

*Very truly yours,
Manager Game Department*

Five months later, another letter arrived, this one from Parker Brothers.

Dear Mr. Darrow:
*Our New Games Committee has carefully considered the game
which you so kindly sent in to us for examination. While the
game no doubt contains considerable merit, we do not feel that it
is adaptable to our line.*

*The games we have planned and developed far in advance,
make a very attractive addition to our line, and are quite
sufficient under present conditions. Therefore, we are returning
your material to you, under separate cover.*

*We thank you sincerely for your kindness and courtesy in writing
to us, and hope that you will remember us when you think of games.*

*Very truly yours,
(Le Roy Howard)
PARKER BROTHERS (INC.)*

*P.S. Of course, you know, you are invited to send in any other
ideas for games that may occur to you. All games submitted will
be for 1935 consideration.*

The letters were cold and impersonal. But Darrow still believed his
monopoly game had commercial potential. He would continue to make,
sell, and market the sets—for Dickie's sake, if nothing else.

CHAPTER 8

PARKER BROTHERS, FROM DEPRESSION TO BOOM

"The cry was raised against the great corporations."
—FRANKLIN ROOSEVELT

ON OCTOBER 24, 1929 the Dow Jones Industrial Average fell abruptly, losing 11 percent of its value, ending a long rally. Investors panicked, and five days later the Dow closed down 12 percent and saw record-setting volume, with investors desperately trying to flee the markets. More than thirty billion dollars had been lost in a matter of days, and there was more to come, with the market plunging from a 1929 peak of 381.17 points to a close in 1932 of 41.22. The American and global economies, which had been flexing their muscles after emerging from World War I, were in free fall.

Parker Brothers continued to pay dividends to its investors in a feeble attempt to remain in their good graces. But the payments were draining the company of its cash cushion. It was a rude awakening for the Parker family, who had become accustomed to luxuries and their business's bottom line. Executives reasoned that a nation struggling to pay its bills and put food on the table was unlikely to spend money on frivolous pursuits. Furthermore, a new national culture—one focused outside the home—was developing, fueled in part by the public's recently acquired ability to collectively experience news and entertainment via radio broadcasts. Technological and economic disruption made the future of the board game industry unclear.

Across the state, Parker Brothers' longtime rival Milton Bradley was also in a precarious position. The company had never really recovered after the death of its namesake in 1911, and by 1932 the company would be severely curtailing production, with no plan in sight for reversing its fast downward course.

In the fall of 1931, Sally Parker, the youngest of George and Grace's three children, married Robert Barton in a celebration that included a New England dinner party and a barn dance. Barton came from a family of prominent Baltimore-area lawyers and often spoke of being a relative of the legendary Confederate general Stonewall Jackson. Despite the dismal economy, Barton earned an enviable living working in a lucrative law practice. He was a Harvard man who avoided drinking at industry events, sometimes, he told people, because he didn't want to chance leaking a company secret. Some employees jokingly called him "the judge" for his serious and somber nature.

In 1932, Parker Brothers' sales figures were disastrous: Revenues were half of what they had been prior to the Great Depression. In addition, the company's management structure was antiquated and ill equipped to handle the turbulence of the downturn. The firm that George Parker had founded as a teenager nearly fifty years before was on the brink of implosion.

The turmoil at Parker Brothers mirrored the unrest of national politics. After the stock market crash, debate raged over whether President Herbert Hoover was being too interventionist in his government's attempts to speed up the economy—or too passive. The ability of average Americans to accumulate and generate their own wealth was coming under fire, with proponents of the New Deal dubbing Wall Street executives "Princes of Property." While campaigning for office in 1932, Franklin Roosevelt gave a nod to the trust-busting era that Henry George had inspired.

"Clear-sighted men saw with fear the danger that opportunity would no longer be equal," Roosevelt told a San Francisco audience. "That the growing corporation, like the feudal baron of old, might threaten the economic freedom of individuals to earn a living. In that hour, our antitrust laws were born. The cry was raised against the great corporations."

In 1933, George Parker decided to step down. The realities of the Great Depression were painfully undeniable by then, and he felt that a newer, younger leader might better be able to handle the difficult economic climate. He asked his son-in-law to take the job. "I don't have any sons left," he told Robert Barton.

Barton had no experience with the game industry and was still new to the Parker brood, but he told his father-in-law that he was willing to accept his offer on one condition: He was to be granted complete control of the firm. With his options limited, Parker agreed, and remained on at the company as chairman—an office fixture known for his thick white mustache upturned at the ends, pointed beard, and elegant suits.

George Parker (seated) and his staff in the 1930s. His son-in-law, Robert Barton, second from the left, would take control of the company as it reeled during the Great Depression. (Philip Orbanes)

As soon as Barton stepped into Parker Brothers' small Salem office, he began assembling a new staff and shrugging off skeptics at the firm who viewed him as an outsider. He quickly became known for his meticulous eye and insistence on cleanliness. When he traveled to the company's distribution plants, he even inspected their restrooms. Barton's moves helped stem some of the company's hemorrhaging, but it was not enough. In his first year on the job, Parker Brothers' sales declined for the third year in a row, with the firm suffering a loss in excess of one hundred thousand dollars. Barton and his employees needed a plan, and they needed it fast.

•

IN PHILADELPHIA, FAR from Barton's office, Charles Darrow was successfully selling the game now officially being called Monopoly. He had even secured a spot in F.A.O. Schwarz's catalog, a notable achievement for a rube in the game business. It is unclear why the toy store picked up Darrow's game and not Daniel Layman's Finance, which bore a striking resemblance to Monopoly and was outselling it at a clip of ten to one.

Hearing about F.A.O. Schwarz's popular new game, Sally Barton excitedly told her husband and father about it. Parker Brothers had rejected Darrow's game earlier because they had found it too complicated, too wonky. And who would want to play a real estate game now, when housing was at the root of so much distress for many American families? But with his firm poised for collapse and nothing to lose, Barton decided to listen to his wife and buy Darrow's Monopoly.

Traveling from Boston to Manhattan, Barton summoned Darrow to the Parker Brothers showroom in the gray, triangular Flatiron Building. Quickly agreeing on the basic terms, the round-faced, jolly Philadelphian and the lean, meticulous executive drew up a contract that allowed Parker Brothers to buy Darrow's version of the game for a reported seven thousand dollars, plus residuals. The version included artwork by Darrow's friend Franklin Alexander and all of the details that the Quakers had added to the game, including the Atlantic City locations, the hotels, the color groupings of the properties, the Income Tax, 10% space, and the "Marvin Gardens" misspelling that had originated with the Todds. Barton arranged to purchase Darrow's remaining inventory, and Darrow headed back to Philadelphia, pleased with the proposed business arrangement. It was March 1935. Darrow had just missed the race riots uptown in Harlem, and the Dust Bowl would hit Oklahoma in just a few weeks.

One year later, the still influential George Parker announced that he had ordered his plant to stop producing Monopoly—as he was certain the game was heading into an "early slump." Almost immediately, however, he realized the folly of his decision and reversed his order. Monopoly, like Finance before it, was defying an industry notion that business-themed games did not sell—that they were archaic, technical, and often boring. As the Parker Brothers catalog proudly advertised, "MONOPOLY: THE GREAT FINANCIAL GAME . . . is sweeping the country because it appeals to every American's love of bargain and business dealing. Give a Monopoly party and guests want to play all night!"

An early white box edition of Darrow's Monopoly game. The blockbuster sales helped save Parker Brothers—and Darrow—from the brink of financial destruction.
(Philip Orbanes)

With the popular edition of Monopoly costing $2 and the deluxe edition costing a dollar more, the game was an undisputed smash. In its first year at Parker Brothers, it sold 278,000 units. In 1936, 1,751,000 units were sold, resulting in millions in profits. That same year, Parker Brothers also released a Stock Exchange expansion pack, priced at 50 cents, that allowed players to buy and sell stocks such as General Radio, American Motors, Motion Pictures, and United Airways in addition to real estate. An outside artist, Dan Fox, was hired by the firm and added onto Alexander's design work, and is believed by many to be the uncredited artist behind the Mr. Monopoly character.

Reports emerged that Parker Brothers was receiving so many telegraphed orders for Monopoly that its overwhelmed employees were filing them in laundry baskets. Overwhelmed, the company placed an order for three million dice with manufacturer Jesse Melvin Koppe of Providence, Rhode Island. No longer considered sinful, dice had become ubiquitous within the American game experience.

It's difficult to pinpoint exactly why, after being around in various versions since the early 1900s, Monopoly exploded in popularity in the 1930s. Was it because players wanted to live vicariously and handle large sums of money—something that so few could do in the 1930s? Was it because of the game's streamlined design? Or its comic strip appeal? Or was it merely because the game could be mass-produced and -marketed now, making it accessible to people in a way that hadn't been possible before? Barton and the team at Parker Brothers did not spend a lot of time musing about the whys. They were too busy keeping up with demand.

Edward Parker, the grandnephew of the founder, recalled years later, "During the Depression, people did not have enough money to go out to the shows . . . So they stayed home and played Monopoly. It also gave them a feeling of wealth. But what kept it going is the chance for individual gain. It appeals to the competitive nature of people. The player can always say to himself, 'I'm going to get the better of the other guy.' People also can play Monopoly without it being the end of the world. Sort of a release from the tensions of everyday life."

Some crazed players wrote to Parker Brothers to dispute the written rules that were included in each set. In one exchange, a player identifying himself as Iron Duke from Brooklyn, New York, wrote: "Do you idiots know how to play this game, or are you trying to disrupt homes and destroy families with your damn rules?"

From the beginning, though, much of the public disregarded Parker Brothers' written rules, which were similar to those used by the Quaker and Philadelphia players and had essentially been product tested for thirty years, since Lizzie Magie had patented her Landlord's Game. Instead, people created their own house rules—rules that often made the game long and exhausting and gave rise to its reputation for being boring. In reality, when played according to its written rules, the typical Monopoly game lasts less than ninety minutes.

To this day, many Monopoly players often discard the rule that states that if a player lands on a property and does not wish to buy it from the bank, the property goes to auction. Property auctions afford players the opportunity to bluff on prices, but they also lead to more direct combat between players, which may be why the rule is so often disregarded, especially by those playing with children.

Another common change to the Parker Brothers rules involves injecting more cash into the game—usually through the Free Parking space or by distributing more money to each player—which prolongs the game time. Many players also spurn the deal-making and trading aspects of the game, even though they heighten its action and lead to some of its most memorable moments.

Parker Brothers wasn't the only one benefiting from Monopoly's overnight popularity—the game had dramatically changed the fortunes of the Darrow family as well. Suddenly, they had more money than they knew what to do with. Charles Darrow told one reporter that he had made more than five thousand dollars in royalties his first year and that sales had been twenty-five times greater than expected during Monopoly's first few years. He was on track to become the rare board game millionaire, a real-life manifestation of a Monopoly player who got rich quick.

The Darrows' first priority was their son Dickie, whom they placed in Vineland, the progressive care facility in New Jersey. They also purchased a farm in nearby Bucks County, Pennsylvania, so that Dickie could come home for holidays and occasional weekend visits. Esther raised orchids in her new greenhouse, and she and Charles spent their days gardening and tending to the land. Charles also puttered in his office.

One journalist after another asked Charles Darrow how he had managed to invent Monopoly out of thin air—a seeming sleight of hand that had brought joy into so many households. "It's a freak," Darrow told the *Germantown Bulletin*, a Philadelphia paper. "Entirely unexpected and illogical."

•

BEFORE LONG, PARKER Brothers needed to manufacture tokens for the game en masse. It called on Dowst Manufacturing Company, a firm on Chicago's West Side that was already producing the toys that went inside Cracker Jack boxes. Dowst was a revolutionary company that had transformed some of the basic concepts of typesetting into die casting, using molds to fashion metal into new and different shapes. Several of the early Parker Brothers Monopoly tokens were already being

Charles Darrow, the long-credited inventor of Monopoly in a promotional shot. (Associated Press)

manufactured by the firm for other clients, some with a small loop for them to be worn as charms. The iron token had previously been used by Chicago-based Flat Iron laundry, and Cracker Jack consumers in the 1920s may have received a battleship as their prize.

Some of the early tokens—including the iron, the top hat, the thimble, the shoe, the cannon, and the battleship—were emblematic of their time. The electric iron was one of the first electronic appliances to make its way into homes, thereby liberating women from the dangerous and time-consuming chore of heating an iron in a stove fire. The top hat was a holdover symbol of Jazz Age elegance, the thimble was a vital tool for sewing, and the floppy and dilapidated shoe was a common sight during the Depression. The cannon and the battleship served as reminders of World War I and the role that America had played in the conflict.

The details of the game itself aside, after signing the contract with Darrow, Barton decided to bulletproof his claim on the game, lest Parker Brothers have another tiddlywinks or Ping-Pong situation on its hands. Barton needed to find out from Darrow precisely what the origin of Monopoly was, and he needed to have it in writing. In a letter with the signature Parker Brothers letterhead, Barton wrote to Darrow.

March 20, 1935
Charles B. Darrow, Esq.
40 Westview Street
Mt. Airy, Philadelphia, Pa.

Dear Mr. Darrow:
I trust that you had a more comfortable night on the train and that you made proper connections to arrive in Philadelphia this morning. It was a pleasure to have you with us yesterday and we certainly appreciate your courtesy in coming up here.

After thorough consideration this morning, we have concluded that we will take some of your present stock and box it up for a $3 edition . . . Under the circumstances we will make very little money out of doing this but at the same time we want

*to be entirely fair to you and so, for every game of yours that
we box up and sell as a $3 number, we expect to pay you an
additional five cents . . .*

*Please remember that we are particularly anxious to have you
write us a rather detailed history of the game beginning with
the time and place where you first received the idea and working
up to your final contract with us. The history is exceedingly
interesting and we may well want to use it for publicity purposes
in one or more of the trade journals. Also, if any patent questions
do come up, we will be fully prepared for them and will not have
to bother you. Please let us have this as soon as you can . . .*

*I believe I told you that we wired our men last night and by
now are undoubtedly selling "Monopoly" in all sections of the
country. I hope for the sake of us both that these sales will be
immediate and large.*

> *With kindest regards, I am*
> *Sincerely yours,*
> *Robert B. M. Barton*
> *President*

The next day, Darrow responded.

March 21, 1935
Mr. Robert B. M. Barton, President
Parker Brothers, Inc.
Salem, Mass.

Dear Mr. Barton,
The history of monopoly is really quite simple.
*Friends visiting at our house in the later part of 1931
mentioned a lecture course they had heard of in which the*

*professor gave his class scrip to invest and rated them on the
results of the imaginary investments. I think the college referred
to was Princeton University.*

*Being unemployed at the time, and badly needing anything
to occupy my time, I made by hand a very crude game for the sole
purpose of amusing myself.*

*Later friends called and we played this game, unnamed at
that time. One of them asked me to make a copy for him which
I did charging him for my time four dollars. Friends of his
wanted copies and so forth.*

*By mid summer of 1933 it was obvious that we should
cover a valuable product with a copyright so applied for this
on October 24th of that year. The publication upon which the
copyright was asked came out as of July 30th, though the
actual game had been in circulation some time. At least two
months prior to the date of the application for a copyright.*

So much for the outline of the history of monopoly.

*I can amplify the first paragraph to the extent that there was
a book written early in the century that took the same plot and
developed it. The story of a boy attending a commercial school in
which the boys were rated monthly by their progress or lack of it
in investments made on the stock exchange listings with scrip
money. I can not remember the name of either the author or the
book, but the story nevertheless has always stuck in my mind.*

*At the time my brain child was born, I was far more
thoroughly unemployed than I even like to imagine now. Not
only unemployed from a financial point of view but a morale
point of view. I simply had to have something to do. The theme of
this paragraph (number three) can be pathetic itf {sic} you choose
with an undernote of "Work and Win" or something like that.*

*During that period of time, when I was selling to friends
and friends of friends there was a tremendous thrill in every
sale. One game a day was our objective and when we reached it,*

there was rejoicing. Remember that I drew each figure on oil cloth with a drafting pen and a sketching pen in india ink. Colored each plot of ground with odds and ends of oil paint. Put in the lettering by hand, cut houses and hotels out of scraps of wood and painted them and then typed all of the paper work. It was a big eight hour job for four hours.

Later (prior to applying for a copyright) I had Patterson and White print on oilcloth the black lines and a conventionalized form of my original drawings. These blanks I would color in by hand. On this basis I could produce six games a day. The result was still crude but much better than past efforts.

Presently Wanamakers {sic} wrote to me saying that they were getting requests for monopoly. Then I came to the conclusion that some form of protection was in order. I could not afford a patent and I did not think a patent possible so it had to be a copyright. After putting in an application for the copyright and feeling some degree of security from theft of my idea, I called upon Mr. MacDonald and showed him monopoly. He by the way has been a splendid friend through all of my experiences with him. A brutal critic but a fine friend.

I think this gives you about what you want. If any point is obscure or if thereis {sic} anything I can add be sure to advise me.

Very truly yours,
Charles B. Darrow

It's impossible to know what was running through Darrow's mind as he wrote his letter. Perhaps the class scrip story is true, but to call the game "my brain child" and "my idea" when it had essentially existed in the public domain for thirty years was somewhere between a stretch of the facts and a lie.

Parker Brothers executives stewed over what to do. After Barton and Darrow had met and corresponded, a vice president at the firm wrote to Barton to say that after Parker Brothers had published Monopoly, another game publisher had told him "frankly and I think without prejudice that the original trading game came out in 1902." In addition, the vice president wrote, "lawyers had investigated the situation and found that Darrow had appropriated the discarded name MONOPOLY— and further, that Finance was on the market quite some time before MONOPOLY. Also [the game publisher] says he has been selling ten times as much Finance as MONOPOLY and that he has sold approximately two or three thousand of MONOPOLY this past year."

The Parker Brothers vice president told Barton that he should prepare a statement that the company could use when answering questions from others in the business. Barton then sent a letter to Darrow asking if he was willing to affix an affidavit to the history of the game. "We have been doing well with MONOPOLY," he wrote. "And we want to do everything that we can to protect its reputation and position in the trade. Please help us just as much as you can."

Creation stories are thought to make patents less vulnerable and were a routine part of the patent business at the time. But Parker Brothers executives also knew that Monopoly's creation story was good public relations. Little was more irresistible to a prospective customer than a compelling Horatio Alger backstory, especially during the Depression. When hearing a rags-to-riches tale, people didn't just hear the story for itself—they became emotionally connected to the storyteller and his or her product or invention. They also identified with the storyteller. If an everyman such as Darrow could become a millionaire overnight, so could they.

Darrow never submitted an affidavit.

Nevertheless, the company moved forward. It needed a patent for Monopoly in order to seal its hold on the game.

Darrow had obtained a copyright for the Monopoly board—but not for its written rules or the name "Monopoly"—on July 30, 1933. At that time, an inventor had only two years after claiming that he had published an idea to file for a patent for it. It mattered not when Darrow had first obtained the copyright, but when the game had first been published. So when Darrow claimed that was on July 30, 1933, he started a two-year clock that would stop on July 29, 1935—a deadline that Parker Brothers did not make. But the company opted to file for a patent anyway, perhaps banking on the likelihood that people wouldn't notice the earlier Darrow date. Saying nothing about the 1933 copyright, it dated the copyright of the game's written rules to 1935, a time gap that would prove critical a generation later in assessing the ownership of the megahit game. Then on August 31, 1935, Parker Brothers and Darrow filed for a patent for Monopoly.

Rumors floated that year at the annual Toy Fair in New York, as well as in everyday game industry chatter, that Finance, now published by Knapp Electric Inc. of Indianapolis, would be discontinued or consolidated with Monopoly. David Knapp, the company's president, told Barton of the rumors, but said that he was sure Barton's "business ethics are above the average." Barton replied that the rumors "have no foundation in anything that we have sold."

On December 31, 1935, Darrow, Barton, and Parker Brothers got their wish. Monopoly had its patent stamp, published in black and white on the board that had been developed by the Quakers from a board originally invented by Lizzie Magie. But only one name appeared on the board: C. B. Darrow.

Dec. 31, 1935.

C. B. DARROW

2,026,082

BOARD GAME APPARATUS

Filed Aug. 31, 1935

7 Sheets—Sheet 1

Fig.1.

Fig.2.

Fig.3.

Fig.4.

Fig.5.

Inventor:
Charles B. Darrow.

by Emery, Booth, Townsend, Medina and Buschner
Attys.

On December 31, 1935, Charles Darrow received his Monopoly patent, sparking controversy decades later as details surrounding Lizzie Magie's Landlord's Game and other early pre-Parker Brothers games surfaced. (United States Patent and Trademark Office)

It's still unclear how Parker Brothers received approval for the Monopoly patent, given the two Landlord's Game patents that had come before it. It's also unclear how the patent was issued in an astonishingly fast four months. Typically, the U.S. Patent Office rejected applications that had strong similarities to ones that were already on file. And even when an application was approved, it took many months or even years to process.

Parker Brothers did add some of its own flair to the game. Earlier players had relied on simple tokens made of wood or miscellaneous objects like buttons to represent them on the board. Parker Brothers used the Dowst metal tokens. For the most part, however, the game was only a new iteration of games that had come before it.

Despite now holding a patent for Monopoly, Parker Brothers would benefit from erasing all mentions of Darrow's July 1933 copyright date. It did not want to risk having its December 1935 patent challenged.

As part of their efforts, Barton and his team at Parker Brothers purchased Finance from Knapp Electric, acknowledging that a competitor in the industry was clearly aware that Monopoly had a predecessor. At the time, with thirty thousand copies sold, Finance was still outselling Monopoly significantly but for a large lump payment, Knapp also skirted having to sell the game amid rumors of its discontinuation (toxic in the toy and game industry) and having to look into the game's origins himself.

Next came Easy Money, published by rival game maker Milton Bradley. Easy Money was similar to Monopoly but, among other differences, had Give or Take cards instead of Chance or Community Chest. In a legal challenge to Milton Bradley, Parker Brothers claimed that Easy Money infringed on its Monopoly patent. That legal action had a seemingly strange result: Milton Bradley was allowed to continue to produce Easy Money through a royalty agreement with Parker Brothers.

Though at first blush the unusual agreement didn't make sense, it was actually beneficial to both companies. The deal allowed Milton Bradley to keep selling the game, while Parker Brothers no longer had to worry about Milton Bradley suing it for patent fraud. The royalties that Parker Brothers received from the Easy Money deal were probably quite small, but the company couldn't afford to sue or buy out a large rival like Milton Bradley.

Perhaps a bigger threat to Parker Brothers in its quest to gain sole control of Monopoly was Rudy Copeland, an outspoken man from Fort Worth, Texas, who in 1936 tried to market a version of the game that he called Inflation. Copeland's deep knowledge of the monopoly game showed that its popularity had reached far beyond the Northeast and Midwest and into Texas. "The NEW game" and "Interesting Thrilling Instructive," Copeland proclaimed of Inflation, priced at $1.50.

The object of Inflation, Copeland said, was "not only to afford amusement to the players but also to illustrate to them how proposed Share-the-Wealth Plans, Excessive Old Age Pension Plans, etc., will increase taxes and place a heavy burden on all citizens and, at the same time, make it possible for the shrewd manipulators to gain a dominating position in economical affairs of the country." Copeland's board featured a large circle printed on a square white board. In one corner was an Uncle Sam figure with dollar bills flying out of his hand. In another, a red banner read, "Share the Wealth." Also occupying spaces were Roosevelt's National Recovery Administration and an emblematic blue eagle, commonplace on posters and in papers at the time—Copeland's board was customized with a political flair.

"If a man has good luck and is a shrewd manager, he may beat the game of 'inflation,'" Copeland stated. "If he isn't, he will be no better off than theretofore and distribution of the wealth of the country will not have availed him anything." Instead of houses and hotels, the game included twenty cottages and ten apartments—the limited numbers designed to "encourage rapid improvement." The currency was called "boloney money."

In 1936, Texan Rudy Copeland challenged Parker Brothers over his right to produce Inflation.
(Tom Forsyth/Anspach archives)

Inflation came to the attention of Parker Brothers attorneys, and on June 1, 1936, they filed a complaint alleging patent infringement against Copeland in Texas's Northern District court. The lawyers charged "that Charles B. Darrow of Philadelphia, PA, on and prior to the date of Aug 1935 was the original, sole and first inventor of a certain board game apparatus not known or used by others in this country before his invention or discovery thereof." Barton needed to maintain the Parker Brothers stronghold on the game if he was to avoid what had happened with Ping-Pong and tiddlywinks earlier in the firm's history.

Parker Brothers sued Copeland first, but then Copeland countersued Parker Brothers, claiming that its copyright claims on the game were fraudulent because Monopoly had been widely played and in the public domain before Darrow claimed to have created it. Parker Brothers was not about to cede anything, however—by the end of 1936, it had sold 1.8 million copies of Monopoly and cleared over two million dollars in profits. A settlement was reached. Parker Brothers agreed to pay Copeland at least ten thousand dollars. Copeland agreed never to discuss the matter again.

Barton also visited Layman's old college friends the Thun brothers in Pennsylvania and asked them if they were going to make an issue of Parker Brothers selling Monopoly. Unaware of the Quakers' board, the Thuns told him no, but declined his request to buy their board. However, their friend Paul Sherk sold Barton his. Barton told him that the purchase was to stock the Parker Brothers archives, but it's more likely that it was part of his Monopoly acquisition plan.

When advertising Monopoly in its catalogs, Parker Brothers went out of its way to tell consumers about its patent. The advertisements stated that the game's "novel and original features, which are protected by United States and Foreign Patents and Copyrights, exist only in MONOPOLY and ensure the constant immense popularity of this extraordinary and unique game."

With Layman, Milton Bradley, Copeland, and the Thun brothers and Sherk taken care of, Barton still had one more major player standing between him and Parker Brothers' total control of the lucrative game: Lizzie Magie.

•

IN NOVEMBER 1935, George Parker, now almost seventy years old, traveled from Salem, Massachusetts, to Arlington, Virginia, on a rare business trip. His mission: to visit Lizzie and her husband, Albert.

Although George and Lizzie had been born in the same year, they could not have been more different. George was a wealthy, famous, and successful businessman about to embark on a happy retirement. Lizzie was an aging educator still clinging to Henry George's theories and still struggling to publish her short stories and games.

George told Lizzie that his company had come across a copy of her Landlord's Game, and while he didn't appreciate its political messages, he wanted to purchase her patent. As part of the deal, he promised to publish not only the Landlord's Game but also two more of Lizzie's games. She was elated. Finally her ideas about economics and politics were going to reach a mass audience—and under the banner of one of the most prestigious game companies in the world.

Lizzie and George signed a deal. She received five hundred dollars. And no residuals.

Two days after the ink had dried on the agreement, Lizzie sent a message to George.

FAREWELL TO MY BELOVED BRAIN-CHILD

Farewell, my beloved brain-child. I regretfully part with you, but I am giving you to another who will be able to do more for you than I have done. I shall do all I can to add to your success and fame, which will, in some measure, add to my own. I charge you do not swerve from your high purpose and ultimate mission. Remember, the world expects much from you. And remember, and be proud, that though others have fought for your possession I would not yield you to them utterly. It was not until the great game king, George S. Parker, did us the honor of seeking you out and offered you a broader opportunity than I could ever do that I would part with you, and I do so now only because I believe that it will be both to your interest and mine as well as to the credit of your new manager, who, I trust will not forget the hope with which he has inspired me. I hope from time to time, to do something for you myself, through Mr. Parker. And now good bye and good luck! My blessing goes with you, my beautiful brain-child.

Elizabeth Magie Phillips.
November 8, 1935.

On the back of the message, Lizzie scribbled, "This may amuse you, Mr. Parker, but it is something I keenly feel. E.M.P."

Lizzie had high expectations for the future of the game she had held so close, and she clearly revered Parker. The critical holiday season was near, and through the sale of the Landlord's Game, she might once again propel her name and ideals into the spotlight.

Four years after Parker Brothers published Monopoly, it published a version of Lizzie Magie's Landlord's Game. The game, like its inventor, Lizzie Magie, faded into obscurity. (The Strong)

When a prototype of the Parker Brothers version of the Landlord's Game arrived at Lizzie's home in Arlington, she was delighted. In a letter to Foster Parker, nephew of George and the company's treasurer, she wrote that there had been "a song in my heart" ever since the game had arrived. "Some day, I hope," she went on, "you will publish other games of mine, but I don't think any one of them will be as much trouble to you or as important to me as this one, and I'm sure I wouldn't make so much fuss over them."

The 1939 Landlord's Game board. (Tom Forsyth)

Much to Lizzie Magie's dismay, the other two games that she invented for Parker Brothers, King's Men and Bargain Day, received little publicity and faded into board game obscurity. Her newer, Parker Brothers version of Landlord's Game appeared to have, as well. And so did Lizzie Magie. One of her last jobs was at the U.S. Office of Education, where her colleagues knew her only as an elderly typist who talked about inventing games and who, as one of a handful of remaining followers of Henry George, taught some single tax classes out of her home. The once-popular single tax meeting and lecture circuit that had spanned New York City, Philadelphia, Atlantic City, and Washington, D.C., had all but faded out of existence.

by Elizabeth Magie Phillips
FAMOUS ORIGINATOR OF GAMES

As part of her deal with Parker Brothers, Lizzie Magie was briefly featured as an inventor of games, but over time her connection to Monopoly faded away.

After the Landlord's Game's disappointing return to the market, Lizzie once again wrote an article, titled "A Word to the Wise," for one of her beloved Georgist periodicals. Published in a 1940 issue of *Land and Freedom*, it read:

> *What is the value of our philosophy if we do not do our utmost to apply it? To simply know a thing is not enough. To merely speak or write of it occasionally among ourselves is not enough. We must do something about it on a large scale if we are to make headway. These are critical times, and drastic action is needed. To make any worthwhile impression on the multitude, we must go in droves into the sacred precincts of the men we are after. We must not only tell them, but show them just how and why and where our claims can be proven in some actual situation.*

•

THE CRAZE OVER Monopoly was going global. Buyers overseas wanted to strike up deals with Parker Brothers to publish their own local versions of the game. Victor Watson, head of the British game maker Waddingtons, called Robert Barton at his Salem office—reportedly the first-ever transatlantic phone call for both companies. Watson wanted to purchase the rights to sell a British version of Monopoly in the United Kingdom. His son Norman had become addicted to the game after playing it in late 1935, and Watson was convinced it had British appeal.

Soon thereafter, Barton granted Watson the rights, and the two drafted a deal that allowed Parker Brothers to expand its blockbuster hit into Europe while providing Waddingtons with the opportunity for making ample profits. Previously known mostly for card games,

Waddingtons substituted British locales—Piccadilly, Bond Street, Mayfair—for Atlantic City ones. "Wherever Monopoly was played," a Waddingtons historian noted, "the players found they could not leave it alone and it became an addiction." At the time, the stories about the game's non-Darrow origins were not relayed to Waddingtons. Victor Watson Jr., who later took over the company, said he believed the reason was that Barton "knew all along that Charles Darrow had not invented it."

Parker Brothers thought that the war was over. It had squashed the competition—Easy Money, Finance, Inflation, and the Landlord's Game—and was expanding internationally. Darrow's riches were secured, and Lizzie Magie was content in her belief that Henry George's ideas would soon gain broad public exposure. Someone's assumptions were terribly wrong.

CHAPTER 9

CONFLICT, INTRIGUE, REVENGE

"He had it handed to him on a silver platter, so to speak, and
was smart enough to see the possibilities in it."
—EUGENE RAIFORD

DANIEL LAYMAN, THE fraternity boy turned advertising man who had sold Finance for two hundred dollars, was flipping through the pages of *Time* magazine one day when he saw a story about Charles Darrow and how he had invented Monopoly. Knowing that the story wasn't true, Layman wrote a letter to the editor. Much to his surprise, *Time* published it in February 1936.

When asked later whether he had tried writing to Parker Brothers, Layman said that he didn't write to the company. "I had no complaint against Parker Brothers as such," he said. "But I did feel that I could if I wanted to, or anybody else could, manufacture a game and call it Monopoly and do it perfectly legally and sell all I wanted under that name, that Parker Brothers couldn't possibly stop me. That was my only feeling."

Darrow's sale of the game to Parker Brothers had rattled many of its early players. In Atlantic City, Ruth and Cyril Harvey, the Quakers who had modified the game, were perplexed. How could anyone own Monopoly? The game had been around for years, casually passing from one player to the next. Whenever anyone asked Cyril about what had transpired, he used the word "stealing" to describe what had happened.

Some angry players in the Friends community advised the Harveys to take Darrow and Parkers Brothers to court. But some of the Quakers felt that went against their beliefs. "Quakers aren't supposed to go to law," Cyril said. Ruth was of the same opinion. She felt that they hadn't invented the game either, so it wasn't theirs to lay claim to. Other Quaker players agreed, even as the fate of Monopoly continued to distress the community.

The Raifords, who had learned the game from the Harveys, were more emotional about losing credit for their adaptations to the game, and that difference of opinion came between the two couples. "They were more hotheaded than we were," Cyril later said. "See, we're Quakers and they weren't. Sometimes other people get hotheaded quicker."

One morning, Ruth told Cyril that she didn't think they should loan out their handmade game boards anymore, now that the commercial version of Monopoly was on the market. They could be doing something wicked, something morally dangerous, she said. Cyril agreed.

The couple also stopped playing the game. "I mean, how could we?" Cyril said. "We didn't feel safe to play on [our board]," he said, making a nod to the game's legal uncertainty and the taboo around chance games that still lingered in some Quaker circles. Now age eleven, their daughter Dottie was "thoroughly disgusted" with what she saw. "It seemed unfair that [no] one knew my mother had made the exact board being sold in stores," she said.

The Harveys moved away from Atlantic City in 1937, one of many families who left the seaside town as its glamour faded and jobs in the area evaporated. The family then moved around frequently, losing pieces of their monopoly games with each shift—small casualties of relocation. One of their boards ended up in the attic of Jesse Raiford and his wife Dorothea's daughter, Joanna, to be forgotten about for decades, collecting dust.

Meanwhile, the Darrow press continued. His face appeared in numerous magazines, and he even went on television, making cameos on the increasingly popular game shows that proliferated in the 1950s. He and Esther went on safari and continued raising orchids, while always saving some of their Monopoly earnings in case another Great Depression hit.

•

ONE TUESDAY NIGHT in 1964, Eugene Raiford turned his television to WRCV-TV to watch the evening news, announced by NBC's popular Vince Leonard. Suddenly, a familiar face appeared on the screen. It was Charles Darrow, the man the Todds had introduced to Eugene and his wife, Ruth, decades earlier, the man with whom he'd spent nights playing the monopoly game. Darrow told the interviewer that he was the inventor of Monopoly.

Eugene bolted upright, remembering all of the hours in the early 1930s that he and Ruth, the Todds, and the Darrows had spent rolling the dice and traversing the Atlantic City properties together. Why, he'd even explained many of the rules to Darrow.

Eugene had heard the Darrow invention story before, but now he decided to do something about it. Calling to Ruth, he asked her to type a letter for him and started to dictate. He wanted to set the record straight.

"In newspaper accounts in 1933 there were conflicting statements," he dictated as his wife began typing. Then he recounted how a Princeton economics professor had used the game as a teaching tool and how one of his students had taken the game to Indianapolis, where a young teacher had learned how to play it. He recalled how she'd then taken the game to Atlantic City, where Quaker players had modified it and added local property names, and how another player there, Jesse Raiford, had added prices to the properties and then taught it to Eugene, his brother, in the fall of 1932. "We still have the houses and hotels he made for us," Eugene stated. Finally, he described how he and his wife had gone on to teach the game to their friends the Todds, who in turn had taught it to the Darrows.

"It was not too long after that that Mr. Darrow 'invented' the game and later made a business arrangement with Parker Brothers," Eugene went on. "The newspaper accounts were correct in saying that he was an out-of-work, who thought a lot about what he could do to improve his financial situation, but were incorrect in saying he invented Monopoly. He had it handed to him on a silver platter, so to speak, and was smart enough to see the possibilities in it."

After Monopoly became a commercial sensation, Eugene said, those involved with the game were "naturally quite irritated but felt we could do nothing about the matter because we had not invented the game either, even though, we had a part in making the game what it is today."

Eugene didn't expect to gain anything by writing his letter. He just wanted to vent his feelings and point out an example of the fact "that everything in this world is not what it seems to be." He sent the letter off to the television station and sent a copy to his friend Charles Todd. Nothing much came of it.

Both sets of Raifords—Eugene and Ruth in Philadelphia and Jesse and Dorothea in Atlantic City—had held on to their homemade game boards and houses, and through the years, people asked them about Darrow's Monopoly story. "I thought your husband had something to do with that," they'd say to Dorothea. The younger generation of Raifords sometimes liked to brag that the Raifords had invented the game, but Jesse and Dorothea always set them straight, saying that although they had contributed to the game, they hadn't invented it and didn't know who had.

Years later, when Jesse and Dorothea tried to tell others about what had happened with their monopoly game, their story was usually met with skepticism. But what annoyed Dorothea the most was when people asked, "Why didn't your husband put it on the market?" "He only made it," she'd reply. "He had no authority, no right to put it on." Dorothea Raiford thought about writing to Parker Brothers herself but never did, and she never played on one of Parker Brothers' Monopoly sets.

•

CHARLES TODD DIDN'T hear from Charles Darrow after he handed him his written rules to the monopoly game. He found that strange—he'd thought they were becoming good friends. But Darrow seemed to be avoiding him. Then one day, Todd saw Darrow in a most unusual place—on a poster in a local bank advertising a demonstration of a great new business game called Monopoly, by Charles Darrow.

The sight of the poster infuriated Todd. He was angry not just with Darrow but also with himself. He felt that he had placed the game the Raifords had taught him in the wrong hands and that there was no way to repair the damage. "It upset me more to know I was the one who had started the whole lie machine," he later recalled.

Todd was so angry that he "destroyed everything related to the game" and tried to confront Darrow. But when either Charles or Esther Darrow saw Todd walking down the street, they crossed to the other side or ducked into a store. Todd felt that he couldn't sue Darrow over the game because he hadn't invented it himself—he had copied it from the Raifords. Todd couldn't understand how Darrow had received his patent.

One night, the Todds were listening to the radio when Darrow came on to tell his by-now-famous tale about the invention of Monopoly. "Darrow went into a great long story," Todd recalled, "weeping about how his family was starving to death and how he sat up night after night there in the basement working up this game." Todd wrote a letter of protest to the show's commentator, who wrote back to say that, as Todd recalled, he "did not select the people that go on his show and he had no record of anything, that they were selected for him and his job was to interview them."

Todd said he wrote to Parker Brothers as early as 1937 explaining how the game had been passed on from player to player, how the Todds had learned the game from the Raifords, and how they had then taught it to the Darrows. "We taught him all he knew," Todd continued. He also noted that "monopoly" was what the game had been called when he'd played it in 1931.

"Darrow didn't have anything to do with originating the game," Todd wrote. "He stole it."

His letter to Parker Brothers went unanswered.

•

MEANWHILE, BACK IN Virginia in the 1930s, Lizzie Magie had been shocked to see a version of her Landlord's Game, now called Monopoly, appear on the market. She was even more shocked when she saw the round, bespectacled face of Charles Darrow gracing advertisements as its inventor. This was not the deal she thought she had struck with George Parker. Darrow had not invented the board game, and she knew that Parker Brothers was well aware of that fact, as it had purchased her 1924 patent to the Landlord's Game.

In spite of the striking similarities between the two games, Lizzie's name was nowhere to be found on the Monopoly box. Her contribution hadn't been completely erased—her tiny patent number appeared on the game's early sets. But few players noticed the number, and those who did had no idea of its significance.

After her husband's death in 1937, Lizzie would still cling to her Georgist beliefs, serving as the headmistress of the Henry George School of Social Science, which she operated out of her home. She viewed the Landlord's Game as an extension of her teachings, and Parker Brothers' failure to acknowledge her was a slight not only to her but also to her idol Henry George. The vast majority of Monopoly players had no clue that the game was a protest *against* capitalism, not an endorsement of it.

"I conceived the game of *Landlord* to interest people in the single-tax plan of the great economist, Henry George," Lizzie said to a reporter. How could Parker Brothers allow Darrow to claim that he was the game's inventor?

The daughter of a newsman and a onetime news maker herself, Lizzie knew how to get revenge. In the winter of 1935–1936, she communicated with reporters at the Washington *Evening Star* and the *Washington Post*.

•

BOMBS WERE DROPPING all around the London offices of MI6, the British Secret Intelligence Service. It was March 26, 1941, and earlier that month, Hitler had ordered an expansion of the concentration camps at Auschwitz. Blocking out the explosions, an agent took to his type-writer and wrote to Waddingtons, the British game company that was producing England's version of Monopoly. On the other side of the war, Germans had realized the potency of using games as a teaching tool for the Hitler Youth, including Juden Raus (or "Jews Out") and Bombers over England, a game that rewarded players for dropping bombs on the English countryside.

In his letter, the agent recapped the conversation he'd had with Waddingtons' top executive, Victor Watson, earlier that day and stressed the need for secrecy. Waddingtons had just been enlisted in one of the Allies' most peculiar missions. A similar effort involving game companies was under way across the Atlantic.

During World War II, the Allies used a variety of objects, including games, to smuggle goods in to prisoners of war. Radios were hidden in cribbage boards, silk maps in decks of playing cards, and compasses in buttons or in the lining of clothing. Table tennis sets proved to be particularly useful, as maps could be easily folded up and tucked into the handles of wooden paddles. Cigarette cases, cigars, books, cotton handkerchiefs that changed color with the aid of certain liquids, a pencil that held a map, a cigarette holder–telescope, games of Snakes and Ladders, and reversible uniforms that allowed soldiers to disguise them-selves as German officers—all these came into play.

In America, military officers purchased Monopoly boards and steamed off their top layer to create a center cavity. Inside, they placed maps. The process was tricky—some boards steamed open more easily than others—and bypassed the direct involvement of Parker Brothers.

Other game companies participated in the war effort. Milton Bradley turned its game-making factories into ones that manufactured missiles, submachine guns, rifles, and joints used in aircraft landing gear. The company also continued to manufacture some games for soldiers—as their founder had done nearly a century earlier during the Civil War. Now under new management, Milton Bradley would become profitable in 1942 and remain successful for years.

The Geneva Conventions allowed POWs to receive some letters and goods, including games, to help them pass the time. But relief groups such as the Red Cross did not want to risk their integrity as aid organizations by participating in smuggling activities, so the Allies set up fictitious relief agencies, such as the British Local Ladies Comfort Society and the Lancashire Penny Fund. The addresses of blitzed buildings were sometimes used as well.

Waddingtons knew how to manufacture some of the specialized smuggled goods and how to modify the Monopoly boards in which they could be hidden.

Clank, clank, clank went the keys of the agent's typewriter.

Dear Mr. Watson,
Reference our conversation today. I am sending you, under separate cover, as many maps as I have in stock of the following: –

Norway and Sweden
Germany
Italy

I shall be glad if you will make me up games on the lines discussed today containing the maps as follows:-
One game must contain Norway, Sweden and Germany.

One game must contain N. France, Germany and frontiers.
One game must contain Italy.
I am also sending you a packet of small metal instruments.
I should be glad if in each game you could manage to secrete one
of these.
I want as varied an assortment containing these articles as
possible. You had then better send me 100/200 games on the
straight.
In those that are faked, you must give me some
distinguishing clue and also state what they contain.
In the above I also include, of course, packs of cards,
calendars, photographs and any other ideas you have.
I will send you in the next post some packs of cards for you to
pack in fancy boxes, etc. and insert in bridge sets.

The Germans were aware of what the Allies were up to and issued propaganda accordingly. They said that the English had "opened up a non-military form of gangster war" by violating the rules of the Hague Conventions. In order to safeguard the homeland, Germany would retaliate by opening up "death zones," and it warned that "escaping prisoners of war, entering such death zones, will certainly lose their lives."

Heartwarming as the tale of Monopoly saving the lives of soldiers may be, it's also unlikely that the games were used directly in aiding escapes. It would be virtually impossible to know the scope of the Allies' use of Monopoly boards or how many POWs were helped by the hidden maps and goods—if any at all. No sets explicitly used for this purpose have ever been found, a fact that gives some game historians pause. However, the mission was believed to have been entirely classified, and materials related to it were destroyed as World War II ended and the Cold War began, in case it became necessary to use such tactics again.

But the spread of this legend, as well as the United States' embrace of Monopoly after the war, spoke to the solidified place the game had in the American psyche. Monopoly was no longer just a popular pastime; it had become representative of what was good about America and a positive symbol of capitalism.

One theory has it that the secret service operatives smuggled maps to POWs so that they could escape in the event that the war ended in anarchy. Another holds that just the idea of plotting an escape helped prevent POWs from becoming submerged in the mental darkness that can plague wartime prisoners—giving them relief from the sense of hopelessness and stigma associated with being captured by the enemy. The board games with their smuggled compasses and maps also served as reminders to the prisoners that people on the outside were thinking of them and trying to get them out. Then, there were the actual games. "The importance of providing amusement for the forces in their leisure hours and in long periods of waiting and monotony in out of the way places," Prime Minister Winston Churchill wrote to the president of the Board of Trade, the man in his cabinet tasked with economic affairs, in the summer of 1943, "and for the sailors penned up in their ships for months together, cannot be overstated."

"It made an enormous difference to one's esprit to know that there were people in England trying to help one," John Powell Davies, a navy flier, said of the Monopoly mission. Davies was among those who spent time in Germany's Colditz Castle prison, a high-security facility for recaptured escapees and important prisoners.

Neither was the irony of the Get Out of Jail card lost on the prisoners, among them Lieutenant Colonel James Yule, who worked as an army intelligence officer. Captured in Norway and sent to a prison camp there, he escaped. Captured a second time and sent to Colditz, the handsome mustachioed solder aided in the escape of other prisoners. "Without *Monopoly*," he later joked, "there wouldn't be an England."

•

WITH OVER ONE million units sold, 1946 was the single best year for Monopoly sales since Parker Brothers had introduced it a decade earlier. The growth of many companies roared after World War II, but even in that climate, the game did spectacularly well, due at least in part to demographics. A greater number of families with more disposable income yielded more board game sales.

Analysts then, as now, marveled at a peculiar trend in board game sales: When the economy was good, sales grew, as expected. But when the economy went south—the Great Depression then, the 1970s recession and the 2008 global financial crisis in more recent years—sales were also good. The fact that games continue to sell even in depressed climates has been attributed to everything from the boredom of the unemployed to families' need for cheap entertainment to a psychological hunger for joy in times of despair. The truth may include some combination of all of those factors.

After the war, magazines and newspapers brimmed with advice for would-be inventors on how to become the next Charles Darrow and make a fortune in the game business. Reportedly, Parker Brothers at the time would not publish a game unless it thought that it could sell at least five thousand copies in its initial print order. A modestly successful game sold twenty-five thousand to fifty thousand copies.

As Parker Brothers ascended in the market, so Robert Barton ascended in the ranks of the Toy Manufacturers Association, a trade and lobbying group that had formed two decades earlier. By 1941, he was a vice president of the organization, and in 1952, in Midtown Manhattan, where the association held its annual meeting, he was elected president. With his perfectly combed brown hair, long narrow face, round glasses, and immaculately pressed suit, Barton posed earnestly for his portrait. By that time, he had overseen Parker Brothers for two decades, leading the company to record profits and acquiring one of the industry's most successful games. And U.S. Census data continued to play to Barton's advantage as families moved to the suburbs and Monopoly sets became as ubiquitous as gleaming refrigerators and blenders—another essential in the modern postwar home.

The Toy Manufacturers Association played a critical role in voicing the concerns of game companies and ensuring that government policy worked in their favor. It was a relatively sophisticated lobbying apparatus for the time, and its methods were to be imitated by myriad industries in the coming decades.

After World War II, the association's annual premiere showcase event, the Toy Fair, saw a boom in attendance. More than eight hundred exhibitors flocked to magnificent hotel showrooms in New York City to display more than one hundred thousand items, including mechanical cows, air-powered helicopters, and the largest construction sets ever offered. To meet the demand, toy manufacturers stepped up their production, expanding factory space or adding staff. In 1949, Foster Parker declared that the year had been the company's busiest to date and that there had been more interest than ever in its old standby, Monopoly.

"A game may become popular in two months," *Kiplinger's* wrote in October 1949. "But sometimes it takes two years as in the case of 'Monopoly.' This is often regarded as the outstanding game in modern history. Nobody knows how many sets of 'Monopoly' have been sold except Parker Brothers and they don't tell. An estimate of 4 million sets was once made, however, and the company didn't challenge it."

With the introduction of television, the art of board game sales shifted from invention and innovation to promotional efforts—something that Barton was early to understand. For the first time, toy and game companies were able to reach children directly via television sets rather than indirectly through their parents in newspapers or through toy distributors. Some research has indicated that the brand loyalties and biases developed in childhood get carried into adulthood and are hard to change—seeds planted in children for when they grow up and fill the toy chests of their own offspring. Parker Brothers enlisted some of Madison Avenue's top advertising firms to transition the business from one that relied on informal word of mouth and the casual wooing of toy distributors to one that had its products marketed on the radio and television alongside cigarettes from Philip Morris and cars from Pontiac.

By 1959, Parker Brothers and one of its advertising agencies were spending an entire year generating elaborate campaigns to blast at consumers during the Christmas season, when the bulk of games were sold. Roughly 80 percent of the firm's advertising budget was used from late October to late December, generating 60 percent of the year's sales. In addition to broad-themed, national campaigns, sometimes the firm did a pointed advertising campaign, teaming up with a local department store in a metropolitan market. Parker Brothers also found that it paid to spend some of its advertising budget in January and February, when the dreary weather kept children and families huddled indoors. Decade by decade, the art and science of board game success was based more and more on marketing and less and less on costly research and development, a quiet but critical shift.

The Parker men, dressed in suits and ties, gathered regularly around their ad agencies' tables, laden with boxes and game boards. Edward Parker, one of the founder's grandsons, oversaw the firm's advertising, but Robert Barton and Channing Bacall Jr., another Parker grandson, also participated in the meetings. The company instructed its regional salesmen to pump up its holiday line as early as June and routinely bought significant blocks of airtime and print advertising space months and months ahead of its competitors.

In the 1950s, the Parkers added a subtlety to their advertising campaigns that would have unintended consequences decades later in court. Game advertisements, they decided, should focus not only on the game itself but also on the company that had produced it. Versions of the phrase "Famous Parker Brothers Games" had been around since the firm's earliest days but now took center stage. The company was selling not just a game but clean, wholesome family fun—and it was the best at what it did. Without realizing it, Parker Brothers was entering into the early phases of a new advertising debate: trying to convince consumers to buy products because of the name of their producer.

Monopoly was still the company's unofficial flagship game, but Parker Brothers was also adding other titles to its catalog. In 1959, in time for the holiday season, it introduced Risk, a game of planetary conquest, on which it lavished a massive advertising budget. Risk had been invented two years earlier in France, where it was called La Conquête du Monde, by the French film director Albert Lamorisse, best known for his 1956 film *The Red Balloon*. Parker Brothers had heard about La Conquête through its affiliation with France's Miro Company. Twenty years after Parker Brothers had first introduced Monopoly, though, it was still king in the company's eyes—a new record of longevity for a modern game title.

CHAPTER 10

THE CASE FOR ANTI-MONOPOLY

"I start out with the idea that everyone is bad and it's just a matter of proving it."
—JOHN DROEGER

RALPH ANSPACH TRIED to push out of his mind all thoughts of the threatening letter from Parker Brothers demanding that he "cease and desist" using the name Anti-Monopoly. He continued to promote his game, which now cost $8.75. He wanted to keep expanding sales beyond the Bay Area and make the game a truly national, even international, phenomenon. By March 1974, a second production run of ten thousand units was in the works. By the end of the year, he would sell seventy-four thousand sets, and another two hundred thousand the year after.

Ralph usually declined to comment publicly about Anti-Monopoly's competition, but he did talk in a general way about Monopoly and games similar to it. "There's a family of games [sold] as a simulation of money making and business activities," he told the *St. Louis Post-Dispatch*. "If one really observes the message, it is not simply money making that is emphasized, but money making by monopoly. As an economist, I know that this is illegal. These games thus glorify illegality." He himself was hardly anticapitalist, he went on. "If anything, I'm pro-business. But I am for independent and competitive business . . . I also know, however, that there is more to life than making money."

As had been the case with Monopoly before it, Anti-Monopoly's origins became part of its marketing tale. "We started the corporation with $5,000 and two living rooms," Ralph said. "We took our game around to stores in the San Francisco area. Some of them took it on consignment, and some of them took a chance." Ralph said that since they put Anti-Monopoly on the market "it was an immediate success," and "the stores sold out of 2,000 games in 10 days."

Originally, Ralph had planned to take 5 percent of every sale and put it into an Anti-Monopoly foundation. He wasn't quite clear about what exactly the foundation was going to do. Perhaps offer an annual prize to a top real-life trustbuster. Or perhaps provide funds for small businessmen who were victims of monopolies. But now, with the specter of the Parker Brothers letter hanging over his head, Ralph feared that the small businessman who needed the money might be none other than himself.

Ralph hoped that the Parker Brothers lawyers would take a look at legal precedent and drop their threats against Anti-Monopoly. With that in mind, he asked his lawyer whether he should put a large disclaimer on his game boxes to distinguish them from Monopoly boxes. His lawyer advised against it and said that the disclaimer could be perceived in court as a tacit admission that there was, indeed, a confusing similarity between the two names. Ralph then offered to change his game's name to Anti-Monopolism or Anti-Monopoli, but Parker Brothers refused.

To combat the game giant on a more serious level, Ralph knew that he needed a lawyer who would be interested in going up against a corporate powerhouse and defending a counterculture board game—not an easy bill to fill. He and his wife figured that they could pay some legal fees, but with two kids and the costs of the new business pressing on Ralph's modest professor's salary, they did not want the bills to get too unwieldy.

Ralph reached for the phone book and began to make some calls. After a few misses, he reached Warren, Rubin, Brucker & Chickering, a small firm in Oakland that had a good reputation. Bob Chickering, who specialized in trademark law, and his litigator colleague, Herb Rubin, agreed to meet with Ralph. They listened to his story with great interest. There was something intriguing about the idea of challenging an iconic American brand.

They decided to take the case, with Rubin taking the lead. A jolly, heavyset man who kept candies on his desk, Rubin told Ralph that they would first try to work things out peaceably. That would save everyone a lot of time and money.

Rubin then brought in John Droeger to handle the antitrust portion of the case. Having an antitrust component meant that the team might be able to argue Ralph's case before a jury rather than a judge— something that would increase his chances of victory, his lawyers thought. Droeger had just won a big antitrust case against Dow Jones over advertising sales rates, and Rubin asked him to look into whether Parker Brothers had committed any antitrust violations against Anti-Monopoly. One mark of monopolization, Ralph's lawyers reminded him, was using litigation as a weapon to eliminate competition. Using litigation didn't necessarily mean that a company had violated antitrust laws, but the possibility did provide a different lens through which to view the threatening letter sent by the Parker Brothers attorney.

Rubin filed lawsuits often, so the idea of escalating tensions between a client and an opponent was nothing new for him. And as for Ralph, the reality of being ensnared in a legal battle with one of the world's largest conglomerates hadn't quite sunk in yet. Legal bills were not much of a concern for Parker Brothers and an even smaller concern for its behemoth parent company, General Mills. For the Anspachs, however, even modest legal bills risked crimping the household cash flow. Still, realizing that if they struck first, they could secure California as the venue for the case and thus save on travel expenses, Ralph and his team formally filed against Monopoly. The legal showdown between the rival board games had officially begun.

Soon thereafter, Parker Brothers asked Ralph for a sworn deposition. Assuring Ralph that all he had to do was stick to the truth, Rubin nonetheless warned him to watch out for tricky questions. The Parker Brothers lawyers might try to trap him into saying something that could be held against Anti-Monopoly. Ralph gulped, beginning to sense what he was up against.

•

THE LITIGATION TACTICS of Parker Brothers counsel Robert Daggett (no known relation to the early monopoly game players Pete and James Daggett) were fierce enough to earn him the nickname Bulldog. An accomplished, rotund man of average height who enjoyed a good drink, Daggett was a star at Brobeck, Phleger & Harrison, one of the largest and most powerful law firms in San Francisco and the nation.

On the day of the Anti-Monopoly deposition, Daggett was well prepared. He had joined forces with Ollie Howes, the lawyer who had written the threatening letter to Ralph. Despite Howes's aggressive correspondence, Ralph was surprised to find that in person, he had a mild demeanor. Also on the Parker Brothers team was Richard Berman, counsel for General Mills. A cloud of tension hung over everyone even before they entered the conference room. Only days earlier, Howes and Ralph's attorneys had butted heads in written correspondence and in phone calls.

Ralph found himself in Daggett's austere but imposing offices that felt so foreign compared to his own homespun headquarters. And the triumvirate of lawyers in their crisp pressed suits were intimidating. Ralph, hair a mess, was wearing his usual rumpled shirt.

He was determined to act as if he were perfectly at ease, but deep down, he was concerned, and not just about the deposition. That night, he had a flight to catch to Minnesota, where he was intending to meet with game distributors and Anti-Monopoly's new manufacturer. He had been planning to head straight to the airport after the deposition, but now he was wondering how long the deposition might take and if he might miss his flight.

In a large conference room, Ralph took a seat beside his pleasant and plump counsel, Herb Rubin. On the other side of the huge table sat the row of Parker Brothers attorneys. Ralph raised his hand and took an oath before a notary. Then he pulled out his secret weapon: a chopped liver and onion sandwich. Its stench invaded the air as he unwrapped it and began to chew. Pickles and a soda were also involved.

At twelve forty-five, the deposition began and Howes led the questioning. Nerves frayed, Ralph knew that one slip, one discrepancy, was all the Parker Brothers lawyers needed to destroy his whole case before it even began.

Ralph started to describe his twelve years working as an economics professor at San Francisco State. But within seconds, Howes stopped him to ask about his other employer: Anti-Monopoly.

Ralph told him how the game had begun. He explained about his wife Ruth's background in child psychology and how that had helped him to develop the testing of the game. He told of his plans to set up an Anti-Monopoly foundation and said that before creating the game, he had had no marketing experience in the game industry. He mentioned his posse of Anti-Monopoly assistants, pleased by the thought of their unconventional roots. "It's a young group," he concluded.

Then Howes asked Ralph about the Computer Industry Association. Ralph had purchased advertisements in one of its publications. The association also took game orders and wrote about Anti-Monopoly in its newsletter. "When they heard about this game," Ralph said, "they thought that this is just the kind of game that would be useful in awakening the American public to the evils of monopolism." This was the first of many left-wing political jabs that Daggett, Howes, and Berman would hear from Ralph that day.

The professor went on to state that early Anti-Monopoly sales had been strong and that he'd sold out his first production run in a matter of days. He'd been expecting to sell yet more games when he hit a snag in production. "Well, in some cases, we ran into, I don't know what the legal term is, interference, apparently by people from General Mills Fun Group," he elaborated.

The name of a game buyer in New York came up, and Ralph said that he had heard from him and others like him that Parker Brothers was threatening them, warning them about potential legal problems involving Anti-Monopoly.

"I recall in one conversation I asked [the game buyer] the same kind of questions you are asking me now," Ralph said, as he tried to find out more about why his game was encountering hiccups. "But he responded that he did not want to discuss it further because he was afraid of harassment and so on."

"Has he been approached by anyone at Parker Brothers?" Howes asked.

"I don't know," Ralph said. "But he indicated to me that he was afraid and he was afraid of giving names to other people."

"How did he indicate that he was afraid?"

"He was afraid," Ralph said, "because people had told him certain things in the industry and he was afraid that if his testimony to me were traced to his having passed on some of this information, that he could get in trouble with some of the people with whom he deals. You see, I am afraid, when an industry becomes monopolized, it is easy to get an atmosphere of this kind started."

The Parker Brothers attorneys were now about two hours into their grilling, and Ralph still had plenty of time to catch his flight to Minnesota. The pungent aroma of liver and onions still hung in the air.

At some point during the deposition, Berman, the trademark lawyer for General Mills, leaned back in his swivel chair, and Ralph caught sight of an airline ticket poking out of his pocket. It was the same, distinctive color as the ticket Ralph had and he knew that Berman had plenty of reason to be booked on the same flight to Minnesota, where his company was headquartered. The last thing Ralph wanted was to sit on the same plane as his rival's lawyer, and, more important, he didn't want the man to catch wind of his new games manufacturer, Mankato Corporation, one of the few game makers based in the Minneapolis area. Rubin had warned him not to reveal the manufacturer's name for fear that General Mills would pressure Mankato not to produce the game.

After a short break, Ralph nervously returned to his seat, unsure of what to do about his impending flight. He told Howes what he had thought of his threatening letter. It "reminded me of the demands of the rebellious students," Ralph said, making a nod to the political turmoil on campuses like Berkeley and San Francisco State. He added, "now that I meet you, I don't see how you could have written it, because, you know, you caused great anguish to my wife, for example, with that kind of a letter. That is a very, very threatening letter."

On and on the dance went, into a third and a fourth hour. There was another recess, during which Ralph ran to his car to grab a copy of his earlier version of Anti-Monopoly: Bust-the-Trust that Parker Brothers lawyers wanted to see. Ralph then told the attorneys that he thought Monopoly was "a fine game, except its values are a little bit off."

As the proceedings wore on, Ralph's rollicking tone began to irritate the Parker Brothers lawyers.

"I have noticed," Howes said as they were examining the Anti-Monopoly game board, "that you have smiled throughout this interrogation, which certainly isn't burdensome, but I wondered why you remarked"—he pointed to one of the spaces on the board—"that this one was amusing. Was it because it refers to the 'Tired of the Boardwalk Barons and Pudgy Felines of Pennsylvania Avenue'?"

The words were written on the space.

"Yes," Ralph said, chuckling. "I thought that was amusing."

"What do you understand by 'the Boardwalk barons'?"

"Boardwalk barons," Ralph said, "I understand, are, you know, in monopolistic times people who—"

"And 'Boardwalk' is a term used in Monopoly," Howes countered.

"Well, there's some association there. I think of it as, you know, a monopolistic people who develop land monopolies and gouge the consumer."

"What does the reference to 'Pennsylvania Avenue' conjure up in your mind?"

"Well, I thought of that for a while," Ralph said, referring to his

Anti-Monopoly board. "I think it's rather witty. I think they are talking about the fat cats who apparently seem to have been involved or at least are alleged to have been involved with our leaders, fat cats rather than—"

Howes cut him off. "And the 'Pennsylvania Avenue' reference in connection with a board game to you means Washington, D.C. and does not mean the Monopoly game board?"

"No, no. Washington D.C., Pennsylvania Avenue," Ralph said. "The White House."

This exchange boosted Ralph's confidence some, even as he was still trembling inside. He thought he was starting to get through to the Parker Brothers lawyers. But he didn't forget what Rubin had told him—one slipup and the entire case could be thrown into disarray.

Hour five. Hour six. Rolling into hour seven. The departure time of Ralph's potentially awkward flight with Richard Berman was inching closer and closer. But during a break, Ralph made a few phone calls and was able to reschedule his flight to one leaving later that evening. Shocked at his success, Ralph was glad that he had eaten his sandwich. Dinnertime had come and gone.

By the time the lawyers were finished, it was eight forty-five P.M.—the deposition had taken eight hours. Feeling exhausted but victorious after his first battle with Parker Brothers, Ralph headed to the airport and flew to Minnesota.

•

SOMETIME LATER, RALPH sat in his study, surrounded by documents and Anti-Monopoly boxes, unsure of where his case was going. Then his son Mark, always the avid reader, burst into the room.

"I found something!" he shouted excitedly.

In Mark's small hands was a red book with drawings of a doll, a teddy bear, and a Monopoly board on its cover. The book was titled *A Toy Is Born* and had been written by Marvin Kaye. Published in 1973, it must have made its way into the Anspach house when Ralph was collecting research material on the toy and game industry.

"Dad!" Mark said, "Charles Darrow didn't invent Monopoly. A woman did!"

Ralph sat up.

Mark handed the book to Ralph and pointed to a passage in the third chapter, "Over the Rainbow Without Passing Go." It read: "The creation of Monopoly is generally attributed to Charles B. Darrow, but game historians point to the Landlord's Game, patented in 1904 by Lizzie J. Magie and featuring purchasable properties, including utilities, a 'public park' corner corresponding to Monopoly's 'Free Parking,' and a 'Go to Jail' space. Darrow evidently added several new elements to the pattern of the Magie game."

From there, the book went on to tell the well-known story of Charles Darrow. There was no further mention of Lizzie Magie.

Ralph couldn't believe it. Who was Lizzie J. Magie? And 1904? That wound the clock back much further than Darrow's 1935 patent.

Then, Ralph's phone rang with tragic news. His forty-three-year-old lawyer, Herb Rubin, had just died of a massive stroke.

•

STARTLED AND SADDENED, Ralph again met with his lawyers at Warren, Rubin, Brucker & Chickering. John Droeger, the man who had been brought in to handle the antitrust portion of his case, would now be his lead litigator.

The two men clicked quickly, with Ralph appreciating Droeger's proud history as a rogue. Before becoming a lawyer, Droeger had served in the U.S. Army in the mid-1940s and had been honorably discharged in 1946. But when the army drafted him to fight in the Korean War, he refused to go. While serving a year and a half in jail for draft evasion, he taught himself law. He had also taken a few law courses at the University of Utah and Stanford University, and after his release he passed the California bar exam. Moving to the Bay Area, he met his future wife, Joanna, and the two started the Brighton Express, a restaurant that became a hangout for the likes of Janis Joplin, Lenny Bruce, and Christopher Isherwood. Perhaps the most famous thing about the restaurant, however, was Joanna's dessert creation: mud pie.

Droeger loved liberal causes and embraced Anti-Monopoly both as a game and as a legal mission. "I start out with the idea that everyone is bad," he said, "and it's just a matter of proving it." He suggested that they pursue two main lines of attack. The first was the "dirty hands" argument—if he could prove that Parker Brothers had acquired its trademark in a fraudulent manner, then the mark would be considered no good. But that argument seemed like a long shot to both men, as it would be hard to prove in court.

Droeger's second line of attack was more promising. People can't trademark something that's in the public domain, so if he and Ralph could prove that Monopoly had been widely played long before the 1935 patent date, they might have a case. Herb Rubin had begun researching the game's origins prior to his untimely passing, but that work remained incomplete. Ralph and Droeger had no idea if it would be possible to track down the game's history, especially since Charles Darrow was long dead, but they decided that they had to try.

As an economist, Ralph understood the mechanisms of the antitrust issues that his Anti-Monopoly game gave a nod to. But he wasn't a lawyer, and he soon realized that if he was to keep pace with the Anti-Monopoly litigation, he would have to turn himself into a de facto paralegal. So, even while up against court deadlines, family pressures, work as a professor, and the labors involved with launching a fledgling business, Ralph gave himself a crash course in trademark law.

Trademark lawyers use the term "genericide" to refer to product names that become so successful that they lose their trademark and become generic words adopted into the common language. As Ralph learned, it's an unintended and negative result of something becoming too popular. Words such as "aspirin" and "heroin" (once belonging to Bayer) and "escalator" (once belonging to Otis) are floated as cautionary tales among trademark lawyers of product names that became so widely used that they lost their trademark. Other examples include "kerosene," "zipper," "yo-yo," and "thermos."

On the opposite end of the spectrum from genericide is a brand that is distinctive, a product that could only be made by, and attributed to, one company. Courts rule where on the generic-distinctive spectrum products lie. Among distinctive trademarks, too, judges determine how strong or weak a mark is. Sometimes, if a judge looks at a trademark and feels that it's weak, other brand names can closely resemble it and still not be ruled infringements.

When company executives see that their trademarks are endangered, they sometimes fight back. Band-Aid's makers eventually added the word "brand" to their television slogan, so that it went, "I am stuck on Band-Aid brand, 'cause Band-Aid's stuck on me." Similar efforts were made to protect Kleenex as a specific brand of tissues and Xerox as a unique way to make photocopies.

Research aside, Ralph continued to try to sell his Anti-Monopoly games. But between his role as a professor, his family obligations, and his frequent Anti-Monopoly-related trips—with their long flights, crummy hotel rooms, and unhealthy food—he was exhausted. Sales of his game had plunged since his fight with Parker Brothers had begun, a development that he blamed on the alleged Parker Brothers intimidation of potential game distributors and sellers. In just a few short months, Ralph had witnessed the explosive success of his game, threatening legal notices from General Mills, his attorney's sudden death, a pile of legal bills, and a lawsuit that could prove to be unwinnable.

•

ON THE SCORCHING morning of August 20, 1974, Ralph made his way to a television studio in Portland, Oregon, where he hoped to drum up more support for Anti-Monopoly. Less than two weeks earlier, Nixon had resigned as president of the United States, and Ralph reasoned that his fall, together with the public's disillusionment over the Vietnam War, could lead to a rise in sales for his antiestablishment game.

In the television station studio, sweat lining his brow, Ralph described how he and his family had come to create Anti-Monopoly. He spoke of the game as a commentary on the 1970s, an era filled with monopolists run amok in a world with what he thought were weak antitrust laws, the Sherman and Clayton Acts shadows of their original ambitions, the Federal Trade Commission stale.

Afterward, the television show host opened up the lines to phone calls from viewers. Dressed in his trademark rumpled suit, Ralph was perspiring even more than usual under the hot studio lights.

An elderly woman came on the line, identifying herself as Mrs. Stevenson. She told listeners that she didn't understand why Parker Brothers was harassing Ralph about Anti-Monopoly. A friend of hers had played the monopoly game with her friends and family long before the Great Depression hit. Whenever Charles Darrow's name had come up in conversation, her friend Joanna had thrown a fit, Mrs. Stevenson said.

Ralph listened carefully to the caller. But as she spoke, the TV show host passed him notes written in big, bold letters warning him not to respond on air to potentially libelous conspiracy theories.

Darrow hadn't invented the game, Mrs. Stevenson continued. He had stolen it. Her friend Joanna, who had grown up in Quaker circles, knew more.

Ralph felt a mix of confusion, shock, and hope. The Quakers had played a role in helping him and his immigrant family adjust when they had first come to New York City, as they had helped many others at the time, but what did they have to do with Monopoly?

Ralph asked Mrs. Stevenson to stay on the line so that he could ask her more questions when the show wrapped. Off the air, she didn't have much to add to what she'd already told him. She had no last name for Joanna. No address. No phone number. They hadn't stayed in touch. And no idea where Joanna could be all these years later.

She did provide Ralph with one important detail, however. She told him that Joanna had studied engineering at New York University during the 1940s.

Given the attitudes about women in that era, Ralph wondered if Mrs. Stevenson's memory was faulty. It seemed unlikely that New York University had allowed women into its engineering program in the 1940s. But upon calling the school, he learned that the school had taken women into its aeronautical program when there was a shortage of men during World War II.

Ralph asked if there were any Joannas in the university's database. The researcher on the line said that the university had lost the records of its female aeronautical students from that time.

Ralph went to the New York Public Library and scoured aviation journals, hoping that the name Joanna would pop out at him from the piles of academic publications on propellers, pistons, and planes.

Nothing.

Next, he sought out helicopter companies that did business in the New York area. Among them was a company in New Jersey. He picked up the phone and punched in the number.

A man on the other end said that a Joanna had once worked at the company. Astonished and elated, Ralph begged for her contact information, or even her last name. But the man said that while he remembered Joanna fondly, he didn't have her contact information and couldn't recall her last name.

It was good to know that she existed, Ralph thought as he hung up the phone, but he was still far from finding her or from finding out what she may or may not have known about Monopoly. Seeking out early players of the game was proving to be a tricky, exhausting, and fruitless endeavor. He was getting nowhere.

Stalled, the Anti-Monopoly team redoubled its efforts to try to find other elderly people who had played the game. Droeger suggested placing a classified ad in the *Christian Science Monitor* saying that they were seeking information about the game's pre-1935 origins. It was akin to looking for the loathsome needle in a haystack, but it was worth a try.

Droeger placed the ad. Then they waited, Droeger with little hope.

An agonizing couple of weeks passed without a nibble. Had anyone even seen the ad? Were any of the early Monopoly players even still alive?

•

MEANWHILE, RALPH AND his legal team found something else of interest. Anti-Monopoly was not the first game to come into Parker Brothers' crosshairs. Through their review of the records that Rubin had summoned from court clerks, Ralph learned that Parker Brothers had regularly sent letters to other financially themed board game producers, accusing them of infringing on its Monopoly trademark. The practice looked as if it dated back as early as the 1930s.

Parker Brothers had sent a letter to a company called Transogram, which sold a game called Big Business. It removed its game from the market immediately. Letters were also sent to the makers of Sexopoly, Space Monopoly, Black Monopoly, and Theopoly, a game designed by priests. All stopped using those names at Parker Brothers' request. Parker Brothers also voiced an objection to a real estate advertising campaign in Florida called "Park Place" and to an Oregonian marketer's wish to name an apartment complex Marvin's Garden.

Before his sudden death, Rubin had discovered the 1936 Parker Brothers case against Texan Rudy Copeland, but had never gotten around to doing much with it. The file sat cast aside, along with the rest of his unfinished business. Droeger revisited it and read about the Inflation case. Both he and Ralph were shocked at its eerie parallels to their own case.

The bombastic and lively Copeland had initially responded to Parker Brothers' legal threat by charging that Darrow was not the inventor of

Monopoly—the game had already been in the public domain for years, he said. His game Inflation featured New Deal Highway, Wall Street, and National Recovery Administration spaces. Players built cottages and apartments on properties, and a large sum of money could accumulate in the Jack Pot. However, whoever landed on that spot had to pay a 25 percent tax on the winnings to the game's treasurer. In short, the game had the echo and feel of Monopoly.

As they read through the court papers, Droeger and Ralph learned that Copeland had called on witnesses who had had connections to the game prior to 1935, the year of Darrow's patent. A list of those names was included in the documents. The Anti-Monopoly team had their Rosetta stone.

They knew what they had to do: track down any and all players involved in the Copeland case. Their hope was that those players would be able to testify that they had played the game before Parker Brothers had published Monopoly.

Ralph and Droeger found other critical documents among the Inflation papers as well. One listed related patents, including two labeled "Magie 1904" and "Phillips 1924"—names Ralph recognized from the small red book that his son had so eagerly brought into his study. Knowing that patents are easily retrievable, he searched for Lizzie Magie's name and found her 1904 and 1924 Landlord's Game patents. Looking at the image of her board, Ralph felt as if a hand from another time was reaching out to him. It had been more than twenty-five years since Lizzie had died in obscurity, but her ink-and-paper protestation against the monopolists had survived. Staring at it and her patents, Ralph struggled to piece together exactly what she had been trying to say.

•

THE ANTI-MONOPOLY CASE was starting to receive more media attention, especially in the Bay Area, where sympathetic progressives rallied behind their board game hero. The Monopoly vs. Anti-Monopoly story line was irresistible to journalists, who immediately cast it as a battle between small and big business, West Coast and East Coast, new and old.

Ralph's sons, Mark and William, embraced the trial. Both took after their parents in their ravenous academic appetites, and they relished the bookish legal banter and stream of lawyers and reporters who swept in and out of their Keith Avenue living room. In the boys' eyes, their father was becoming a real-life manifestation of the heroes they read about in books and comics such as *The Adventures of Tintin* (about a Belgian reporter who traverses the globe solving mysteries). Ralph also involved his sons in tactical decisions related to Anti-Monopoly's legal and media strategy.

Still, William was occasionally teased at school for going up against the beloved brand. Ruth and Ralph banished General Mills cereal from their kitchen cupboards, and their mounting legal bills, tallied on a board that hung in the kitchen, were a worry to the entire family.

And as the Anti-Monopoly fight wore on and on, Ruth began to feel that something was wrong. She felt tired all the time, often falling asleep on the couch or taking naps while Mark and William played. Sometimes she lost feeling in her arms, causing her to drop whatever she was carrying, and she purchased plastic dishes to spare herself the humiliation of more shattered plates. Strangest of all was the sensation she felt when she put her foot down and couldn't feel the ground beneath her. She was only in her thirties and had always been healthy and energetic. What could be wrong?

Ruth had pledged her steadfast support for the cause, and was continuing to act as Anti-Monopoly Inc.'s secretary and treasurer, as well as take care of the children, but Ruth and Ralph worried about her health. The couple visited several doctors and explored a variety of possible diagnoses and cures, including hypnosis for pain, but concerns over her health soon joined the Anti-Monopoly case in the growing list of household concerns.

Proceeding with the case, Droeger and Ralph successfully tracked down Daniel Layman. He had retired from the advertising industry and was now living on a suburban street in sunny Pasadena, California.

Much to Ralph's amazement, Layman still had the Finance game board that he had made decades earlier. In his personalized version of the game, neighborhoods were grouped by ethnicity: O'Leary Avenue, Delancey Street, and Maguire Street, each denoted with a clover, were $140 apiece; Cohen Boulevard, Epstein Road, and Goldberg Square, each denoted with a Star of David, were $80 apiece. The two cheapest properties, Wayback and Rubeville, had outhouses and cost $50 each; American Power and Light and United Gas International cost $75 each. In the middle of each row of properties was a railroad space: New York Central, Pennsylvania, Southern Pacific, and Santa Fe.

Layman told Ralph and Droeger about Finance's early history. Then he examined the booklet of rules that he had written decades before. He had intended to apply them to Finance, but they were actually the rules that his fraternity brothers at Williams College, the Thuns, had taught him for the monopoly game they had been playing for years. Ralph asked if he could speak with the Thuns, and Layman said he could put him in touch. They had remained friends, and Louis Thun had once sent Layman a package with an article about Darrow from an airline magazine. They "forgot to mention that when Mr. Darrow died, he was working on the invention of the wheel," Thun wrote in his accompanying letter.

Layman also told Ralph that economist and educator Scott Nearing had played the monopoly game early on. Ralph felt shocked—he had heard of Nearing's famous academic freedom case and knew about his work as a radical.

Then Ralph asked a crucial question: When he first played the game, did Layman and his fellow players call it "Monopoly"? Proving that the name "monopoly" had been in the public domain—i.e., had been a generic word—prior to Darrow's 1935 patent was critical to his case. If it had been generic, then Ralph could argue in court that Parker Brothers should not have received a trademark in the first place and had no legal case against Ralph's use of the word "Anti-Monopoly."

"Every single person who referred to this game at that time called it monopoly and nothing else," Layman said.

Bingo.

In some ways, the actions of Layman and Darrow had not been all that different. Both men had seen a popular game, played it, and marketed it. But Layman had never filed for a patent, and had never claimed to have invented the game. Darrow had.

Layman agreed to testify in the Anti-Monopoly trial. Standing on his lawn, he raised his Finance board up to his chest as Ralph clicked the shutter on his brand-new Polaroid SX-70 camera, another photo to add to his growing Anti-Monopoly evidence arsenal.

•

FINALLY, RALPH AND Droeger received some replies from the *Christian Science Monitor* advertisement. Through those replies and the continuing research from the Rudy Copeland list of players, they learned that the monopoly game had once been played in some of the most influential intellectual pockets of the Northeast, including Columbia University in New York City.

Ralph flew east to meet with a woman named Alice Mitchell, who told him about her husband, George; the monopoly games they'd played; and George's colleague at Columbia, the famed economist Rexford Tugwell, who had first taught George the game. Ralph asked Alice if she still owned the original board she had made. She produced a cloth approximately the size of a card table. She had painted everything on the board, she said, except for the words in one corner that read, "Graduate Student's Club at Johns Hopkins University." Alice agreed to testify under oath that she had played the monopoly game before Darrow had produced it.

Ralph then got in touch with Ruth Raiford. She had seen his advertisement in the *Christian Science Monitor* weeks before, but it had taken some nudging from her friend Dottie Harvey, the now-grown-up little girl who had watched her mother, Ruth, paint so many monopoly boards in Atlantic City, before she contacted him. Later, Ruth Raiford would put him in touch with both Dottie and Dottie's father, Cyril, and with her sister-in-law Dorothea Raiford, widow of Jesse Raiford, the real estate agent who had attached prices to the game's properties.

Ruth also had an old oilcloth board game to show Ralph. When she pulled it out, he could hardly believe it. The board looked almost identical to the Monopoly board he and his family had played on that fateful night just a few years earlier. The color groupings were almost identical, and so were the Atlantic City property names. Ruth pointed to a space on the board and began to chuckle. Marven Gardens was spelled with an "e," consistent with the real-life spelling of the name—Charles Darrow and Parker Brothers had gotten it wrong.

Ralph asked Ruth if she knew of a woman named Joanna who had worked at an aircraft company.

"Yes," Ruth replied. "That's my niece Joanna." Joanna Raiford McKain.

Ralph's heart leapt. He had finally found her. Joanna lived only a few blocks away from her mother.

Ruth had one more suggestion for Ralph.

"You should speak with Charles Todd," she told him.

CHAPTER 11

ANSPACH CONNECTS THE DOTS

*"All the ancient histories, as one of our wits say, are just fables
that have been agreed upon."*
—VOLTAIRE

AS THE ANTI-MONOPOLY trial gained attention in the mid-1970s,
Parker Brothers commented publicly, albeit briefly, on the case. Robert
Daggett, who continued to represent the company, told reporters that he
could prove that Ralph had chosen the name Anti-Monopoly to capital-
ize on Monopoly's trademark, because sales of Ralph's game when it was
called Bust-the-Trust had gone nowhere. With his comment, Daggett
played into the idea that Ralph was a crackpot opportunist, a loony left-
wing professor looking to make money off of an American icon.

Ralph was too busy trying to track down the early monopoly players
to take much notice of his opponents' remarks. The testimonies he had
obtained were helpful, but questions remained. For the moment, all he

really had was a hodgepodge of elderly people remembering long-ago days spent over handmade game boards. What he needed was a linear narrative of Monopoly's inception. The hunt continued.

In the meantime, depositions of the early monopoly players had to be taken—and taken carefully. Ralph told potential witnesses that he wanted to learn about Monopoly's origins, but avoided saying that the makers of Monopoly were trying to put him out of business. Even the mention of Anti-Monopoly could put him at risk—he could be charged with witness tampering, in which case the witness's testimony would be thrown out.

Taking the depositions of the older Quaker players was not without awkward moments. Both sets of lawyers needed to be in attendance, meaning that the legal rivals had to travel and spend significant amounts of time together against their respective wills. Usually, that meant Ralph, John Droeger, Parker Brothers lawyer Ollie Howes, and a court reporter whom none of them had met before piling into a car together, even as they were conspiring about how to destroy each other in court. The sequence of events for setting up a deposition usually included Ralph making a preliminary phone call, then making a scouting trip to see if someone would make a good witness, then he and the lawyers traveling together to take the sworn deposition.

Ruth Raiford had put Ralph in touch with her old Quaker friend Cyril Harvey, a retired teacher. Cyril's wife, Ruth, had passed away some time before. Cyril agreed to be deposed, and in 1975, forty years after the boisterous monopoly nights in his home in Atlantic City, he and his daughter, Dottie, sat down with Ralph, Droeger, Howes, and a court reporter in Haddonfield, New Jersey.

In an early question to Cyril Harvey, Droeger described the game in question as a "real estate trading game," knowing that if he asked about Monopoly by name, it could be considered a leading question.

Immediately, Howes jumped in to ask Harvey if he understood what "a real estate trading game" meant.

"Yes, I guess that's right," Harvey said. "Oh, that's right. He had to ask the question that way."

"Why did he have to ask the question that way?" Howes asked.

Everyone was curious to hear the elderly man's answer. Was Ralph or Droeger guilty of witness tampering?

"Well," Harvey said. "I'm just being facetious. I mean, he couldn't just start out and use the word."

"Did he tell you that?" Howes pressed.

"No," Harvey said. "I have heard enough Watergate to figure some things out . . ." The televised Watergate hearings had, for better or for worse, given the public an education in the fine points of questioning witnesses.

"Watergate is making a hell of a difference in our profession," Droeger interjected. "Isn't it?"

On the deposition questions went.

"I'm not surprised at the time it took with Watergate," Harvey commented at one point during Howes's questioning. "This is infinitesimal in comparison."

Droeger, oddly enough, came to his opponent's rescue. "Oh, he's just being very thorough. We're going to earn our money here today."

One of the lawyers produced a copy of an early Finance board, published by Knapp Electric.

"I never saw anything like that before," Harvey said, looking at the board. "That is something."

Both sides tried to use the Finance board to ask Harvey about the differences between it and his Atlantic City board. But Harvey couldn't remember the details of the game that he had played some forty years ago.

•

ACTING ON THE tip from Ruth Raiford, Ralph tracked down Charles Todd. He felt nervous about calling him. Many of the potential witnesses he had tried to find had turned out to be deceased or unable to remember much about their monopoly days. He also worried about the risk of accidentally tampering with a witness—a mistake he especially didn't want to make with Todd. Raiford had led him to believe that Todd's testimony could be critical.

Ralph dialed Todd's number in Augusta, Georgia, and his wife, Olive, answered. She told him that they had been expecting his call ever since Ruth Raiford had alerted them to his interest in Monopoly's origins. They would be happy to speak with him.

On his way to the Todd home, Ralph wondered, as he had wondered before, why Parker Brothers had had Darrow sign for the Monopoly patent. It appeared that Darrow had never applied for a patent during the two years that he had sold the game on his own, nor had he sought to register the word "Monopoly" as a trademark. Yet Darrow had put a copyright on his game board once it had been acquired by Parker Brothers. Why? It didn't add up. Had Parker Brothers needed Darrow to get the patent for some reason?

Ralph arrived at the Todds' well-kept, fifteenth-floor condominium, unsure of what, if anything, would come of the meeting. The couple ushered him into their living room.

"Now tell me," Ralph said. "What really happened with Monopoly?"

Todd described how he had reconnected with his childhood friend Esther Darrow and how he had taught her and her husband the game.

Ralph asked Todd if Darrow could at least be credited with Monopoly's design. Todd replied that his old friend deserved credit for nothing—he had copied everything off the Todds' board. Olive Todd then stood up, walked to the corner of the room, and began rummaging through an antique chest. She pulled out an Old Maid game box and a blue oilcloth and handed them to Ralph. His heart beating fast, Ralph examined them. Was this the very set that the Todds had used to teach the Darrows the game? he asked. It was.

Philadelphia monopoly

Philadelphia monopoly was played by Charles Todd, an acquaintance of the Atlantic City Quakers in 1932. He taught the game to Charles Darrow who licensed it to Parker Brothers. Both then falsely claimed that Darrow had created it in order to monopolize Monopoly™ with an invention patent.

Todd misspells Atlantic City's MARVEN GARDENS

A copy of a board played by Charles Todd in Philadelphia in 1932. Todd taught the game to Charles Darrow, who later sold it to Parker Brothers. (Anspach archives)

Even more than Ruth Raiford's board, the Todd game board looked virtually identical to the Monopoly boards stocked on store shelves and stowed in millions of homes. It had Atlantic City street names and the "Marvin Gardens" spelling error. What Darrow had later claimed was a flub on his part had actually been Todd's mistake. And copied errors, Ralph had learned from Droeger, could be critical in proving plagiarism.

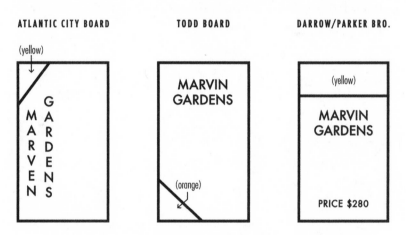

Comparison of the Atlantic City, Todd, and Parker Brothers boards. (Anspach archives)

"Incredible," Ralph said as he examined the contents of the Old Maid box with awe.

The Todds smiled.

In the box were hand-carved houses and hotels and Chance, Community Chest, and property cards. Printed in typewriter font were directions such as "Take a walk on the Boardwalk" and "Pay visiting nurse $5.00."

Now Ralph had not only a direct link to Darrow but also an explanation of how Darrow had taken the game from what had essentially been the public domain. The Todds were the bridge between the monopoly games played by the Quakers and left-wing intellectuals and the man who became internationally famous for "inventing" the game. In Charles Todd's version of the story, Darrow hadn't created Monopoly—it had been handed to him. Suddenly, Ralph Anspach's battle against Parker Brothers no longer felt like a lost cause.

Much to Ralph's relief, Charles and Olive agreed to be deposed.

Weeks later, Ralph and the lawyers crowded into the Todds' apartment. On clicked the recorder as a court typist began to take notes.

In a gravelly voice, Charles Todd evenhandedly told his tale. He spoke of boards made of canvas, colored with crayons. "It's been a long time since I've played the game," he said.

The lawyers asked Todd if he had ever called the game anything but "monopoly."

"No," he said and added that the game had been "entirely new" to the Darrows. "They had never seen anything like it before and had great interest in it."

When Todd was shown a version of the board with Philadelphia street names, he said he didn't recognize it. The only versions of the game that he knew were those with Atlantic City property names.

Ralph asked Todd if he would be willing to submit the oilcloth board as evidence and tell his story under oath.

Todd said that he had been waiting years for the opportunity.

•

WITH THE TODD and Raiford interviews completed, Ralph pieced together what he had learned. Meanwhile, Ruth Anspach's muscle problems and fatigue had worsened. Together she and Ralph sought out medical opinions. One doctor told her that she had a single lesion, but not multiple lesions or multiple sclerosis—it was not too serious, but another said she had MS. While the official diagnosis remained unclear, her illness fluctuated from day to day. Sometimes she felt completely youthful and energetic; other times she could barely get out of bed. She worried over the logistics of maintaining a household, supporting the Anti-Monopoly crusade, and not letting her boys know how sick their mother was.

Ralph's focus on the trial intensified as he continued to receive letters containing kernels of Monopoly history. As word about the Anti-Monopoly vs. Monopoly trial spread, he heard from many early players who remembered the game from their years at Columbia, Wharton, the University of Michigan, Haverford College, and Yale, as well as from intellectuals who had played the game while living in New York's Greenwich Village in the late 1920s.

The pieces of this early monopoly game resemble U.S. presidents, and college life, namely at Cornell and Haverford. (Malcolm G. Holcombe)

One game board played on by Harvard Law students had had Boston locales. Another early player wrote, "I have always understood that Scott Nearing invented the game and have been annoyed by the fact that someone else patented it." Ralph interviewed a married couple he had heard about from a court reporter who mentioned offhand that his boss had played the game. The Parker Brothers attorneys rolled their eyes at that, but Ralph followed up on the lead, which turned out to be useful. The couple had indeed played the monopoly game extensively with many friends in both New York and Pennsylvania. Unfortunately for Ralph, many of those friends were now deceased.

One player saw Ralph's advertisement in the Yale alumni magazine and wrote to say that he had played monopoly in the early 1920s in Reading, Pennsylvania, on a board that someone had brought from Princeton. "The purpose of the game was to illustrate the evils of the capitalist system," he wrote, and also mentioned that he was a friend of Louis Thun, one of the twin brothers who had played the game at his Williams College fraternity. Ralph then knew that he had to contact Louis Thun, whom Daniel Layman had mentioned as well.

Once again Ralph flew east. He had dinner with the no-longer-mysterious Joanna, her husband, and Dorothea Raiford. From their conversation, Ralph deduced that the game could have been brought to Atlantic City as early as Christmas 1929, just after the catastrophic collapse of the stock market. He placed ads in the Atlantic City *Press* and visited the Atlantic City Friends School, the small building that connected so many of the early Quaker monopoly players.

Next he flew to Reading, Pennsylvania, where he tracked down a printer who had worked at Patterson and White, the printer that Darrow had used for his initial run of games, pre–Parker Brothers. Then came a visit with Louis Thun in the Reading area. The Thun brothers' old friend

Paul Sherk joined in the conversation. They told Ralph that they had played a game called monopoly extensively between 1916 and 1935.

Ralph couldn't believe it—1916 was almost twenty years before the Darrow patent and over a decade before the Atlantic City Quakers had played the game. The more Ralph kept searching, the further back the clock kept winding.

Sherk told Ralph that his cousin had copied the monopoly game from someone who had brought it to Reading from the University of Pennsylvania in 1916. Then he pulled out a game board. It didn't have the word "monopoly" printed on it, but it had the same circuitous path as the Parker Brothers game and was essentially the same board. Included were many of Lizzie's Georgist touches: George Street, and Fairhope Avenue, a nod to Arden's single-tax-colony counterpart in Alabama. It also had New York locations such as Wall Street, Madison Square, the Bowery, Broadway, and Fifth Avenue.

Louis Thun told Ralph that he didn't know where the game had originated. But he did remember that Robert Barton, the head of Parker Brothers, had visited him decades earlier to ask if he could buy his board. Thun hadn't sold, but his friend, Sherk, who had also owned a board, had—for fifty dollars. Both men had been under the impression that Barton wanted the board for the Parker Brothers archives.

The board that Ralph saw would help his case, but he still needed to find an early board with the word "monopoly" printed on it. Having the name in writing would dramatically improve his case. He also needed to trace the origins of the game back further—back to the University of Pennsylvania and Wharton professor Scott Nearing.

According to several people Ralph had spoken with, Nearing had been among the earliest players of the monopoly game, leading Ralph to wonder if he might be its lost inventor. If not, he might at least know

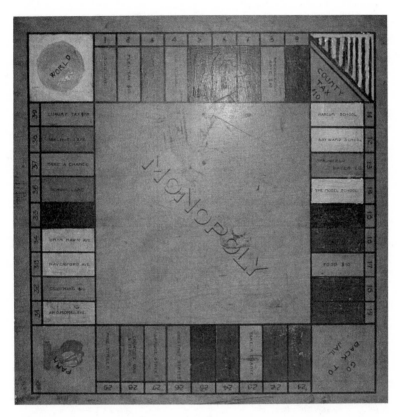

Forty years after the start of Ralph's quest for early monopoly game boards, one would surface with the word *monopoly* printed across it. This board is believed to have been played 1917–1925 in Pennsylvania. (Malcolm G. Holcombe)

what the game's connection was to Lizzie Magie, the name on the 1904 patent.

After his rejection at the hands of the University of Pennsylvania, Nearing had moved to a farm, where he had lived modestly off the earth, maintaining a vegetarian diet and pacifist views decades before they became the cultural rage. Now in his nineties, he was living in Harborside, Maine. Ralph contacted him.

Nearing told Ralph that he and his brother Guy had first played the game while living in Arden, Delaware, around 1910, and that it had been called the Landlord's Game back then. Everyone had played the game on homemade boards, he said, but beyond that, he couldn't recall much. He suggested that Ralph call Guy, who might be able to tell him more.

Now Ralph wondered if Guy might be the game's originator and contacted him. But he was too late. Guy had recently suffered a stroke that had done irreparable damage to his memory.

Back home in California, Ralph did what most academics would and dove into library stacks to research Arden, where he was surprised to learn about its single tax origins. In his collegiate seminars on the history of economic thought, he taught about Henry George and single tax theory, with no idea, of course, of its connection to the development of Monopoly. Ralph thought that Georgism was right in some respects but off target in others, and by the 1970s a tax overhaul akin to George's vision seemed virtually impossible. In any case, how did such staunch anti-monopolists as the Georgists end up playing a game that would become one of the most beloved corporate brands of the twentieth century? he wondered.

Ralph spent endless hours, occasionally stroking his beard or taking a puff of his pipe, poring over anything and everything that might help his case: case law, depositions, patents, newspaper articles and books about the toy and game industry. On and on he pressed. If he didn't get to the root of Monopoly's history, his case could fall apart. His own curiosity had overtaken him as well, with the game occupying his mind morning, afternoon, and night.

Among the documents that Ralph took a closer look at were Lizzie Magie's patents for the Landlord's Game—one from 1904 and the other from 1924. And the more he looked at the patents' drawings of Lizzie's game boards, the more striking their resemblance to Monopoly seemed: the Go space, the square board with its perimeter of properties, the railroads. Ralph picked up on the fact that Lizzie had infused her game with single tax principles. Oddly, her game politically resembled Anti-Monopoly more than it did Monopoly.

There was something very strange about the Darrow patent, Ralph thought. It had shoved Lizzie Magie into the bowels of history while allowing Parker Brothers to promote its 1935 patent and the Darrow story. Could Lizzie Magie have been Monopoly's real originator?

One day while at his office at San Francisco State, Ralph opened an envelope from Boutwell, Crane, Moseley Associates. Lizzie's former boss at the U.S. Office of Education, William Boutwell, now worked for his own firm and had heard about the Anti-Monopoly game and lawsuit.

Boutwell's letter described how, back in his days at the Office of Education, he had "found on my staff a pert gray-haired lady named, as I recall—this can be checked—Mrs. McKee. She was a great one for inventing games."

He continued, "She was also the only person I ever knew who was a devoted Henry George single-taxer. To advance the single-tax cause she invented a board game which could be played with two different sets of rules—life in a single-tax economy and life under capitalism. I remember taking the game home—she had somehow managed to have it manufactured—and playing it with friends. When one played it by single-tax rules no one could monopolize wealth, but when played by capitalistic rules money concentrated with one player.

"She sent the game to Parker. In the office we were outraged because Parker soon published only the monopoly side of the games."

Boutwell concluded, "I have seen various accounts of who invented Monopoly. I'm still convinced that the game was created by the gray-haired lady in my office and she never received proper credit or compensation from Parker."

Immediately, Ralph picked up the phone and called Boutwell, who confirmed his written account. Furiously, Ralph jotted down notes.

•

RALPH FOUND AN old photograph of Lizzie in the Washington *Evening Star*, a face now put to the patent. Elderly in image but not in spirit, she was holding up game boards from the Landlord's Game and another game that had the word MONOPOLY written across its center four times in bold black letters. It was 1936, and on a table in front of her was a "Darrow" board, fresh out of the Parker Brothers box. The image of Lizzie painted by the reporter couldn't have been clearer. She was angry, hurt, and in search of revenge against a company that she felt had stolen her now-best-selling idea. Her hair was snow-white, yet her eyebrows had stayed dark brown, her face now resembling that of her father in his later years.

The distinctive jawline of Lizzie's youth was still on full display. Parker Brothers might have the rights to her 1924-patented Landlord's Game, but they didn't tell the story of her game invention dating back to 1904 or that the game had been in the public domain for decades. She had invented the game, and she could prove it.

The Evening Star reporter wrote that Lizzie's game "did not get the popular hold it has today. It took Charles B. Darrow, a Philadelphia engineer, who retrieved the game from the oblivion of the Patent Office and dressed it up a bit, to get it going. Last August a large firm manufacturing games took over his improvements. In November, Mrs. [Lizzie Magie] Phillips sold the company her patent rights.

"It went over with a bang.

THE EVENING STAR. WASHINGTON, D. C., TUESDAY, JA

Designed to Teach

Game of "Monopoly" Was First Known as "Landlord's Game."

Mrs. Elizabeth Magie Phillips, Clarendon, Va., and the "monopoly" game she patented in 1904. To her left is the miniature model, to the right the new "landlord's game" she is now perfecting. —Star Staff Photo.

VERY likely your grandma and grandpa played Monopoly.
Why not?

It isn't new. Truth to tell, Mrs. Elizabeth Magie Phillips, 2309 North Curtis road, Clarendon, Va., then Lizzie J. Magie of Brentwood, Md., took out a patent on the game on January 5, 1904—a good three decades ago!

Except that it was called "The Landlord Game," at the time (and also 20 years later, when Mrs. Phillips improved the game somewhat and took out a second patent on it), you might notice little difference in the 1904 version and the one you tried to buy this week.

According to the specifications of the earliest patent, "the object of the game is to obtain as much wealth, or money as possible, the player having the greatest amount of wealth at the end of the game, after a certain predetermined number of circuits of the board have been made, being the winner."

Method of Teaching.

This innocent statement of the purposes of the game was somewhat of a subtle blind for putting across ideas then stirring the mind of Mrs. Phil-

lips. For, as well as a game to amuse it was one to teach.

A follower of the principles of the famous "single taxer" of the nineteenth century, she still holds the Henry George School of Social Science classes in her home. Thirty-two years ago, she created "The Landlord's Game" as a means of spreading interest in George's system of taxation. The game, as now called "Monopoly," still smacks of the Georgian principles.

As first devised, the game didn't catch hold. Four times Mrs. Phillips improved and patented new, similar ones. The latest, of September 23, 1924, comes out pretty boldly in its specifications.

"The object of this game," it states, "is not only to afford amusement to players, but to illustrate to them how, under the present or prevailing system of land tenure, the landlord has an advantage over other enterprisers, and also how the single tax would discourage speculation."

The winner is, in this newer game with the same title of "The Landlord's Game," the one who first accumulates $3,000. It had become more blunt, less leisurely, in the 26 years of its evolution.

Engineer Popularizes Game.

Even this game, however, did not get the popular hold it has today. It took Charles B. Darrow, a Philadelphia engineer, who retrieved the game from the oblivion of the Patent Office and dressed it up a bit, to get it going. Last August a large firm manufacturing games took over his improvements. In November Mrs. Phillips sold the company her patent rights.

It went over with a bang.

But not for Mrs. Phillips. It is understood she received $500 for her patent and she gets no royalties. Probably, if one counts lawyer's, printer's and Patent Office fees used up in developing it, the game has cost her more than she made from it. However, if the subtle propaganda for the

single tax idea works around to the minds of the thousands who now shake the dice and buy and sell over the "Monopoly" board, she feels the whole business will not have been in vain.

Although she has never played "Monopoly" as such, Mrs. Phillips has a set for doing so, along with sets of other games she has invented, in her living room. A card game, called "Mock Trial," is one of her other creations. At present, she is working out a new board game which she hopes will prove as successful as this astounding grandchild of her first game of finance and economics, "The Landlord's Game."

In 1936, at the height of the Monopoly craze, Lizzie Magie spoke out in the pages of the Washington *Evening Star* against the Darrow creation story. The paper reported that she received $500 for her invention. (Anspach archives)

"But not for Mrs. Phillips. It is understood she received $500 for her patent and she gets no royalties. Probably, if one counts lawyer's, printer's and Patent Office fees used up in developing it, the game has cost her more than she made from it."

No stranger to boldness, Lizzie had nothing to lose by speaking out against Parker Brothers and Darrow. "There is nothing new under the sun," she said to the *Washington Post* in a story that ran the same day as the *Evening Star* interview.

Lizzie went on to tell the reporter that if Darrow's Monopoly spread the notion of how the single tax worked, then her work would "not have been in vain." But the vast majority of commercial Monopoly players even then had little to no idea they were learning about single tax theory. She hadn't played Monopoly, but owned a set, which sat in her living room alongside other games, including Mock Trial, the theatrical card game she had sold to Parker Brothers years ago.

"At present, she is working out a new board game which she hopes will prove as successful as this astounding grandchild of her first game of finance and economics," the *Post* reporter wrote.

•

AT PARKER BROTHERS headquarters, Barton and his team understood that Lizzie posed a problem. The *Evening Star* and *Washington Post* articles put a face on someone whom Robert Barton hadn't thought he would ever have to deal with: Monopoly's real originator. Darrow's fame was unquestionable, as he appeared alongside all things Monopoly, and the game's popularity was continuing to soar. Nonetheless, Lizzie's claim was not only a public relations debacle but also a threat to all the work that Barton had done to gain exclusive rights to the game. Millions of dollars were on the line.

Parker Brothers was not about to have a second Ping-Pong situation on its hands. Monopoly would remain a Parker Brothers title no matter what.

CHAPTER 12

BARTON UNDER OATH

". . . because the game was completely worthless . . ."
—ROBERT BARTON

AT SEVENTY-ONE YEARS old, Robert Barton was not eager about the prospect of being deposed in the Anti-Monopoly case. By 1975, he had long been retired from the game business and enjoyed spending his free time at his home on the water in Marblehead, Massachusetts. Barton was among the few people still alive who knew precisely what had happened with the Monopoly patent back in the 1930s. His words, which had once helped clinch the Monopoly deal—and had saved Parker Brothers from destruction—now held the potential to unravel it.

Barton headed into compact and colonial downtown Boston. The deposition was to commence May 8, 1975, at nine thirty A.M. in the State Street Bank Building. At stake for the Anti-Monopoly team:

whether or not Barton would talk openly about Monopoly's origins and confirm the findings of their research.

"Now, sir, on the subject of Mr. Charles Brace Darrow and the game 'MONOPOLY,'" Ralph's attorney, John Droeger, said, "do you recall approximately when you first became aware of Mr. Darrow and his game?"

"To the best of my knowledge," Barton said, "in very early '35 or very late '34."

"And can you tell us the circumstances?" Droeger asked. "Did he come to Parker Brothers, did you go to him, or were you introduced by a third party?"

"To the best of my recollection," Barton said, "he submitted his game to us sometime in '34, and it was put through our regular R&D department and turned down. I had very little to do with it. I didn't see the game, and I do not remember how it was turned down other than that my father-in-law thought it was much too long and would not be successful. The first time that came to my attention was in early '35 when one of my wife's friends called her up, I think after Christmas, to say that she'd been playing Monopoly and it was a very fine game and did we have it, and if not why didn't we get it."

"I see," Droeger said. "And then did you initiate contact with Mr. Darrow?"

"I did," Barton said and then described how he had written to Darrow, probably sometime in early 1935, to say that Parker Brothers had reconsidered and was interested in meeting him in New York. At that time, Barton said, Darrow had already produced an initial run of the game through a local printer, and the printer had not affixed a copyright notice to it, even though that would have been routine procedure at the time. As part of his deal with Parker Brothers, Darrow turned over most of his unsold games to them.

"Can you tell us everything that you can recall of your first meeting with Mr. Darrow?" Droeger asked. "Was there any agreement reached at that meeting with respect—"

"Immediately," Barton said, recalling that in their Depression-era meeting in the Flatiron Building, Darrow had entered into his contract with Parker Brothers on the spot.

Droeger then presented the letter that Darrow had written to Barton relating his version of Monopoly's origins. He handed it to Barton and asked him to read it.

"Do you recall receiving that letter?" Droeger asked.

"No, I honestly cannot say that I do," Barton said. "But I have no doubt that I asked Charles Darrow to give me the history of the game for publicity purposes."

"I see," Ralph's lawyer said. "Now, it appears the letter is in response to a request for some kind of elucidation; and I thought perhaps you'd made that by a prior letter. Mr. Howes has informed me while we were off the record that the contract that you made with Charles Darrow was dated just a few days before this letter. Do you recall having asked him to give the background of his game?"

"No," Barton said. "But it was customary in the publishing business to require all the information that we could about an author's game so we could use it for advertising and publicity."

Barton then said that he couldn't remember if he had responded to Darrow's letter or not.

"Now, sir," Droeger said, "do you know what you got in your deal with Charles Brace Darrow? For example, you must have got some rights and some property, I would assume. Do you recall as you sit here today what you actually got by way of consideration from him?"

"Yes," Barton replied. "We acquired full right, title, and interest to a game which he was actually publishing called '*Monopoly*.' And if I remember the simple contracts that we used to draw in those days, we also acquired his assurances of cooperation in helping us defend his right to the game and in helping us publicize it and so forth. In other words, to make a success of its publication. We usually put all those things."

"For years," Barton continued, "we had a paragraph in the contract stating that if the game was attacked, and we were defending it, he would appear as a witness anywhere provided we paid for expenses. That was about all the publisher could ever acquire in those days. We also warranted that he also did have full right, title, and interest to the game."

"Essentially," Droeger said, "you got what he had, in other words?"

"That's about all we could take."

Barton further described acquiring Darrow's stock of the games on consignment and mentioned that at the time, he hadn't thought Parker Brothers would be able to sell them. "That I remember perfectly," Barton said, "because when I think that shortly thereafter we were selling 10,000 a day, it always made me smile."

Barton explained that 95 percent of game submissions in those days were rehashes of older games. These were examined by the Parker Brothers staff, who usually sent them back to their inventors without Barton's or his fellow executives' knowledge. The remaining 5 percent of ideas went to him or his father-in-law, George Parker, and other executives for review. If they liked a game, they accepted it, and if they didn't, they sent it back to its inventor, along with a rejection letter.

Droeger asked about Finance, the game that Daniel Layman had sold to Knapp Electric. Barton had negotiated the Finance deal himself and had paid ten thousand dollars for the game, which in Ralph's eyes was proof that Monopoly had existed before Darrow under a different name. Droeger showed Barton copies of the contracts the company had signed as part of its deal. Barton said that they had changed the game to make it easier to remember and had added the Parker Brothers branding.

"Now, sir," Droeger said, "I understand that, also, in this era, the mid-1930s, Parker Brothers acquired some rights in games from a Mrs. Elizabeth Magie Phillips. Now, do you recall acquiring any games or rights in games from Mrs. Phillips?"

"I do," Barton said. "We purchased her game called 'The Landlord's Game,' all of her rights in it including her patent."

"And that was done pursuant to written agreement?"

"I would think so," Barton said, "but I cannot remember because my father-in-law handled that purchase."

"That would be Mr. George Parker."

"Right," Barton said.

"Do you know whether Mrs. Phillips had any prior dealing with Parker Brothers before the game was purchased in 1935, I guess it was?"

"To the best of my knowledge and belief," Barton said, "she had not."

The answer sidestepped the firm's prior publication of Lizzie's game Mock Trial.

"Do you remember when your father-in-law negotiated this deal with her?"

"Now again," Barton said, "this is the best of my knowledge and belief."

"Sure," Droeger said.

"Sometime after we purchased *Monopoly* and he thought that we should try for a patent, engage the services of Mr. Townsend in Boston, Mr. Townsend, in conducting a patent search, discovered that she had a patent on this type of game and that no additional patent could be issued unless we owned the basic patent, which was hers."

"Do you remember the amount paid to her for rights in the game that she owned?" Droeger asked.

"I have no idea," Barton said. "But it could not have been very much because the game was completely worthless. I know that we published a small edition of it merely to make her happy."

Barton's lack of interest in Lizzie Magie and her original Georgist-themed game could not have been made clearer. Barton added that as far as he knew, Parker Brothers had never acquired any rights from her regarding the trademark Monopoly because she had not used it.

"Now, sir," Droeger said, "in 1936, Parker Brothers became involved in litigation with a gentleman named Rudy Copeland in the Northern District of Texas. Do you recall that Copeland lawsuit?"

The lawsuit had taken place roughly forty years earlier, but Barton clearly remembered going with the Parker Brothers attorney to meet the loud Texan and his attorneys in Indianapolis. "I remember going out there and meeting this infringer," Barton said. "He was my idea of a true professional Southerner."

Droeger asked him what he meant.

"I mean professional to the extent that everybody is a damn Yankee and so forth," Barton said, "and he had the hat on and the South could do no wrong. I further remember him stating that if we came down there, we'd just be damn Yankees and when we got in Texas to court, we would find out what was what.

"His attorneys seemed very embarrassed about it all. And then I did something which I despise doing, but if you go down in the gutter you get in the gutter. And I said, 'Well, if that's the way you want to fight the case, on the Civil War, I'll ask our Texas attorney to have me admitted. I'm a member of the Maryland and Massachusetts Bar. And I'll tell the court that my grandfather was adjutant for Stonewall Jackson and that I had four great-uncles die in the War whose names are on the rotunda at Charlottesville, and we'll see who wins the Civil War all over again."

Barton said he recalled the Parker Brothers attorney at the time, a quiet man, just sitting in the corner with "a grin from ear to ear" as Barton spoke.

"And it shook this fellow up," Barton said of Copeland. "And after he left, his own attorney went all over with us our purchase of Monopoly and our purchase of Finance from the Knapp Electric Company, the whole thing.

"When we got through, he said, 'Had I known all of this at the start, I wouldn't have represented the man. I'll tell you that right now.' But he said, 'You've got a situation down there in Texas. I don't know what it will cost you to fight the suit and so forth. I can probably settle the thing for you.'"

That very day, Copeland agreed to settle the lawsuit for ten thousand dollars. The next afternoon, Barton and his lawyer delivered the check and bought Copeland's game, Inflation. Barton said that he didn't remember Copeland's counterclaim about the Darrow patent being invalid.

After a short recess, the interrogation began again. It was time to learn about what had transpired between Barton and Darrow.

"Now, sir," Droeger said, "after your purchase, that is, Parker Brothers' purchase, of Charles Brace Darrow's interest in the game 'MONOPOLY,' did you ever receive notice or information or claim from any other person to the effect that Mr. Darrow was not the true inventor of the game?"

"No," Barton said.

That contradicted Charles Todd's claim, and those of several other early players, that he had written to the company and never received a response.

"If there had been such a communication addressed to Parker Brothers, would it have in the normal course been brought to your attention?"

"Yes," Barton said.

Then Droeger asked Barton what magazines he had read at the time, and Barton answered *Playthings* and *Toys and Novelties*, two trade publications. Droeger held up the June 1935 issue of *Playthings*, which carried an advertisement for Finance. He read aloud a description of the game: Players could buy and sell real estate, build houses, collect rent, buy and sell railroad and utility stocks, get rich, or go broke.

"Wouldn't you agree that's a pretty good description of MONOPOLY?" Droeger said.

Ollie Howes stepped in. "I object to the form of the question," he said.

Droeger withdrew the question.

"Did Charles Brace Darrow ever submit any other games to Parker Brothers for their possible use?"

Barton recalled Darrow's follow-up game to Monopoly: Bulls and Bears. It was "a complete failure," but Darrow had had "little or nothing to do" with its invention, Barton said.

The questioning over the reason for acquiring Finance resumed.

"We covered the waterfront whenever we bought anything," Barton said. "But we knew that Charles Darrow had based his game *Monopoly* on both the *Landlord's Game* and possibly something of this kind. We knew that perfectly well . . . We knew that he based *Monopoly* on this type of play. Whether he got it all from Magie Phillips, whether he got it from somewhere else, we didn't know. And we cared very little about it."

Droeger asked whether at the time there was any question about who had invented Finance.

"The only question I can think of might be relating to Mrs. Magie Phillips' patent," Barton said, "which we had purchased in complete good faith. And I think it's for this reason that we covered the waterfront. Remember, in making this thing we are in an adverse position. We are trying to buy this game as cheaply as we can get it. Knapp Electric is trying to get the price as high up as they can get it. So we claim everything and they claim everything." Barton added that he had never had discussions with Knapp Electric about what it knew about the origins of Monopoly or Finance.

"So it's your belief," Droeger said, "as you sit here today that no one had ever called a game Monopoly before Charles Brace Darrow?"

"That is true," Barton said. Parker Brothers had never done an investigation of whether or not the name had been used before, he went on, because if it had been used, Parker Brothers "would have known of it in the industry."

"Now, sir," Droeger said, "have you ever met anybody by the name of 'Thun,' T-h-u-n, particularly a Mr. Louie Thun or a Mr. Ferdinand Thun?"

"Never heard of the name," Barton said. He also said he hadn't heard of Paul Sherk, the man whose game board he had purchased in the 1930s.

Droeger confronted him with Daniel Layman's letter to *Time* magazine, a publication that Barton said he read regularly.

"I can't say I have a recollection," Barton said of the letter. "But I almost certainly read it."

"Do you know whether there was any follow-up, any communication, with Mr. Layman to find out what he was talking about?"

"None whatsoever," Barton said.

The room was tense, with the Anti-Monopoly team hoping to back Barton into a corner and the Parker Brothers lawyers relying on him not to implicate the company or lie under oath.

"Were there ever any discussions with Mr. Darrow through the years about how he got the game?" Droeger said. "Did you ever say, 'Look here, Charles Darrow, what is the true origin of this game? We want it straight from you now,' or words to that effect?"

"No," Barton said. "He had given us his version of the history of the game, so we were not about to question the veracity of one of our leading licensors. I don't think any publisher would under such a situation."

The next line of questioning concerned Lizzie Magie. Barton said that the company had sought her out and that she had never indicated to them that Monopoly infringed on her rights to the Landlord's Game. Parker Brothers had first learned of Magie's game when it had done its initial patent search, Barton testified. "She was a rabid Henry George single tax advocate," Barton said, "a real evangelist. And these people never change."

"And was the game that was published by Parker Brothers—let me put it this way," Droeger said. "The very attractive game that had her silhouette on the cover, was that game a single taxer game?"

"It was," Barton said. "But, to the best of my knowledge and belief, we took some slight editorial privilege."

"I see," Droeger said. "You deradicalized? Would that be a fair statement?"

"Well, you could at least end the game. Let's put it that way."

"The game of life never ends," Droeger said. "The single taxer will never go away. However, I think they do change."

Droeger asked Barton about a pamphlet that recounted the Darrow story called "Seventy-five Years of Fun, The Story of Parker Brothers Inc." and whether anyone had reviewed it for accuracy.

"I suppose that if you wanted to take it apart with a witness on the witness stand, you might find a little inaccuracy just as you are," Barton said, "the way with what the law calls 'puffing' as permitted in advertising, if you know what I mean."

"Surely," Droeger said.

He rested, and Howes took over to cross-examine. He was brief. Within two hours, Barton's turn at the stand was over, leaving Ralph and Droeger baffled. Barton's claims of ignorance of pre-Darrow monopoly games didn't add up. Barton had, however, revealed several new details about the Magie deal. He had admitted that Parker Brothers had bought her out and that the company had tried to do the same to all of its competition.

Next up to be deposed: Ralph Anspach. Again.

•

ON JUNE 12, 1975, Ralph once again returned to Robert Daggett's pristine offices on Sutter Street in downtown San Francisco. He was expecting another sear session, maybe even one that could last another eight hours, but he was more emboldened than he'd been the first time around. To prepare, he had gone through the pile of letters he'd received either in discovery or from the Quakers and other early monopoly game players and bracketed the word "monopoly" whenever it appeared so that he could pull the material out easily when needed. He had conducted enough research to know that the Darrow invention story was sour, even if he did have many hurdles ahead as far as proving it went.

In a letter to his Anti-Monopoly supporters some time earlier, Ralph had written, "We will show in court that the alleged inventor of the game did not invent it, and that Parker Brothers has been aware of this since at least 1936 . . .

"What was done here was much more serious than depriving a real inventor of his rewards. In that case, one person loses and another gains but it makes little immediate difference to the public since this is only a matter of replacing a legal monopoly with an illegitimate one. Here, however, the public as a whole has been deprived of its property."

In the conference room, Ollie Howes began by questioning Ralph about Charles Darrow. "Is it true that there have been published statements," he said, "attributed to you and that you have written letters to third parties in which you have asserted that the game which Charles Darrow sold . . . was not in fact invented by Mr. Darrow, is that correct?"

Ralph said that it was, and that Monopoly's trademark was invalid because the game had been played prior to its publication by Parker Brothers. He recounted his Portland television appearance the year before. "The lady told me a strange story," he said and described how his exchange with Mrs. Stevenson had led him to the mysterious Joanna and other early monopoly players.

"In your investigations in this case have you found any game boards made by persons other than Darrow or Parker Brothers that have the word 'Monopoly' displayed on them?" Howes asked.

"No, I have not," Ralph said. "And I would not have expected to, since people don't put trademarks on homemade games." He mentioned the Landlord's Game passage in *A Toy Is Born*, the book that his son Mark had discovered.

Next, Howes confronted Ralph about the similarity between the name "Anti-Monopoly" and the name "Monopoly." The General Mills lawyers, working on behalf of Parker Brothers and its new parent company, knew that the consumer-confusion angle was critical to winning their case.

Ralph said that he had never heard of anyone trying to return an Anti-Monopoly game because they had purchased it instead of Monopoly by mistake. Howes moved on, digging into Ralph's rejected Anti-Monopoly trademark application. Ralph explained what his earlier lawyer had told him about patents often being rejected by lower-level patent officers attempting to avoid granting patents that could be duplicative.

"Nevertheless," Howes said, "it is a determination that somebody expert in this field had made that determination?"

Ralph's lawyer objected.

The deposition didn't last eight hours this time, but it was long enough for Ralph. General Mills now knew the broader contours of what he understood to be the hidden truth about Monopoly, all of which could explode even more in public if the case went to trial.

•

CHARLES DARROW NEVER had another board game hit. Despite a vigorous advertising campaign, the stock-exchange-themed Bulls and Bears did not sell well. But it didn't matter to the Darrows. The family continued to enjoy their Monopoly fame and fortune, traveling the world by cruise ship and raising orchids in Bucks County.

Darrow's artist friend Franklin Alexander never received compensation or recognition for his contribution to the game, but he laughed it off and said he didn't care. The Alexanders and the Darrows remained friends well into old age, with Charles and Franklin still enjoying a good fishing expedition and a good chuckle over their poke at pop culture history.

In 1952, Darrow's Monopoly patent expired, seventeen years after it had been approved by the U.S. Patent Office. However, the game's trademark rights and copyright lived on—Parker Brothers remained what some later called "a monopolist over Monopoly." Lizzie's patent number had disappeared from sets decades earlier—an unusual occurrence, as the earliest date of a patent is seldom removed from a product. But given the circumstances, it was only logical that Parker Brothers would not want to draw attention to the game's early years.

Even when in his seventies, Darrow continued to tell reporters his mythical version of Monopoly's origins. The Great Depression had ended long ago, but the Darrows had never forgotten it. Esther hoarded pencils until they were tiny nubs, and Charles still made his son William and later his grandsons work for pay, ten cents an hour to weed dandelions. In a navy blue two-ring binder, Charles marked the purchases and sales of individual stocks he was invested in, and those investments mirrored the properties on the Monopoly board—the B&O Railroad, the Pennsylvania Company, various utilities.

Dickie lived in the Vineland facility in New Jersey, occasionally coming home for weekends or holidays. William studied agriculture in college and eventually bought property adjacent to his parents'.

The Darrow home was filled with trophies from their travels—exotic tribal masks from Africa, orchids from obscure rainforests, and knick-knacks from around the world. Charles and Esther took home movies and photographs of their voyages and showed them to friends who were interested. The Darrows were grateful for the Monopoly fortune, but throughout the years, Esther sometimes commented that no amount of money could bring Dickie's health back.

For the most part, Charles Darrow kept quiet about Charles Todd and the monopoly games that had been played before he stepped in. But he wasn't totally unaware of Lizzie Magie. In an article about Darrow and the game in the *American Magazine*, a reporter wrote, "But [Darrow] wants it known, that part credit goes to a Virginia woman, Mrs. Elizabeth Phillips, who started him on the idea."

Darrow's modest efforts to give Lizzie acknowledgment went largely unnoticed.

•

ON A WARM day in August 1967 in Bucks County, Pennsylvania, Charles Darrow got in his car and drove to the post office to collect the mail, just as he had done every morning for years. Returning home, Darrow took the mail into his office. Over coffee, he sorted through envelopes, daily notices, and financial statements. Then Darrow collapsed, a cerebral aneurysm killing him instantly. His obituary in the *New York Times* and other publications hailed him as the inventor of Monopoly. Members of the Darrow family continued to receive residuals from the game decades after his death.

•

RALPH HAD FINALLY linked together enough of Monopoly's history to create something of a complete story, and it bore little resemblance to the tale that had been told by Parker Brothers. As Ralph saw it, Parker Brothers had not only lied about the true inventor of the game, they had engaged in patent fraud and also tried to erase any signs of the game before 1935.

Ralph flew east to Philadelphia to aid in deposing Darrow's widow. Elderly and elegant, but still mourning Dickie's death four years earlier, Esther appeared with her lawyer in his firm's storied, antique-filled downtown Philadelphia office. Howes and Droeger were also in the room.

Pulling out an oilcloth and photos of early game boards, the lawyers began questioning Esther about what she knew of the game. She said that her late husband had designed its toy locomotives, and when asked if he had also created the "little man with the mustache," she said, "Well, I think so." When asked whether her husband had received any help from friends in developing the game, Esther said that "there were neighbors next door that I can't remember the name of" and that he had played the game with Charles Todd. She couldn't remember why her husband had called his game Monopoly and said that the family had seldom vacationed in Atlantic City, bringing into serious question the long-held belief that the town had served as Darrow's vacation inspiration.

•

WITH A GOOD handle on Monopoly's history, Ralph now shifted his focus from deciphering the true story to spreading it. As with his earlier causes—the Arab-Israeli War, the Vietnam War—telling the truth about Monopoly became a crusade that consumed every ounce of his being.

By now, it was clear that Monopoly's history, visually displayed, was more akin to an organic chemistry formula than the average toy's or game's.

Ralph Anspach, inventor of Anti-Monopoly, became a board game detective, using early, pre-Parker Brothers boards as evidence of the game's controversial origins in his case against Parker Brothers. (Anspach archives)

Not everyone was eager to hear the truth. At William's school, fellow students—and a few teachers—sometimes mocked him about his nutty Anti-Monopoly inventor father. Others told the younger Anspach son that they didn't understand why his family was working so hard to rip apart a treasured icon of American pop culture. Some family friends began to snub Ruth and Ralph—their patience for hearing about legal battles having worn out. Dinner and party invitations trickled to a halt. And Ruth continued to undergo test after test.

Gene Donner, Ralph's public relations man, still cast Ralph as a character in a David vs. Goliath narrative, and reporters still responded. But the Anspachs's growing Anti-Monopoly file of clippings was also sprinkled with negative notes, some painting Ralph as a lunatic.

The case had turned into an exhausting rotation of courthouse visits and lawyer appointments, and Ralph was often out of town, doing research on the road. Ruth, Mark, and William talked constantly about Anti-Monopoly, the game and the legal battle.

One time, William picked up the phone to call a friend and heard a clicking noise. He mentioned it to his parents. Sure enough, Ralph and Ruth began to hear the clicking on the phone line too.

The family discussed whether or not they were being wiretapped. Given all the chatter about the government developing a penchant for the practice, the idea didn't seem entirely far-fetched. Could Parker Brothers or an outside private investigator be listening in on their conversations? Was their paranoia misplaced?

After discussing the matter among themselves, the family decided not to say anything about their suspicions. It would make them sound too crazy. Instead, they would just wait it out and conduct important conversations only in person. Nonetheless, Ralph felt the same way he had during the height of his involvement in the anti–Vietnam War movement. "I have nothing to hide," he said.

•

MEANWHILE, ON A college campus on the other side of the country, a different kind of Monopoly controversy was brewing. Cornell University had become a hub for zealous Monopoly players and, as such, had brought two unlikely friends together shortly after they had arrived on campus in 1973.

Jay Walker was the son of a successful real estate developer in Scarsdale, New York, and had a dorm room filled with then-high-end gadgetry such as an open-reel tape deck, Sennheiser headphones, and an IBM Selectric typewriter. A proud libertarian, Walker quoted Ayn Rand with gusto and boasted his own "Walker Foundation" letterhead. Jeff Lehman was a middle-class kid from Bethesda, Maryland. His father worked in civil service, and his mother had raised five kids and then returned to the work force to practice law. A math major, Lehman was an ardent believer in activist government and New Deal philosophy.

When the two students weren't roaming Cornell's expansive green lawns, they could be found holed up in its large, austere brick buildings, playing games at odd hours. From his dormitory, Walker held Monopoly fests that featured four to six regular players, including Lehman. All were completely unaware that their collegiate predecessors had done the same with different versions of the game forty years earlier.

Walker, Lehman, and their friends liked Monopoly so much and played it so often and with such vigor that they began to modify the rules, adding things to the game that Walker thought had never been done before. They experimented with more-effective deal making, offering immunity for landing on properties, and analyzed which properties were the most likely to receive renters (the strip on the board from the Jail space to the Free Parking space), selling each other options to buy a property or engage in profit-sharing arrangements. Walker proclaimed that anything not explicitly prohibited in the rules should be permitted, a wildly different style of play than most of the players had grown up with.

The players formed the Ivy League Monopoly Association, with Lehman and Walker presiding over its Cornell chapter. They began to train for regional tournaments, traveling and crashing with friends as needed, and spending at least one night sleeping on the floor. As the two friends honed their skills, they became critical of the competition, which they found to be unimpressive, and the "terrible rules" used at the regional tournaments, as compared with the freewheeling rules they used at Cornell.

Before long, the Cornell group had set up its own regional tournament at a fair in Syracuse, drawing over one hundred players (Walker won), and a Monopoly exhibit that drew thousands of viewers. When Parker Brothers heard that Walker and his cohorts were using the advanced Cornell rules for their games, a lawyer sent Walker a letter asking him to stop. It also demanded that the players hand over all rights of authorship over their rules to the company. When Walker and Lehman asked if Parker Brothers was willing to pay them for their hard work, they were told that Monopoly belonged to Parker Brothers and students could not modify the game without its permission.

That spring, the Cornell group conducted a Monopoly marathon on campus featuring four players playing fifty games simultaneously for two days. The proceeds went to local charities. After that success, Walker and Lehman weren't satisfied with running local tournaments anymore—they wanted to go to the game's national and world championship, sponsored by Parker Brothers. They divided their efforts: Lehman continued running the tournament, and Walker entered the world championship. He won his region's local competition and advanced to the national championship, held at FAO Schwarz in New York, the same store where the Darrow version of the game had been sold forty years earlier.

As word of the Ivy League Monopoly scene trickled out in the press, Walker and Lehman were contacted by a book publisher about writing a book on Monopoly strategy. Novices in the book industry, the pair were unsure what to do but saw that Yankee baseball pitcher Jim Bouton was scheduled to lecture on campus about his book *Ball Four*. The two approached Bouton afterward for advice, and he recommended his literary agent, who also represented famed children's author Madeleine L'Engle, author of *A Wrinkle in Time*.

With the help of the agent, the two college students sold their book concept to Dell Publishing for an advance of ten thousand dollars, and Walker hired "a whole set of fancy lawyers" to review their text. He had heard that Parker Brothers had made legal threats to their publisher, claiming that their guidebook infringed on the Monopoly trademark. Infuriated by the challenge to what Walker felt was the freedom of the press, he dumped more money into legal bills to counteract their prepublication challenges.

During Christmas vacation of their sophomore year, Walker and Lehman hibernated in Walker's suite in the Sigma Phi fraternity and put together the book, taking turns writing the chapters. Their finished product was titled *1000 Ways to Win Monopoly Games* and contained "for the first time, the sure-fire skills, strategies and secrets the experts use."

The two students had realized that the return on investment of Monopoly properties was not equal. While the blue and the green properties were the priciest and most coveted among amateurs, the orange and the red ones yielded higher rents relative to their costs and the cost of buying houses and hotels. Years later, a computer enthusiast in Downers Grove, Illinois, analyzed the odds of winning based on 187,000 Monopoly games, and his findings confirmed that the orange properties were potentially more lucrative than the blue ones. Walker and Lehman also understood that Monopoly wasn't purely a game of luck—the art of deal making played a significant role, as it was unlikely that one could obtain a monopoly just by landing on all spaces of a like color. Most people played Monopoly incorrectly, injecting far too much cash into the game, which allowed a single game to go on for hours and hours. People also felt entitled to ask for rent owed after a turn had passed. To Walker and his friends, these were marks of an amateur.

In *1000 Ways to Win Monopoly Games*, published in 1975, Walker and Lehman offered simple tips, encouraging players to buy every property that they landed on and recommending when to build four houses per property rather than a hotel and thus create a housing shortage, as each box was limited to thirty-two houses and twelve hotels. Most people forgot that when a player landed on a property and decided not to purchase it, the banker should then auction it off, accelerating the pace of the game and giving a nod to the system that Lizzie Magie had originally conceived.

The authors advocated not breaking the rules, but rather knowing them inside out and using them with clever aplomb. The earlier a player could trade, the better, as "trading is the key to almost every Monopoly victory." When players paid off a mortgage on a property, they commonly forgot to pay the bank back an additional 10 percent. A player in Jail retained the right to collect rental income, making it an advantageous place to be later in the game to avoid landing on a competitor's built-up property monopoly. Railroads and utilities were good to own, but inferior to colored property groups. Immunity deals, which offered free stays on properties, were fair. "A Monopoly game," Walker and Lehman wrote, "can be a lot like golf. You can play well for several hours, then make one little mistake and lose it all."

Parker Brothers did not acknowledge any of the records set by the players at the Cornell tournaments, asked Walker and Lehman to stop printing their book, and effectively locked Walker out of the Parker Brothers world championship.

"I've offered them pretty much everything," Walker later said. "And every time they turn around and tell me, 'no, no, no, no, no, no.'" Through their agent, Walker and Lehman found a lawyer who was so enraged by the Parker Brothers response that he agreed to represent them at little to no cost.

On April 28, 1975, Walker read a front-page story about Ralph Anspach and his legal battle with Parker Brothers in the *Wall Street Journal*. Within days, Walker looked up Ralph's phone number and called him in Berkeley. Ralph had received his share of prank calls since his legal battle had begun, but Walker's story captured his attention, and the two swapped anecdotes. Both men felt that Parker Brothers' actions were stifling the development of its own game. They began devising a plan.

CHAPTER 13

A MATTER OF PRINCIPLE

*"All for ourselves, and nothing for other people, seems, in
every age of the world, to have been the vile maxim of
the masters of mankind."*

—ADAM SMITH

IN JUNE 1975, John Droeger called Ralph with good news: Parker Brothers, via its parent company, General Mills, had made a settlement offer. This could be it—the end to nearly two years of legal hell, credit card bills, jetlag, and personal strain. General Mills' offer was "very generous," Droeger said.

General Mills offered to make Ralph an executive in its games division, which now clearly included its Parker Brothers acquisition, and to give him more than $500,000—roughly $2.2 million in today's dollars—plus damages. In exchange: He had to hand over the production of Anti-Monopoly.

Droeger regarded the job offer as a chance for Ralph to "change things from the inside" while also earning a hearty salary. Droeger had handled some big settlements in his career, but this would be his largest yet. The settlement would also allow Ralph to finally pay his legal bills. Droeger felt that the offer, especially the cash part, was a good deal for his client and that the Anspachs would be crazy not to take it.

At home, the family deliberated. It was possible, they thought, that General Mills was trying to buy Ralph's silence. If he accepted the offer and became a Parker Brothers employee, he might not be able to talk freely about Monopoly's origins anymore.

The General Mills offer represented a tremendous amount of money for the Anspach family. The proposed six-figure sum was more than enough to pay off the Anti-Monopoly legal bills, put Mark and William through college, and maybe even buy a house that wasn't slipping away.

But for Ralph, it wasn't all about the money. He wanted to prevail in court for the right to make his own Anti-Monopoly game and tell the world about Monopoly's true origins. He was also concerned that if Parker Brothers had the rights to Anti-Monopoly, it would allow the game to wither away, just as it had done with Lizzie Magie's Landlord's Game.

It wasn't all about the money for Ruth, either. She was concerned about General Mills having ownership of a game that they had invented as a form of political advocacy and education.

It was important to Ralph to have consensus among all his family members before making any decision. Ruth was already on board, and when he spoke to Mark and William, they vowed their support for Anti-Monopoly as well.

When Ralph told Droeger that he would not accept the settlement offer, Droeger asked him if he was insane. Droeger asked to meet with the rest of the Anti-Monopoly board of directors and found that they were in agreement with their leader.

In a June 10 settlement meeting with the Parker Brothers lawyers before Judge Lloyd Burke in the United States District Court for the Northern District of California, Droeger said that he had done everything in his power to make his client understand that this was a good offer, but to no avail. The next day, the Anti-Monopoly team formally turned down the settlement. That afternoon at a meeting in his firm's offices, Droeger told Ralph and his colleagues that it was "bizarre" to turn down an offer of a pile of money and a chance to alter the game industry from a coveted position inside the business.

Things only got worse from there. At another conference later that summer, Droeger told Judge Burke that he thought his clients were "crazy" and that he was not going to defend them anymore. Ralph was confused as to why Judge Burke was even there, as it was his understanding that after a settlement offer, a case was assigned to another judge, so that the proceedings could start afresh and without bias. Outside of chambers, the tension between Droeger and Ralph regarding Ralph's epic unpaid legal fees only further intensified. Droeger's partners had been pressuring him about collecting for the tremendous number of hours he'd spent on the case.

Judge Burke did ultimately recuse himself from the Anti-Monopoly case, but the relationship between Droeger and Ralph continued to crumble. In addition, due to a mishandled court procedure, Ralph's hope that his case would now be assigned to a jury rather than to a judge was thwarted. Ralph began to look for another lawyer.

Ralph asked Droeger to hand over all the documents related to the trial. For now, they would go to Benjamin "Barney" Dreyfus, a friend of Droeger's who had done some work on the case early on.

Dreyfus had built his career as a champion for underdogs. His client list included whistle-blowers, Black Panthers, and a woman named

Helen Sobell, who had been trying to visit her husband at Alcatraz, where he'd been serving a thirty-year sentence, having been convicted of conspiring with Julius and Ethel Rosenberg. Dreyfus's core causes were freedom of speech and voting rights, and he was known to often work for little or no money.

Ralph now found himself at the mercy of whichever new judge was assigned to his case. That turned out to be Judge Spencer Williams, Richard Nixon appointee and reputed fan of big business. At the time, Williams was one of the most overturned judges in the entire state, meaning that his decisions were often reversed on appeal. Ralph also heard that Williams hailed from Massachusetts (Parker Brothers' home base), was a fan of Parker Brothers, and had ruled in favor of large businesses in the past. Ralph was in despair.

During a particularly low moment of the trial, Dreyfus sat in the court cafeteria with Ralph and his younger son, William, and told the Anspachs that he thought a trial loss was imminent.

William, after years of putting up with bullying, watching the jokes come in at his father's expense, and now sitting in a courtroom for long hours, finally couldn't handle it anymore. He burst into tears.

"I started crying because I was so upset," William later said. "That was really devastating." He added, "But I think he was trying to be honest."

•

AT SOME POINT before the Parker Brothers–sponsored national and world Monopoly playoffs, scheduled for winter 1975, Jay Walker flew to San Francisco to meet with Ralph. Walker was still irate over being banned from the official, elite Monopoly competitions. The tournaments were invitational, so Parker Brothers had every right to exclude him, but as one of the top players in the country, Walker felt that he should have the opportunity to compete.

Rumors flew that Parker Brothers was spending hundreds of thousands of dollars to transport players from all around the world to Atlantic City for days of glittery competition at the national championship, then Washington, D.C., for the global competition soon thereafter. Just two years earlier, a "life-size" game board had been constructed in the seaside town, its properties traversed by young women in bikinis.

"I call it a farce," Walker said of the upcoming tournament. No one from his region had even been considered for the qualifying rounds. Ralph and Walker decided to join forces, and they began to plot what they called the "Atlantic City caper."

Gene Donner started to work on publicity. Leading up to the tournament, he helped get two stories written in the Atlantic City *Press* about the Quakers and their role in the game's early history. He also purchased an ad in the paper promoting a lecture open to the public to be given by a professor of economics at Atlantic City's Holiday Inn at two P.M. on the day of the tournament. The Holiday Inn was located next door to the building where the tournament was taking place, and the time slot fell in between Parker Brothers' scheduled events.

Atlantic City's decay had only worsened after World War II. With the widespread use of automobiles and the establishment of commercial airlines, the Northeast's middle class now had many vacation destinations to choose from. Atlantic City was no longer glamorous or exotic. A third of its citizens lived on welfare, and public health officials were fighting rampant venereal disease. The only activity that seemed to be on the rise was arson.

Parker Brothers saw the advertisement for Ralph's lecture and changed its schedule to conflict with Ralph's event, making it extremely

WHO

DID INVENT THE GAME OF

MONOPOLY?

--WAS IT A PHILADELPHIAN NAMED CHARLES B. DARROW?

--OR, WAS IT DONE RIGHT HERE IN ATLANTIC CITY BY ATLANTIC CITY RESIDENTS?

A Professor of Economics will give the answer in a free Public Lecture. Come and see some of the evidence and meet those who helped create the game.

DATE: Saturday, Nov. 22
TIME: 2 P.M.
PLACE: Holiday Inn
in the Wildwood Room

As part of his "Atlantic City caper," Ralph Anspach took out advertisements for a lecture designed to undercut the publicity around Monopoly tournaments. (Anspach archives) difficult for journalists to attend his lecture. In addition, at company expense, it shuttled reporters away from Atlantic City and to Washington, D.C., where the world championship was taking place. Parker Brothers seemed to have outwitted the Atlantic City caper.

Undeterred, however, Ralph packed up his actual-size board game replicas in his black artist portfolio and he, Donner, Walker, and another Cornell friend headed to Washington for the tournament. Once there, they found the area surrounding L'Enfant hotel, where the tournament was taking place, thick with security personnel. Parker Brothers had learned its lesson from Atlantic City and was hoping to shield everyone in attendance from the band of Anti-Monopoly misfits.

Ralph's plan was to transplant his Atlantic City scheme: host a lecture in a conference room at a cheaper hotel nearby and invite journalists. L'Enfant was not allowed to give out the names of its guests, but somehow Walker and his friend managed to obtain a list of the reporters, contestants, and other Monopoly-related guests staying at the hotel. They put together press kits and distributed them, only to realize afterward that they had forgotten to insert the "truth about Monopoly" lecture information in the kits, thus defeating the whole point of the endeavor.

All would have been lost had Walker not learned that a breakfast banquet was planned for the Monopoly press. The saboteurs dashed into the L'Enfant dining room before the guests' arrival and carefully tucked invitations beneath the plates. Then they raced back to the conference room that they'd rented at the nearby hotel and set up for the lecture. Ralph pulled out the pre-Darrow boards he had collected, along with property cards and some examples of the early monopoly money. Copies of the sworn depositions he had gathered from Daniel Layman and the Quaker players were laid out as well. Reporters trickled in and began to learn the details of the case that had consumed Ralph and his lawyers for many months. The unraveling of the board game tale that the public knew had begun.

After the lecture, Ralph tried to get back into L'Enfant for the presentation of the championship's top award, the Darrow Cup, but a representative hired by the company asked him to leave. He boarded a plane back to California to finish preparing for his trial, pleased with his work in D.C.

•

Infuriated with Parker Brothers for bestowing the Darrow Cup on its champions, in 1975, Ralph Anspach hatched a plan to sabotage Monopoly tournaments. (Anspach archives)

THE PHONE RANG, interrupting another frigid February day in the Bay Area. On the other end of the line was a man claiming to be a former Parker Brothers employee. He had heard about the Anti-Monopoly trial and wanted to be a whistle-blower. Ralph quickly grabbed a writing utensil and a piece of paper.

"Parker steals games," the man told Ralph, going on to describe a black box at the company offices that contained the "true story" of Monopoly. The whistle-blower did not feel comfortable testifying at Ralph's trial, as he had a game development company that still depended on its relationship with Parker Brothers to survive. The lack of on-the-record testimony was unfortunate for Ralph, but he was emboldened by the tip and began to seek out other Parker Brothers employees, past and present. None of them agreed to testify against the company.

The case and related stresses were wearing on Ruth and Ralph's marriage. The financial arguments continued as Ralph shifted expenses on and off credit cards. Ruth's health was not improving, and increasingly the doctors suspected her condition to be multiple sclerosis. Ralph's sons were inching toward adulthood, and life in the household was not getting any easier. Ralph was frequently out of town, and when he was home, the conversation often revolved around the impending trial.

•

HUMID, CORRUPT, AND crime-ridden. Such were typical characteristics of summers in Chicago, along with sidewalks that could double as skillets and foul moods. But what transpired at the secretive toy design firm Marvin Glass and Associates in July of 1976 surprised even the most blasé Chicagoans.

First, lawyer Carl Person, acting on behalf of his client Christian Thee, served executives and game designers at Marvin Glass with subpoenas. Thee claimed that the company had stolen his invention, an art auction game that he called Artifax and Marvin Glass had marketed as Masterpiece.

Five days later, in an apparently unrelated event, Albert Keller, a designer at Marvin Glass, headed into the office. He had notes in his shoes. He also had a gun. He walked into the fortresslike building and down the corridor of the second floor of the Marvin Glass offices, entering and exiting one office after another. He shot and killed his coworkers Anson Isaacson and Joseph Callan in Isaacson's office. He shot two more employees in another office, killing Kathy Dunn, a twenty-three-year-old designer. Then he shot two more employees, reloaded his pistol, and shot himself in the temple.

By ten A.M., sirens were wailing into the thick Chicago air. When the police arrived at the Marvin Glass offices, they found bodies slumped over desks, surrounded by pools of blood and brightly colored toys. Keller's body was sprawled in the second-floor corridor, one hand still clutching the pistol. Reportedly, a model of a toy police car was nearby.

Employees and executives at toy and game firms across the country were shocked to hear about the carnage. They were baffled as to why the shooting had taken place and how a killer could have been lurking inside the walls of one of the industry's most famed and acclaimed firms tasked with creating childhood joy. Keller had been a deeply troubled man, but his rampage highlighted the fact that the game industry was not just about fun. It was cutthroat big business.

Ralph heard about the Marvin Glass shooting when a reporter phoned him for a comment on the breaking news. What breaking news? he asked.

He listened to what had transpired with a mix of horror and anxiety, knowing firsthand just how dark and sinister the game industry could be. Game ideas weren't just pieces of paper, patents and prototypes. Inventions were often central to the identity of their inventor and, in extreme cases, could become matters of life and death.

The murders at Marvin Glass had been the work of a mentally ill, disgruntled employee, but something at the company had enraged the distraught man. As the legal claims brought against Marvin Glass just a few days before the killings showed, idea stealing—and who knew what else?—seemed to have become common in the industry. A large company could purchase or contract new game ideas through a smaller company like Marvin Glass, where they could be further developed, and then get a patent for the finished product.

•

BY NOVEMBER 1976, the battle was about to begin in the Anti-Monopoly vs. Monopoly courtroom. Robert Daggett and Ollie Howes were confident of a Parker Brothers victory. Former executive Robert Barton was due to appear, and the Parker Brothers legal team had assembled several toy and game store employees who would testify that customers were confused about who made Anti-Monopoly and who made Monopoly. Parker Brothers had brought in additional counsel as well—a fleet of sharply dressed men in suits who contrasted with the motley band of Anti-Monopoly supporters, mostly Bay Area locals.

Ralph's attorneys Barney Dreyfus and Bob Chickering were representing Anti-Monopoly in court. Reporters wielded their notepads and took their seats. Judge Williams sat on the bench.

Daggett called up a woman from Bellevue, Washington. From 1968 to 1976, she said she had worked at a toy and hobby store that sold both Monopoly and Anti-Monopoly. She told the court that when she had first seen Anti-Monopoly, she had thought Parker Brothers had made it because of its name, and that store customers had been confused too.

A toy and game store owner testified that in November 1975 his store had taken out an ad in the *Cincinnati Enquirer* that had read, "Monopoly or Anti-Monopoly, your choice, $4.48," followed by the phrase "by famous Parker Brothers." A similar ad had run in Ohio's *Columbus Dispatch*. The store owner told the court that he had thought that because the games were synonymous, Anti-Monopoly would sell.

"Does the prefix anti, a-n-t-i, mean anything significant to you, sir?" Daggett asked.

"It means against."

"Does anti-abortion mean the same thing to you as abortion?"

"Well," the store owner said. "The prefix 'anti' means anything that you are saying against any other wording or name that you use it."

"It means the opposite, does it not?"

"Yeah, I would—yeah, possibly."

By the time the court broke for lunch, the outlook for Ralph was dreary. Clerk after clerk had filed onto the stand to paint a picture of a game profiting on the tailwinds of Monopoly's success.

In the afternoon, another woman who worked at the New York City Parker Brothers office took the stand. One of her duties at the office was to answer the phones. She recalled that on one occasion when she picked up the phone, Ralph was on the line. His first words to her were "This is your enemy."

She said she didn't understand his humor. Then Ralph explained that he was from Anti-Monopoly and had heard that she would be called as a witness. He said he wanted to know what she planned to say in her deposition. He also said that Parker Brothers was going to lose the case. "He told me over and over that—that Parker Brothers is going to lose," she recalled.

"Did these conversations please you or disturb you or leave you neutral emotionally?" Daggett asked.

"I'm not sure that's relevant, Your Honor," Dreyfus said.

"I think it is, Your Honor," Daggett said.

"Objection overruled," Judge Williams said.

"They disturbed me," she said.

"Will you tell the court why?" Daggett said.

"Well, I had the impression I was being interrogated on the phone," she said. "He didn't scream at me or anything. He spoke moderately, but I had the feeling that I was being manipulated and that—he didn't come out and say that he did not want me to give the deposition, but I just got the feeling that he wanted—he wanted to know everything that I was going to say and my words were going to get twisted around somehow."

Then Jim Esposito, a young, shaggy-haired freelance journalist living in Venice Beach, took the stand. Dreyfus had called him. Esposito, who was writing an exposé about the game industry for *Oui* magazine, recounted his conversation with the national sales manager for Parker Brothers. Esposito said that the manager had told him that anytime Parker Brothers or Milton Bradley released a new game, orders came in all the time from distributors and game store owners who were confused about which company had produced the new game.

This testimony helped dampen the Parker Brothers argument, as it portrayed a confusing business landscape. People were often unclear about which company made what.

Daggett began to cross-examine Esposito, whose story was still in its early stages. "There are several references in your notes to me," Daggett said. "One of which says I have been a member of the Bohemian Club for some years. What has that got to do with this article?" (Judge Williams was reportedly a member of the club as well.)

"Well," Esposito said. "The nature of the article—I deal with a lot of personalities in it. They're people. I like to round off the personalities to present—you know, Mr. Anspach is a professor. You are a lawyer. The Judge is a judge."

"Some days, Mr. Esposito, some days," Daggett said. He continued. "Have you written anything in draft form on Mr. Anspach's charge that Mr. Robert B. M. Barton is guilty of fraud?"

"No," Esposito said.

"You haven't written anything about that?"

Esposito shook his head no.

"What have you drafted respecting Anti-Monopoly and Monopoly?"

"I talked to Mr. Anspach at length about his depositions," Esposito said. "His investigations into, you know, the history of Monopoly, what he uncovered as the history of Monopoly, stated as such. I wrote that up. But I haven't really finalized it yet. I have also written an introduction to my article. That's about the size of it."

"Have you written in draft form anything which even refers to Mr. Anspach's fraud charges?"

"Which charges?" Esposito asked.

"The charge that Mr. Barton fraudulently promoted Monopoly relative to a patent, for example?"

"No," Esposito said.

They wrapped for the day. Ralph was feeling more optimistic about his chances.

In a boost to Ralph's spirits, his family was planning to attend the trial every day. His sons roamed the halls to eavesdrop, hoping to pick up scuttlebutt from the enemy. Many of the older game players had flown in to California, and there were happy reunions in the hallways of the courthouse among friends who hadn't seen each other in many years. Everyone was determined to have the whole true story of Monopoly finally told.

The testimony from nine of the game's early players occupied most of the proceedings. Ruth Raiford took the stand to describe how she had taught Charles Todd, and helped to teach Charles Darrow, the game; Daniel Layman testified about Finance and his game-playing days at Williams College; a still-angry Charles Todd told of his friendship with Darrow and their many monopoly nights together; and friends of the Thun brothers and others testified that they had played the game at Wharton and other elite institutions. Eagerly, the press took notes.

Perhaps the most dramatic moment of the trial came when the silver-haired Robert Barton took the stand and reiterated the points he had made in his deposition in Boston. He conceded that Darrow was not the originator of Monopoly and that Parker Brothers had bought up all the competition. But such was the nature of doing business, he said. Cameras clicked as the stoic figure sat in the witness chair and testified how uninterested he had been in Lizzie Magie's original game.

Another market researcher testifying for Parker Brothers stated that some 15 percent of those surveyed were confused about the difference between Monopoly and Anti-Monopoly.

"Do you consider your findings significant?" Daggett asked.

"Oh, yes," he responded.

Ralph rolled his eyes, and took the stand as a rebuttal witness.

"Mr. Anspach," Daggett said, beginning examination. "You are intimately familiar with what has occurred in this litigation leading up [to] the trial, aren't you?"

"Yes, sir," Ralph said. "Intimately familiar" didn't even begin to describe it. The game and the case had taken over his life. It was all he could think about, day or night.

"You have sent your attorneys to take depositions in New York, haven't you?"

"Yes."

"You have sent your attorneys to take depositions in Washington, D.C.?"

"Yes."

"You have sent your attorneys to take depositions in Augusta, Georgia?"

"Yes."

"Philadelphia, Pennsylvania?"

"Right."

"Salem, Massachusetts?"

"Right."

"In Rochester, Vermont?"

"Yes."

"In Baltimore, Maryland?"

"Yes."

"Arlington, Virginia?"

"Yes."

"And Springfield, Massachusetts?"

"Right."

"So when you reportedly told Randy Bienenstock you couldn't afford to go to Madison, Wisconsin, you were lying?"

"I certainly was not," Ralph said. The litany of places could not have taken more than a few seconds to recite and were a reminder of what an exhausting hunt the last few months had been for Ralph, a blur of starched hotel linens, naps on airplane tray tables, rental cars, notes jotted on napkins, bleary-eyed walks through San Francisco International Airport. "Incidentally, the charge for sending my attorney went on both my American Express card and Diner's Card [sic] on the 12-month payment plan."

The attorneys launched into their closings. Both sides were sick of the litigation and eager to end years of madness.

Dreyfus began by saying that Parker Brothers dealt with Monopoly "almost as an icon, almost an object of worship." He continued, "Mr. Barton spoke with some awe from the stand of his belief that nobody had challenged it for 40 years, the trademark Monopoly."

Dreyfus went on to say that the trial was about the truth and the right to compete, a right that he and Ralph considered to be as precious as democracy itself. If history couldn't get the story of Monopoly correct, what hope was there for anything else? And if he, Dreyfus, couldn't get the ethics of a board game right, what chance did he have in cases for clients such as Daniel Ellsberg or Eldridge Cleaver?

"A trademark is a privilege, a privilege protected by the Government," he said. "It is a crutch. It is a—well, it is sort of a governmental subsidy that permits somebody who owns one to be free from the competition in the marketplace. He doesn't have to worry about that—he has a monopoly.

"Here, we have a monopoly on the word monopoly, a word in ordinary, common usage, Your Honor. And it is not the law. The cases that we have given Your Honor show there is no favor by the law upon the use and maintenance of such a trademark. It is not in the public interest. There is an overriding public policy to the contrary to permit ordinary words to be used by people to whom they belong generally."

Dreyfus then began to read from a letter that Parker Brothers had sent to the makers of Theopoly, asking them to discontinue publication.

Among the items the company objected to were "'panels entitled indul-gence, penance, actual sin, original sin, baptism, limbo and purgatory,'" Dreyfus read. "'We also ask that on the Hell panel you use some other term in place of "just visiting."'"

Parker Brothers was literally trying to assert its control over words as old as the Bible, Dreyfus went on. Should the company be allowed to go on unchecked, there was no telling what it would lay claim to next.

The makers of Theopoly "had a game that should have been allowed in competition, Your Honor," Dreyfus said. "And shouldn't have been threatened by a trademark that is not in the public interest. Now I don't—I can't represent to the Court that we have established fraud in the obtaining of the trademark in the strict sense that the cases prescribe. We have not.

"Right from the very beginning, Mr. Barton was candid enough to tell us he didn't believe the story that [the game] had been invented by Mr. Darrow. And almost immediately, within a week, he sought a lengthy history from Mr. Darrow in Mr. Darrow's handwriting to estab-lish and buttress the story that he didn't believe."

Dreyfus wasn't done. He reminded the court about Rudy Copeland, the early players of the game, and Parker Brothers' efforts to buy out any and all competition. "It is in the public interest to encourage a challenge to a trademark," he said, "particularly one that has become generic."

He to a survey referred conducted regarding words that were now in the public domain. "Look what happened to aspirin, cellophane, thermos bottle. All those, Your Honor, were trademarks; and not only that, they were highly regarded, protected trademarks because they were invented words. They didn't have any common meaning at all. They didn't depend upon a secondary meaning."

Dreyfus said that Ralph had acted in good faith and had made no effort to make his box look the same as Monopoly's. His was the type of competition that the American economy should encourage. "The Court ought to send this brave little entrepreneur out with the Court's blessing to pursue his commercial enterprise . . . against, Your Honor, what seems to be overwhelming odds," he said. "The odds against him are great enough without their seeking the intervention of the Court."

The mood in the courtroom was anxious and anticipatory as Daggett stood up and began his closing remarks, which were characteristically blunt.

"Mr. Dreyfus' conception of the trademark law is dead wrong," he began. "Mr. Dreyfus implies that this is a patent case, not a trademark case. And I want to contrast those two bodies of law in their general reach."

"Now," Daggett continued. "Trademark limits itself to saying do whatever in the world pleases you, but don't do it with anybody else's name."

Daggett argued that since the Monopoly trademark had been in effect for many years, it had become incontestable unless fraud could be shown, which Ralph could not do. The testimony from the Quakers and other witnesses had been intriguing, but it did not prove fraud in the legal sense.

"I say nothing further about that," Daggett said, "beyond pointing out that the statute doesn't say unclean hands; it says fraud."

Then Daggett argued against the name "Monopoly" having become generic.

The Anti-Monopoly team had cited the dictionary definition of "generic," which defined it as either "relating to or characteristic of a whole group or class" or "being or having a nonproprietary name." Daggett countered that a word had "to be the common, descriptive name of an article . . . The most graphic test for the statutory requirement, I think, is this: if a word is generic and, nevertheless, enforced as a trademark, you deprive every seller in the marketplace of the right to call his product what the public calls it, except the one who's got the trademark. And that's not right."

Daggett further argued that there was only one Monopoly game and that other real-estate-trading board games were being sold all over the place under names that did not infringe on the Monopoly trademark. Even Ralph had "started with Bust the Trust" until "his ship caught fire and sank," he said.

"If Mr. Anspach is honestly wrong, a subject of which I will not discuss further in his presence," Daggett said, "if he is wrong and there is a likelihood of confusion, then I think the law of the United States calls upon Your Honor to send Mr. Anspach out that door with the best wishes and encouragement of the Court to carry on in his business—however, using somebody else's name, not mine."

Daggett was done. But before leaving, he said that he had a photocopy of every case cited in the trial brief that he no longer needed. Judge Williams said to leave them with him.

"Another example of they have more money than we do," Dreyfus said.

"Sympathy," Judge Williams said, "has no place for consideration in this court."

Parker Brothers and Ralph began their painful wait for a verdict. With his fate in Judge Williams's hands, Ralph feared that even though he had succeeded in telling the story of Lizzie and the Quakers in court, he still risked losing everything.

Judge Williams ruled that Anti-Monopoly had indeed infringed upon Monopoly's trademark and ordered Ralph to "deliver up for destruction" any remaining copies of Anti-Monopoly. Barton and Daggett were elated, Anspach and his team crushed.

CHAPTER 14

THE BURIAL

"It may be that all games are silly. But then, so are humans."
—ROBERT LYND

TYPICALLY, WHEN A company wins an injunction, the acquired goods are stored in a warehouse until the court proceedings are completely over. However, Parker Brothers decided that it needed to show its strength and teach other potential Monopoly makers a lesson.

On July 5, 1977, with a handful of journalists witnessing the scene, representatives from Parker Brothers buried approximately forty thousand Anti-Monopoly games in a landfill in Mankato, Minnesota. By burying the games, the firm was showing its utmost confidence in its victory. Should Ralph appeal his case and win, Parker Brothers would have to hand over the games. By dumping them into the earth, the firm made it abundantly clear that it thought Ralph had no chance. Under the circumstances, that belief was not unfounded.

Ralph had flown to Mankato to watch the spectacle with his friend Russ Foster, who lived in Minnesota. The two men shook their heads, feeling helpless. What a waste it was. A reversal in court was still possible, but the burial was humiliating.

Ralph had acquired a mountain of debt, his family's patience was frayed, Dreyfus would be leaving the case, and now even the physical evidence of much of his hard work and what he was fighting to produce was gone.

•

IN A SMALL, cluttered office tucked into one of Lower Manhattan's windy, cavernous streets, the phone rang. It was Ralph, calling for Carl Person. One of Ralph's lawyers had mentioned that Person was an anti-trust attorney whom he admired. Person was also the attorney for Christian Thee, the designer who was suing Marvin Glass over his claim to an art auction game he called Artifax, which he said Marvin Glass had sold as Masterpiece.

Ralph had become aware of a linchpin argument in Judge Williams's ruling against him that made the Anti-Monopoly case ripe for appeal. If he and his team were reading the ruling correctly, the judge had misinterpreted an aspect of trademark law, opening the door for another trial. The key issue: When a trademark becomes the name of a product, rather than an indicator of its producer, it loses its significance. And when a consumer saw Monopoly on a store shelf, Ralph and his team believed, it was the name of the game, not the Parker Brothers imprint, that compelled him or her to buy it. Williams had decided otherwise and made several fact-finding errors. In terms of legal reasoning, Williams set up a situation in which Monopoly would be treated like Aspirin, a trademark that had slipped into the public domain. But if that was true, then Anti-Monopoly could not be infringing on Monopoly.

Ralph briefed Person on the case. After Judge Williams's ruling, he had embarked on an exhausting excursion through the California court systems, and he had already won one victory in an appeal decision on genericness as an issue (other arguments were not discussed). Ralph felt he now had the right to dig up his games and wanted to take the case further. For that he needed a long-term lawyer who was willing to take on a complicated case that had no shot at a jury trial. The lawyer also had to be willing to work on a contingency basis.

Person was intrigued. The two agreed to meet in San Francisco.

When they did, Ralph wondered if the man before him was indeed the Harvard Law School graduate who had taken on manufacturing titans, or someone else from New York City's shadier corners who had somehow made his way onto the plane. Person did not look the part. His hair was in disarray and his ill-fitting suit was a decade or more out of fashion. When he opened his briefcase, a rainfall of papers fell out. I'm lost, Ralph thought.

But what Person lacked in presence he more than made up for in legal intensity. The two went out for dinner and discussed the Anti-Monopoly case in greater detail. Person was willing to take the case, but on one condition. He wasn't a trademark lawyer and didn't have a fleet of other lawyers or paralegals working for him, as did his counterparts at large firms. If he was to take the Anti-Monopoly case, Ralph would have to be his paralegal and clock even more hours on the case than he already had. Confident that his legal abilities had stood him in good stead thus far, Ralph was happy to oblige. He was grateful that Person was willing to take the case at all.

Before long, Carl Person became a regular at the Anspach home, often working with Ralph in the living room until two A.M. From time to time, Person would become discouraged, but Ralph would cheer him up, and the two struck up a friendship similar to the one that Ralph had shared with John Droeger.

Ralph also spent a lot of time working with Person in New York City, with Person and his wife often hosting him on the couch of their Upper West Side apartment. Person had an uncanny ability to nap while sitting up and could program himself to fall asleep or wake up when he wanted. Watching him snap in and out of consciousness was one of the strangest things that Ralph had ever seen, but it helped to explain how Person was able to juggle his incredible workload.

•

IN JANUARY 1980, almost three years after the forty thousand Anti-Monopoly games had been buried, Ralph returned to the landfill in Mankato, Minnesota. He wanted his games back. With him, again, was his friend Russ Foster.

The press and a handful of spectators were also there. Perhaps out of a natural unbridled optimism, perhaps out of a sense of having reached the point of no return, Ralph had enthusiastically promoted the exhumation, dubbing it an "archeological spectacular." He had a purpose and a shovel.

Despite the harsh winter weather, all that Ralph was wearing was a tissue-thin trench coat, gloves, and a cotton hat, which was failing to keep his wild, wavy brown hair out of his eyes. As the wind whipped around him, pieces of garbage that weren't frozen to the ground occasionally fluttered up and hit him in the face. Russ lumbered a few feet in front of him, a dark, bearlike figure in a heavy fur-lined coat, topped off with a coordinating hat fit for Siberia. Ralph and Russ kept their heads down and their noses low to avoid inhaling the odor of the rotting matter around them. Peculiarly enough, even though most of the refuse was frozen, it still emitted a suffocating stench.

The onlookers stood several feet away, watching the duo as they traipsed through the refuse. But as time ticked by and nothing happened, they trickled off one by one, accompanied by the sound of engines sputtering back to life as their tanklike cars slowly pulled away.

Resurrecting the buried treasure had sounded simple when Ralph had spoken about it on the phone with Russ. But it was a much more difficult project to execute than he'd anticipated. The search team roamed over the vast, rotting terrain. And roamed. And roamed. Six hours passed. It was hopeless.

Then, through the freezing air, Ralph and Russ saw uniformed figures heading their way, their lights blinding in the bright haze and cold air. They were environmental protection officers, and they asked Ralph and Russ to leave. The two men retreated to Russ's house to thaw out and have a drink. The phone rang. It was a man who claimed to have been involved with the burial. He had seen their excavation efforts on TV and said that Russ and Ralph had been about thirty yards away from where the games were buried.

It was too late for Ralph. He had to return to California.

A few months passed; ice melted, flowers bloomed. Russ and Ralph spoke over the phone. Russ had bad news: The land where the Anti-Monopoly games were buried had been sold to a residential development company. Houses were being constructed on top of the forty thousand board games.

They would remain underground.

•

IN THE SUMMER of 1980, just six months after Carl Person joined forces with Ralph, the Anti-Monopoly case had to go up against Judge Spencer Williams again, on appeal. Dubbed "trial two" by the Anti-Monopoly team, this round of debate centered on whether the public had a product or its producer in mind when it purchased a game. Did people buy Monopoly because it was Monopoly, or because it was a game from Parker Brothers?

How Judge Williams had handled the question had ping-ponged through the court system already, a legal labyrinth that seemed equally riddled with confusion. After Williams had originally ruled in Parker Brothers' favor, the appellate court in 1979 had sent the decision back to Williams for a reexamination of the validity of the Monopoly trademark.

To help prove their case this time, Person and Ralph commissioned a market research survey. Among lawyers, the use of surveys in trademark cases had mixed reviews. Surveys, as any student of politics or polling knew, could be easily manipulated to meet a specific agenda. They were also costly to conduct and at risk of being thrown out by the presiding judge. Surveys were prone to errors, too, as it was often difficult to interpret what a consumer was really thinking.

Edward Canapary, the researcher who had conducted the Anti-Monopoly survey, took the stand. He reported that when people were asked the open-ended question "Why did you buy Monopoly?" or "Why would you buy Monopoly?," 82 percent gave responses that were related to the product itself; 2 percent gave answers that were either related to Parker Brothers or neutral; and 16 percent answered in a manner that was indecisive. Robert Daggett, again representing Parker Brothers, said that he thought the survey had been designed by Ralph so that each question was phrased to "predict, if not require, the conclusion it reaches."

Weeks later, a court reporter called Ralph with the news. Anti-Monopoly had lost again. All they had left was a second appeal. The Monopoly battle had lasted over six years. Ralph had taken out a third mortgage on his home, and his credit cards were maxed out. His sons now had deeper voices, William in high school and Mark off to college, with little to no financial help from Ralph. His relationship with Ruth was rocky, as was her health, and he hadn't spoken with his friend John Droeger since the settlement conference blowup.

If they lost this time, it would likely be all over for Anti-Monopoly and up to Ralph to figure out how to pay hundreds of thousands of dollars in legal bills and how to explain to his sons why he felt the fight had still been worth it.

•

THE MONTHS DRAGGED on, with Ralph meandering back to his routine as a professor and his mountains of trial documents collecting dust in his study. Then, in the summer of 1982, nearly a year after the most recent trial, the phone rang at the Anspach house. It was a court reporter with news.

The United States Court of Appeals for the Ninth Circuit had again ruled against Parker Brothers and General Mills, this time not only declaring that the trademark "Monopoly" was invalid and that the word had become generic, but also reversing the majority of Judge Williams's remaining findings of fact. The opinion also read that a lower court now had to determine whether Anti-Monopoly had taken reasonable care to inform consumers that Parker Brothers did not manufacture the game.

The court added, "It remains unclear how widely played the precursors to modern MONOPOLY were in the 1920s and early '30s." Also, the

Anti-Monopoly team "has simply made no showing as to what the public conception of the term was at that juncture."

Nonetheless, the overall decision was resoundingly positive and enormously significant to Ralph. Perhaps most vindicating was this line: "The court's reference to Darrow as the inventor or creator of the game is clearly erroneous." Since normally it is the district judge who makes rulings on facts (because it is that judge, not the appellate judge, who has the witnesses and documents before him or her), the appellate court had in effect given poor marks to Judge Williams on that score in accepting Ralph's exhaustive research.

At first, the victory didn't sink in. Only slowly would the weight of the last eight-plus years begin to lift off of Ralph's shoulders. That night, the family went out for dinner in an expensive restaurant. After nearly ten years of drastic budget cuts, the Anspachs were finally free of both the Anti-Monopoly case and its debts. Ralph's legal bills would be paid by Parker Brothers.

News of the verdict traveled quickly to the palatial Parker Brothers offices in Beverly, Massachusetts. Inside the company's pristine glass facility, financed by parent company General Mills, employees were shocked to hear that Parker Brothers had lost. Some executives shook their heads and wondered what was wrong with the courts in California. Randolph Barton, Robert Barton's son, said that he was "dismayed and disappointed" by the decision. Spokespersons for Parker Brothers refused to comment on the court's account of the game's origins.

Much had changed at the firm since the case had begun. Randolph Barton, grandson of founder George Parker, had risen to the presidency of the company in 1974, shortly after Ralph had received his first threatening letter from Parker Brothers.

At the 1982 Consumer Electronics Show, Parker Brothers had finally introduced an electronic version of Monopoly. The electronic version was essentially the same as the traditional version, but featured a Playmaster that controlled the rolling of the dice, property ownership, and how players moved around the board.

Parker Brothers was also facing threats from some new players in the game industry. Foremost among them was Nolan Bushnell, the cofounder of Atari, which produced Pong, an addictive digital version of the Ping-Pong game that George Parker had reeled over nearly a century earlier. Bushnell, perhaps even more than Parker, understood that successful games had to be easy to learn but difficult to master.

None of this seemed to matter to the Parker Brothers attorneys and executives as they deliberated over their next move. Ralph had been a thorn for nearly ten years. They weren't about to let the ruling of the appellate court stand. They would appeal the Anti-Monopoly case to the Supreme Court.

•

WHILE PARKER BROTHERS lawyers frantically worked long hours to prepare for a fight in the nation's highest court, other employees engaged in a massive publicity drive to drum up support for their cause. Soon other companies with significant trademarks told reporters that they were "up in arms" over the court decision to strike down Parker Brothers' victory, and scholars argued over whether the courts could start to punish those who had created unique, popular products by deeming their trademarks generic. The Parker Brothers spin on the case was that the appellate court hadn't known what it was doing.

Others who joined Parker Brothers in its fight included the American Bar Association, Procter & Gamble, and the U.S. Trademark Association. The notion that a trademark becomes invalid when it denotes mostly the product, not the producer, was blasphemous to them and many other companies. "You don't have to know Crest is from Procter and Gamble to have the trademark identify the source," the executive director of the U.S. Trademark Association told the *New York Times*.

The sparring between Anti-Monopoly and Parker Brothers evoked references to Pac-Man, E.T., and Wheaties as lawyers for Parker Brothers argued that the Anti-Monopoly ruling, if untouched, "immediately jeopardizes many of the most successful marks on consumer products." "This is sheer nonsense," Carl Person said in reaction to the dire predictions.

Parker Brothers hired Nathan Lewin, an acclaimed lawyer who had argued numerous cases before the Supreme Court, to take the case on its behalf. On January 27, 1983, Lewin filed several amicus, or "friend of the court," briefs from titans of corporate America on behalf of Parker Brothers. The briefs took issue with the Ninth Circuit appellate court's decision, "because it causes confusion and uncertainty in the administration of trademark law."

Four days later, Person, who had relatively little experience before the Supreme Court, fired back. He wrote to the court saying that Lewin's amicus briefs did not reflect the uniform view of trademark lawyers. "It is Mr. Lewin, not the Ninth Circuit, which has created the alleged uncertainty and confusion," Person wrote. In addition, Lewin had mentioned an earlier Anti-Monopoly survey, regarding possible confusion over the games' names, but not the one that had proved Person and Ralph's point, that people buy Monopoly because of the product, not the producer.

In New York City, Ralph huddled with Person in his tiny office, the two working late into the night on documents tied to the Supreme Court filing. Once again, they pulled out research relating to Lizzie Magie, the Atlantic City Quakers, the Darrow invention story, and the confusion over the Monopoly and Anti-Monopoly names. Finally, documents in hand, Ralph boarded a train from New York to Washington, D.C., to personally deliver the papers.

Peculiarly enough, Jeff Lehman, the Cornell student who had coauthored the controversial book about how to win at Monopoly, had gone on to law school and was working as a clerk for Justice John Paul Stevens. Upon hearing about the Monopoly appeal, Lehman recused himself from the case.

Ralph stared up at the white pillars of the storied Supreme Court building with awe, and then ascended the steps to drop off his filing. He was only a few blocks away from where Lizzie had filed for her first patent on the Landlord's Game eighty years earlier.

CHAPTER 15

REDEMPTION

"They monopolized Monopoly. Actually the game was in the public domain. But now the truth is coming out."
—RALPH ANSPACH

ALMOST A DECADE to the day after Ollie Howes's threatening letter had shown up in Ralph's mailbox, a very different piece of Anti-Monopoly news arrived at the Anspach home in Berkeley. Calling from New York City, Carl Person said that the Supreme Court had refused to hear Parker Brothers' case. The Ninth Circuit appeal victory stood firm, and Parker Brothers reportedly entered into a series of six-figure settlements with Ralph that exceeded his legal fees and the costs associated with the loss of his forty thousand Anti-Monopoly games. These settlements more than doubled the settlement offer that Ralph had turned down years earlier and had far more beneficial terms, including ensuring that Anti-Monopoly stayed on the market.

Ralph didn't know whether to believe Carl or not. He had become so accustomed to false hope. But finally, he realized that at last the

Monopoly war was won. At last he would be able to sell Anti-Monopoly without interference from the company he had grown to despise.

•

DURING THE REAGAN era, Anti-Monopoly's countercultural bent didn't resonate with the public the same way that it had a decade earlier. Bigger—houses, cars, shoulder pads, hair—was better. The cynicism of the Watergate era had faded into the roaring economy of the 1980s, and Anti-Monopoly sales in the United States stalled. Ralph later lamented the lost window of opportunity for selling the game. "Justice delayed is justice denied," he said.

After decades of marriage, the raising of two boys, and a legal battle that had lasted almost a decade, Ruth and Ralph divorced. Years later, both wondered whether their obsession with Anti-Monopoly had blinded them to fractures in their marriage. They also wondered if there had been anything they could have done differently, or if the loss of a common enemy—be it Nixon, the war in Vietnam, or Parker Brothers—had been the reason the marriage had ended. But staying together, both agreed, would have been even more difficult than embarking on new lives apart.

In the original Anti-Monopoly game, players separate things that are bound together into independent pieces, lending the dissolution of Ruth and Ralph's marriage a bitter symmetry. Mark and William were now out of the house, but their parents' divorce, compounded with Ruth's illness, which they now knew for certain was multiple sclerosis, had taken a toll. That fateful Monopoly night they had shared together in the early 1970s felt as though it had happened a century ago.

•

It still didn't seem right to Ralph. Through all of this, he felt, the Atlantic City Quakers hadn't received ample credit for their contributions to the creation of Monopoly. The streets of Atlantic City were lined with tributes to Darrow—a plaque near Park Place, mentions in the local museums, false retellings of the legend by city officials and tour guides. Yet the Quakers and their hours of playing and perfecting the game went largely unnoticed, even after Ralph's trial. Through the course of his Monopoly research, they had become real people to him and revived the connection to those who had welcomed him when he immigrated with his family as a child.

In the late 1980s, he decided to try to get a plaque acknowledging the Quakers placed in the seaside town. The Quality Inn on Pacific Avenue agreed to host the commemorative marker, as the hotel stood on the former site of the Atlantic City Friends School, torn down in the mid-'80s.

On September 11, 1989, the plaque was hung in the hotel's Quaker Room. It read,

> HONORING THE TRUTH ABOUT MONOPOLY
> In 1931, the game now sold as MONOPOLY, was invented in
> and around the Atlantic City Friends School which once stood
> on this spot. The invention was a cooperative effort centered on
> Ruth Hoskins, Jesse Raiford, and Cyril Harvey. Ruth Hoskins
> was the principal and Cyril Harvey was a teacher of this
> school. Jesse Raiford was their friend.

While the plaque told an incomplete story of Monopoly's history by omitting Lizzie Magie and the Arden players and using the word "invented" perhaps too strongly, Ralph considered it progress in the war against the Darrow folktale. Ralph dedicated the plaque, and Talicor, the new publisher of Anti-Monopoly, sponsored the event. In a hotel conference room, Ralph took to a podium wearing a blazer and a striped tie. He stood before a banner that read, "Talicor: Honors the True Creators of Monopoly and Introduces Anti-Monopoly." The group of early monopoly game players craned their necks to watch Ralph as he spoke—older, grayer versions of the souls who had tread the same soil decades before. The event served as a reminder of who wasn't there: Jesse Raiford, who had died in 1960; Ruth Harvey, who had passed two years later; and dozens of other Quakers who had played the game in its early years.

"Parker Brothers supported the Darrow myth for years," Ralph said, "and bought up a lot of patents and versions of the game that were popular at the time. They monopolized Monopoly. Actually the game was in the public domain. But now the truth is coming out and the people who deserve the credit for Atlantic City Monopoly are getting the credit."

Ralph walked outside the hotel and snapped a Polaroid photo of the three-story brick building with a green and yellow Quality Inn banner above its door. The Atlantic City Friends School was long gone from the corner of Pacific and South Carolina Avenues, but much of its original building had been incorporated into the hotel. Behind the site rose a bland brick building over fifteen stories high, and across the street stretched a stark, empty parking lot.

After years of decay, Atlantic City had become another experiment in urban renewal. Representatives from large casinos and area politicians had argued that in order to rebuild the city, it was first necessary to destroy it. Hotels like the Traymore and other decadent pieces of the city and its Quaker-constructed past were demolished, Ardenite William Price's beloved Marlborough-Blenheim imploded spectacularly to make room for a modern Bally's. Thousands of residents were displaced as casino moguls designed businesses that isolated their guests as much as possible from the city's harsh streets. By the end of the 1980s, Atlantic City had become one of the top tourist destinations in the United States, yet only five of the twelve major casinos in town were posting a profit, and what little bounty was earned was seldom passed on to locals.

Local papers reported that elderly residents were being robbed on Oriental Avenue and that the city's youth pelted the tourist buses with rocks. Land speculation pushed people out of their houses, and local churches and synagogues left the city, never to come back. Void of customers, hundreds of businesses shut their doors.

Yet despite the bleak cityscape, Dorothea Raiford, now eighty-eight years old, said that for the first time since she had lived on Atlantic City's streets, she would be able to look at a Monopoly board and smile. A fifty-five-year-long wait had come to an end.

"I feel wonderful," Raiford told a news reporter who asked her about the new plaque. "I'm just glad I lived long enough to see it. It finally happened."

•

IN THE YEAR following the Supreme Court's refusal to hear the Monopoly case, the decision "put the fear of God in people," according to one trademark lawyer. The Anti-Monopoly case was cited in a New York federal court ruling upholding a decision stating that Nestlé's Toll House cookie, like Monopoly, was generic. A similar invocation was used to find Eastern Air Lines' Shuttle generic as well.

Critics argued that the finding of the appeals court disregarded the basics of trademark law. By 1983, "shredded wheat," "elevator," and "aspirin" had been deemed generic because they had become common-place terms, but Formica, Teflon, and Coke had been upheld as trade-marks. An already confusing body of law had become even more so.

In the wake of the Anti-Monopoly decision, trademark lawyers and lobbyists took to Capitol Hill to push for legislation that would strengthen copyright protection for corporations. Fearful of succumbing to Parker Brothers' fate, companies began airing advertisements that stressed that they represented a specific brand. One brochure stated, "So please: *copy* things, don't 'Xerox' them."

Republican senator Orrin Hatch of Utah argued that quality brands were under fire because of the decision and proposed an amendment to the federal trademark laws that would outlaw the consumer motivation test, which asked people why they bought a certain product and had helped earn Ralph his victory. The provision was tucked into a bill that protected the manufacturers of semiconductor chips from piracy, and it easily passed. In the eyes of Ralph and Carl Person, the new law made it easier for a company to lay claim to something that otherwise would be perceived as generic, and hurt competition. "People were afraid all of the other marks would go the way of Monopoly," Person said, years later. "It just helps the rich get richer."

As part of its agreement with Parker Brothers, Anti-Monopoly could not reopen litigation in the matter, but Person ensured that Ralph's right to sell Anti-Monopoly would still be protected under the new act in what became known as "the Anti-Monopoly amendment." (Ralph later joked that because of the law's backers, it should have been called the "pro-Monopoly" amendment.) The longer-term concern, however, wasn't one of trademark protection for Anti-Monopoly as much as it was one of fair use. If a game inventor wanted to create a new game that made some kind of comment on Monopoly, it could cost hundreds of thousands of dollars in legal fees just to get the idea started, a fate that befalls many tech entrepreneurs today.

And even after the Supreme Court outcome, Ollie Howes and the other Parker Brothers attorneys held that the Ninth Circuit appeal ruling applied only to the Ninth Circuit region. Howes knew that Ralph could sell Anti-Monopoly anywhere he pleased, but the court had not yet ordered that the Darrow Monopoly trademark be canceled, and other inventors did not enjoy the same freedom regarding the Monopoly trademark that Ralph was guaranteed.

Had Ralph never pursued his Anti-Monopoly case until the end or taken a settlement of some kind, it's extremely unlikely that Monopoly's true history would have been unearthed, or at least not as fully. Even so, the beloved Darrow legend lives on. It only makes sense. The Darrow myth, while largely a false narrative, is irresistible, an inspirational parable of American innovation. It's a "nice, clean, well-structured example of the Eureka School of American industrial legend," the *New Yorker*'s Calvin Trillin wrote in 1978. "If Darrow invented the story rather than the game, he may still deserve to have a plaque on the Boardwalk honoring his ingenuity." It's hard not to wonder how many other unearthed histories are still out there—stories belonging to lost Lizzie Magies who quietly chip away at creating pieces of the world, their contributions so seamless that few of us ever stop to think about their origins.

Commonly held beliefs don't always stand up to scrutiny, but perhaps the real question is why we cling to them in the first place, failing to question their veracity and ignoring contradicting realities once they surface. And in the case of Monopoly, there didn't seem to be any reason for the public to question its creation story in the first place. If Ralph's legal battle had percolated even a few years later than it did, several of the key players he needed to testify to win his case would have been dead, their witnessing of the truth lost.

As the revelations of the game's controversial origins gained more attention in the courts and in the press, Parker Brothers quietly began to massage its Monopoly history. A 1985 version of the Monopoly rule-book opened with the header "The 30s, the Depression, and Darrow" and said that Darrow had "presented" a game called Monopoly to Parker Brothers executives. Similarly, a 1988 history called *The Monopoly Companion*, written by a former head of Parker Brothers' research and development department, acknowledged that Darrow had not invented the game, but didn't fully discuss his limited contribution to it. In 1996, on the official Monopoly website, Hasbro Inc., which purchased Parker Brothers in 1991, wrote, "It all started back in 1933 when Charles B. Darrow of Germantown, Pennsylvania was inspired by *The Landlord's Game* to create a new diversion to entertain himself while he was unemployed." And even in 2014, on Hasbro's website, a timeline of the game's history begins in 1935. While clever and lawyerly, these corporate retellings are most illuminating in what they don't mention: Lizzie Magie, the Quakers, the dozens, if not hundreds or thousands, of early players, Ralph Anspach, and the Anti-Monopoly litigation. Perhaps the care and keeping of secrets, as well as truths, can define us.

Some argue that Parker Brothers, and later Hasbro, has been an able steward of the game, and that we owe the consistency and potency of the brand to these companies. "Would the world have been better off with Monopoly in the public domain?" said game historian David Sadowski in an interview. "I think not. Most likely, there would've been a plethora of competing games, with differing rules and visual signatures." Perhaps, but then again, games like checkers and chess, which have long been in the public domain, act as counterpoints to that argument.

Consumers are consistently able to obtain those games in standardized versions.

The Monopoly case opens the question of who should get credit for an invention and how. Most people know about the Wright brothers, but don't recall the other aviators who also sought to fly. The adage that success has many fathers but we remember only one rings true—to say nothing of success's mothers. Everyone who has ever played Monopoly, even today, has added to its remarkable endurance and, on some level, made it their own. Games aren't just relics of their makers—their history is also told through their players. And like Lizzie's original innovative board, circular and never-ending, the balance between winners and losers is constantly in flux.

While Lizzie Magie's 1904 patent clearly laid the foundation for what most people today know as Monopoly, many others modified it, and Charles Darrow brought it to the world's attention. Does Monopoly belong to Lizzie? The Quakers? The Darrows? Parker Brothers? Or all of the above and anyone and everyone who plays it?

Now well into his eighties, Ralph has retired as a professor but still oversees Anti-Monopoly, which is currently being published by University Games. Once a year, he and some of the other surviving original board members meet for dinner in San Francisco, just as they did in the 1970s, when they had fewer wrinkles but more anxiety about the game's fate. Ralph's sons, Mark and William, intend to carry on the business and legal affairs of Anti-Monopoly Inc. for another generation.

Most important to Ralph, the outcome of the Monopoly legal battle preserved his right to freely talk about the game and its history.

His silence, Ralph said, "is not for sale."

WHAT BECAME OF THEM

"The court's reference to Darrow as the inventor or creator of the game is clearly erroneous."
—THE U.S. COURT OF APPEALS, NINTH CIRCUIT

RALPH ANSPACH is retired and has finished a memoir entitled *An American Professor Fought the 1948 Arab Jihad to Destroy Israel at Birth and Explains Why It Continues.* He is happily remarried and he and his wife Silvia split their time between the Bay Area, France, and New Zealand. Anti-Monopoly games are still for sale at antimonopoly .com, but while the game has sold well overseas, Ralph and the representatives at University Games, who handle Anti-Monopoly's sales in the United States, say they've had a hard time finding distribution in the States due to agreements between Hasbro and big box retailers. A computerized version of Anti-Monopoly is slated to be released by Webfoot Games.

RUTH ANSPACH retired in Queens, New York, and she enjoyed spending time with her family in Manhattan. She never lost her interest in progressive politics. She died in March 2012.

WILLIAM ANSPACH graduated from Harvard Law School and currently represents labor unions in New York City. He wrote his law school admissions essay about the Anti-Monopoly battle. He is happily married to his wife, Ronit, an urban planner, and keeps busy chasing after their baby boy, Leo.

MARK ANSPACH is an anthropologist and social theorist affiliated with a research center in Paris, where he earned his doctorate after graduating from Harvard College. Much of his work explores the ritual aspects of economic exchange.

JOHN DROEGER continued to practice law in the Bay Area for years and is now retired in Arizona.

CARL PERSON still practices law at his own firm in New York City and is credited by many for revolutionizing the paralegal field. He has run for many public offices over the years, including New York attorney general and mayor of New York City. Among his pending legal matters is an antitrust suit against Google Inc.

CHARLES DARROW died in 1967.

ESTHER DARROW died in 1991. She was survived by several family members who recalled her as a loving mother and grandmother.

RICHARD "DICKIE" DARROW died in 1971.

WILLIAM DARROW continued to live and work as a farmer in Pennsylvania until his death in 2006. His children continue to play the game from time to time.

FRANKLIN ALEXANDER died at the age of ninety-five "with a smile on his face," according to his family. He worked on political cartoons into his eighties. He is survived by his two daughters, Lyn Russek and Mimi Simson, and several grandchildren and great-grandchildren, including his grandson Hal, who e-mailed me on a whim wondering if I knew whether or not his grandfather had drawn the Monopoly art.

ROBERT BARTON retired after the sale of Parker Brothers to General Mills and died in 1995 at the age of ninety-one.

RANDOLPH BARTON is retired and still lives in Massachusetts. He spends his time with various philanthropic organizations, with his family, and at a second home in Maine.

JAY WALKER, years after sabotaging a Monopoly tournament, became one of the biggest stars of the first dot-com boom as the founder of Priceline.com. By 2000, the *Forbes* 500 was placing his net worth at $1.6 billion dollars, at the time one of the fastest ascents to the fabled list ever. The bubble burst, and Walker's fortune dwindled to only a few hundred million dollars. His roommate and fellow Monopoly player, Jeff Lehman, went on to become the president of Cornell University and is currently the vice chancellor of New York University in Shanghai.

Parker Brothers is a wholly owned subsidiary of Hasbro Inc., as is Milton Bradley. No former Parker employees who worked in marketing or research and development are on the Hasbro payroll. Through a spokeswoman, Hasbro declined to make its executives available for interviews for this book and declined to provide any photographs or images of its Monopoly game boards. My lists of over two hundred fact-checking questions and follow-up contact attempts went unanswered. When Hasbro purchased Parker Brothers in 1991, it's likely that it also purchased a trove of George Parker's diaries and neatly organized game library, which it has declined to make available to researchers for decades, as it declined my request to access them.

Monopoly continues to be among the bestselling commercial board games of all time and lives on in its classic cardboard incarnation, as well as on iPhone, iPad, and other digital platforms, well over a century after Lizzie Magie drew her original game. In an effort to keep the old brand relevant, Hasbro hosted a vote in 2013 that resulted in fans ousting the iron token and introducing a cat. In 2014, it sought out favorite "house rules."

Lawmakers continue to push back the year of expiration of the so-called Mickey Mouse Protection Act. The estates of everyone from Sonny Bono to George Gershwin have weighed in on how long after a creator's death an estate can continue to claim copyright. Under the Copyright Act of 1976, a copyright lasted for the life of an author plus fifty years, or seventy-five years if the work was corporately authored. Since then, copyright protection for works created before 1978 (like Monopoly) has been extended to ninety-five years from the publication date (in the case of Monopoly, 2030). One side of Congress felt that extending copyright protection helped the economy by ensuring that works were preserved and protected overseas. If artists were incentivized to create their own works, the thinking went, they would be less likely to rehash old ones. Opponents saw the extension as a boon to those who currently held the marks at the expense of the public.

LIZZIE MAGIE died in 1948. She and her husband, Albert, as well as her father, mother, and grandfather, are buried alongside each other in Arlington, Virginia, neither her obituary nor her headstone making any mention of her game invention. While she did not have any children, several of her extended family members maintain a genealogy of their connection to the Landlord's Game and the founding days of the Republican Party.

ACKNOWLEDGMENTS

"Let us be grateful to the people who make us happy; they are the charming gardeners who make our souls blossom."
—MARCEL PROUST

THE MONOPOLISTS is the result of more than five years, five apartments, four laptops, jobs at two newspapers, hundreds of miles run to train for three marathons, a Great Recession, research trips to ten states, two Olympics, and hundreds of gallons of coffee. There was high-fiving and heartbreak, tears and triumphs, weddings, funerals, baby showers, and even a few board game nights. In the process of reporting this story, I hacked off over a foot of hair in one anguished swoop, sold off many of my material possessions, was confronted by law enforcement for falling asleep in public places, was charged parking fines, found Monopoly money in my linens when doing laundry, fretted about finances, had nightmares about the various aspects of the story—including one exclusively about semicolons—and felt an eerie sense of connection with my characters, who also became obsessed with Monopoly and its curious origins in a twisted Nancy Drew way that perhaps bordered on unhealthy. I loved, I lost, I learned, I wrote.

They say that writers suffer so their readers don't have to, but so do those dear souls who are close to writers, who empower, encourage, and rip apart story structures in the name of friendship and generosity. I can't say I always completely understand it, but I'm incredibly grateful nonetheless.

Finishing *The Monopolists* was a true battle of endurance that I never could have even dreamed of attempting without an incredible and gracious group of people.

SOURCES

I'M INCREDIBLY GRATEFUL to Ralph Anspach and the Anspach family for taking the time to tell their story. Ralph endured hours and hours of interviews and more fact-checking e-mails and phone calls than he or I ever imagined, and was enthusiastic and upbeat through the whole process. Mark and William, too, were kind enough to meet with me and answer my questions, and I was grateful that I could spend time interviewing Ruth Anspach before she passed away in 2012.

Thanks are also due to Richard Biddle and Edward Dodson with the Henry George School in Philadelphia, the New York Public Library, the New York Historical Society, the Gilder Lehrman Institute of American History, the Robert Schalkenbach Foundation, New York University, the library at Swarthmore University, the Family History Library in Salt Lake City, Elwyn School, Ancestry.com, the Atlantic City Historical Museum, the New Jersey Historical Society in Newark, WorldCat, Google Books, the Delaware Historical Society, the Smithsonian, the United States Postal Service, the Library of Congress, NYU Game

Center, Nerd Nite, the Peabody Essex Museum, the Arden Craft Shop Museum and the kind residents there, Mike Curtis, Bruce Whitehill, David Sadowski, Becky Hoskins, Phil Orbanes, the Allphin family, Byron Coney, Malcolm G. Holcombe, the Strong Museum, Jonathan Will, Roger Angell, Calvin Trillin, Tim Walsh, Christian Donlan, Ian Brown, Jesse Fuchs, Alfred C. Velduis, Stephen Pavlisko, Jeff Lehman, Jay Walker, Richard Stearns, Christian Thee, Evan Kalish, Marty Schwimmer, Zachary Strebeck, Neil Wehneman, Jim Esposito, Carl Person, the Magie family (John Q. Magie and William Magie in particular), and BoardGameGeek.com.

Thomas Forsyth has gone above and beyond as a game researcher and friend. Many thanks to him, and find him online at landlordsgame .info.

CHEERLEADERS

MY MOTHER, CAROL, believed in me, gave me blank notebooks, and lived a courageous life. My father, Myron, is a fantastic father who never questioned why his offspring was spending her time writing about board games. My older brother, Andy, and awesome nephew, Quint, keep me in check, and I love them dearly for it. They taught me how to play Monopoly, and so much more.

Thank you to Aunt Ronda Pilon and Uncle Bob Roschke (and Chicago's best bookstore, the Bookworks), Larry and JoAnn Morse, Michael Morse, the Guernsey family (Carol, Daniel, Aidan, and Owen), the Renfro family (Guy, Linda, Sarna and the Beckers, Trystan, Tal, and Gabe), Jim and Carol, Grandma Maxine, Aunt Jan Nakagawa, and Uncle Steve. From diapers to drafts, my family has been unwavering.

This project simply never would have happened without my power literary agent, Deborah Schneider, and fearless lawyer, Kim Schefler. From the start, they believed in the story and me, and I can't thank them enough for their expertise and friendship.

From the moment we first met at their offices in the Flatiron Building, where Darrow and Barton had done their deal eighty years before, the crew at Bloomsbury USA have created a tremendous home for this book. Nancy Miller and her team embraced this story from the start, and I'm indebted to them. Thanks are due to also to Lea Beresford, Laura Phillips, George Gibson, Sara Mercurio, and Nathaniel Knaebel.

The *New York Times* is a truly incredible newsroom, and I'm humbled and grateful to work there every day. Jason Stallman and Joe Sexton hired and inspire me and are two of the best editors and all-around human beings in the business. Thanks are also due to Jill Abramson, Dean Baquet, and my colleagues on the sports desk who show me every day what teamwork is. Many other *Times* people deserve note: Steve Eder, Jenna Wortham, Sam Dolnick, Susanne Craig, Jessica Silver-Greenberg, Peter Lattman, David Carr, Sarah Maslin Nir, Maya Lau, Willie Rashbaum, Emily Steel, and the benevolent DealBookers and Biz Day reporters across the birches. Fern Turkowitz runs the place, and the world. High five to ladies of the O.G.C. And the *Times* pop-up book club is always in my heart.

Thanks are also owed to the staff of the *Wall Street Journal*, with shout-outs to Ken Brown, Neal Templin, Mike Allen, Rob Hunter, Jason Zweig, Laura Saunders, Bob Sabat, the Money & Investing section, the Page One staff who published my original Monopoly story back in 2009, and the fellow reporters and editors I worked with there who made the *Journal* a special place to be.

Maureen Thompson was a fantastic accomplice in research. Lauren Leto, Pip Ngo, Jeremy Greenfield, Rolfe Winkler, Sue Sataline, Seth Porges, and Blake Eskin are friends who also offered insight on early drafts. Matt Wasowski of Nerd Nite allowed me to lecture to hundreds of drunk geeks in Brooklyn, who emboldened me to pursue this project. Thank-yous are also due to producer and friend Diane Nabatoff and screenwriter Ted Braun.

Danny Strong provided incredible insight and enthusiasm. Great thanks are also due to Aviva Slesin, Anna Karingal, Christina "Lopez" Lipinski, Irma Akansu (Esq.), Jon Levy, William D. Cohan, Gay Talese, Simon Winchester, Erik Larson, Michael Malice, Susanna Chon, Seth Porges (yes, again!), Francine Dauw, Samantha Oliver Wolf, Dexter Filkins, Jan Messerschmidt, Alexander Baxter, Andrew Adam Newman, Wendy Frink, Caroline Waxler, Bob Sullivan, Mika, Eli and Sawyer Gonda, Brad Tytel, Kari Ferrell, Jeremy Redleaf, Adam Spiegel, Chuck Schaeffer, Matthew Williams, Charlie Lyons, Jim Miller, Barry Newman, Lindsay Kaplan, Richard Blakeley, Erin "Thrills" McGill, Jennifer Wright, Randi Newton, Vanessa Livingston, Peter Gaffney, Hamilton Pug, Rachel Weiss, Fred Armisen, Scott Kidder, Danielle Lurie, Jenny Li, my dear book and article club members, Rachel Fershleiser, Nick Douglas, Clarissa Williams, Mister Ooh-La-La, Annie He, Jeff Bercovici, Taylor Katai, Pantea Ilbeigi, Tess Soroka, Pip Ngo, Halley Theodore, Alex Amend, Philip Green, Salman Somjee, Peter Feld, Rana June, Carey Alexander, Troy Pospisil, Andrew Cedotal, Lauren Giudice, Tommy DeLillo, Dara Rosenberg, Sophia Muthuraj, the members of the Invisible Institute, and miscellaneous colleagues from the Gawker Brat Pack.

Those folks provided an array of support—couches, phone calls, food, pep talks, beers, Monopoly games—and I'm grateful.

Early believers include Ron Lieber, Nick Denton, Alex Balk, Choire Sicha, Chris Mohney, Lockhart Steele, Mitchell Stephens, Yvonne Latty, my teachers at New York University and Winston Churchill High School in Eugene, Oregon (go, Lancers!), and the staff of the *Register-Guard*.

COFFEE SHOPS

NEW YORK CITY: Soy Luck Club (R.I.P.!), Café Pick Me Up, the Bean (Broadway, First Avenue, and Second Avenue locations), Ost Cafe, Oren's (Times Square and Waverly locations), B Cup Cafe, Grounded, Think Coffee (Fourth Avenue, Eighth Avenue, and Mercer Street locations), Culture Espresso, the Tea Spot, Caffe Reggio, McNally Jackson, Table 12, Stumptown (both locations), the Ace Hotel, S'Nice (gold star: Eighth Avenue (RIP), Sullivan Street, and Park Slope locations), the *New York Times* cafeteria, Soho House, Atlas, Veselka, The Uncommons, the coffee shop at Housing Work in Soho, Konditori (Park Slope), Venticinque Café, and Kos Kaffe.

CHICAGO: Espresso Thy Art and Intelligentsia.

PORTLAND: Stumptown (SW 3rd) and Powell's Books (Burnside).

EUGENE: Allann Bros. (both locations), Wandering Goat Coffee, Morning Glory Café, Espresso Roma Cafe, Eugene Coffee Company (RIP—formerly known as Jamocha's), and Perk.

SALT LAKE CITY: Coffee Garden.

LOS ANGELES: Mr. Tea, Graffiti, and Urth Caffé.

MIAMI: The Café at Books & Books and Panther Coffee.

An assortment of Starbucks, Pret a Manger, the Coffee Bean & Tea Leaf, and Le Pain Quotidien locations were in the mix as well. Zipcar and Airbnb made this project infinitely simpler. Seamless fed me. Pandora and iTunes filled me with music streams. Mostly David Bowie.

And to everyone I didn't mention: Please accept my deep sense of guilt and know that I adore you.

Thank you.

A NOTE ON SOURCES

THIS IS A journalist's attempt to tell the true story of Monopoly. It is a work of nonfiction. To ensure the accuracy of the narrative, I spent hundreds of hours conducting in-person and telephone interviews and reviewing court opinions, letters, board games, radio and television clips, newspaper articles, catalogs, advertisements, patents, websites, forums, court transcripts, in- and out-of-print books, academic papers, public records, and other primary-source documents spanning over 150 years of U.S. history. In some places, particularly where court transcripts are quoted, I have condensed the conversations but tried to paraphrase when possible to ensure their overall integrity.

It's easy to assume in this age of research that if information doesn't surface via Google search, then it must not exist at all. My profession is among those being disrupted by technology, perhaps in a way that is ultimately for the better, but the reporting of this book was a humbling reminder of the infinite amount of knowledge still tucked away on dusty bookshelves, in attics, or in brains, yet to be documented and only woven together through sweat, obsession, and love of story, even regarding something as seemingly simple as board games. The Internet has yet to do its best work.

For years, rumors have swirled among a small set of game historians of the lost diaries of Lizzie Magie. In a 1906 interview with the *Washington Post*, Lizzie's mother mentioned "stacks of manuscripts" Lizzie had written that awaited publication, and Lizzie herself mentioned a year later in the pages of the same paper that she was working on a book. Her work could be in private hands, incomplete, or lost. I spent years trying to track such documents and any distant relatives to Lizzie down and never saw any diaries firsthand, nor can I confirm their existence. While some members of the Magie family agreed to be interviewed for this book, others declined. One game collector reportedly has a cache of documents, games, and other archival material related to Lizzie Magie, but I never gained access to this material and, as far as I know, others have not either. Ralph Anspach has said that this was the same person who read him passages from Lizzie's diary in which she expressed disappointment over the deal with Parker Brothers. Given the circumstances, I did the best I could to tell Lizzie's story, and I hope that through the years more comes to light about this astonishing woman and her long-overlooked life.

Since I first began reporting on Monopoly's history in 2009, I've questioned my purpose in pursuing this story. When you tell people that you're writing a book about board games, many chuckle, somewhat justifiably dismissing it as a silly pursuit. In many ways, it is. But Monopoly's history is a complicated and controversial one. In that spirit, I've tried to be as detailed as possible in listing my sources in the hopes that this book will be a jumping-off point rather than an entombment in the conversation about the ownership of ideas, the evolution of innovation in this country, and a brand that millions of people have treasured for generations.

But, after all, it is just a game.

NOTES

1. The Professor and the Trust-Busting Game

"The courtiers were shown the board" Charles Robert Bell. *Board and Table Games from Many Civilizations* (London: Oxford University Press, 1969). Bell's compendium is a trove of board game geekery.

Ralph Anspach, professor of economics Ralph Anspach, author interviews, fall 2009 and March 2010. Anspach Federal Bureau of Investigation files: On April 17, 1988, Ralph made a written Freedom of Information Act request to the FBI and the U.S. Army. In letters from the Department of Defense and the Department of Justice dated April 13, 1989, he received responses with "sanitized" information. Two earlier responses dated May 13, 1988, and June 21, 1988, included public records (requested by Ralph) that he included in his archives related to the Anti-Monopoly case (to be referred to hereafter as "Anspach archives"). They place him in the army from May 10, 1944, through May 14, 1946, when he was honorably discharged as a technician, fourth grade. Ralph Anspach, author phone interview, February 12, 2012. One memorable memo dated May 8, 1952, that chronicles Ralph's visit with his brother in France reads, "Gerald Anspach was reported to have told friends in Paris that his brother was 'of an adventurous turn of mind and something of a crackpot.' This, of course, could mean almost anything." William Anspach, author interview, October 18, 2013. Corroborated several times by Ruth, Mark, and William Anspach.

At San Francisco State Calvin Trillin, "Monopoly and History," U.S. Journal: Berkeley, CA, *New Yorker*, February 13, 1978. Trillin gets credit for the fork line, but this author has experienced Ralph's handwriting firsthand.

The seventies were in full throttle Ruthe Stein, "A Liberated Dragperson," *San Francisco Chronicle*, November 17, 1973.

It was into this kaleidoscope Ralph Anspach, author correspondence, September 8, 2012. Ralph Anspach, author interview, February 18, 2013.

With the help of his sons Robert Duffy, "Game to Bust the Trusts," *St. Louis Post-Dispatch*, March 8, 1974. The 1975 Anti-Monopoly patent can be found here: https://www.google.com/patents/US3961795?dq=anti-mono.

At first, Ralph called his creation Ralph Anspach, deposition, *Anti-Monopoly Inc. vs. General Mills Fun Group Inc.*, June 12, 1975.

Rejection after rejection Ibid.

Throughout the summer and fall Gene Donner, author phone interview, February 12, 2012. *Monopolygate* (later renamed *The Monopoly Detective*). Ralph Anspach, author interviews from 2009 to 2014. Donner was also kind enough to provide me with some written materials tied to his time with Anti-Monopoly. Review of *San Francisco Chronicle* coverage of 1973: Thanks to the New York Public Library.

Finally, in the fall of 1973 Anspach, *Monopolygate*.

Anti-Monopoly hit the market Ibid. Mark and William Anspach, author interview, New York City, November 2, 2011. Magazine advertisements, magazine unknown: Anspach archives.

In October Regular Shareholders Meeting notes, Anti-Monopoly Inc., minutes for December 3, 1973, Anspach archives. Letter from Slippery Rock: Anspach archives.

Ralph, Ruth, and the rest Ruth Anspach, author interviews, November 4 and 10, 2011. Mark and William Anspach, author interview, November 2, 2011. Ralph Anspach, e-mail to author, September 8, 2012.

A negative story about the game Ibid.

Ralph also applied for a patent Ralph Anspach, deposition, *Anti-Monopoly Inc. vs. General Mills Fun Group Inc.*, March 22, 1974. The date of the trademark application is December 21, 1973, and the application states that the Anti-Monopoly trademark was first used in interstate commerce on October 23, 1973. Application: Anspach archives. Ralph Anspach to Mssrs. McGurk and Biddle, November 24, 1973, Anspach archives. U.S. Department of Commerce Patent Office to Melvin R. Stidham, June 25, 1974, Anspach archives.

Trademarks—which protect words The definition of a trademark can get very wonky, but the U.S. Patent and Trademark Office offers some relatively clean language: http://www.uspto.gov/trademarks/basics/definitions.jsp.

In February of that year Oliver Howes Jr. to Ralph Anspach, February 13, 1974. Anspach archives.

Ralph viewed the Howes letter John Marshall, "Little Guy Who Beat a Monopoly Is at It Again," *Seattle Post-Intelligencer*, November 8, 1988.

Howes wrote on behalf Ellen Wojahn. *The General Mills/Parker Brothers Merger: Playing by Different Rules* (Washington, D.C.: Beard Books, 2003).

2. A Woman Invents

"I'm thankful" "Would Be Slave Girl Is Glad She Is Alive," *Kalamazoo Gazette*, October 17, 1909.

George's message had resonated deeply "Mr. George on Ireland: A Pamphlet by the Author of 'Progress and Poverty.'" *New York Times*, March 23, 1881.

During the 1880s Carol Easton, "No Intermissions: The Life of Agnes de Mille," *Washington Post*, http://www.washingtonpost.com/wp-srv/style/longterm/books/chap1/no_inter.htm. We're going to get back to board games, and this is all related to Monopoly, I promise!

George was an ardent anti-monopolist "Henry George on Free Trade," *New York Times*, February 15, 1883. No byline.

The anti-monopoly parties also served Matilda Joslyn Gage, *Woman, Church and State* (Amherst, NY: Humanity Books, 2002). "Talking Toilers: Trying to Establish an Anti-Monopoly Branch," *Chicago Daily Tribune*, February 12, 1882.

In the early 1900s U.S. Census, June 14, 1900, available on Ancestry.com.

Lizzie's political views Megan McKinney, *The Magnificent Medills: America's Royal Family of Journalism During a Century of Turbulent Splendor* (New York: Harper, 2011).

In earlier years (Davenport, IA: Andreas, Lyter, 1871). Magie is referred to here as a major, in reference to the lectures he gave about Lincoln: http://ia600308.us.archive.org/22/items/historicalpoliti00magi/historicalpoliti00magi.pdf.

James enlisted James K. Magie to Mary Ritchie, January 1, 1863, New York Historical Society. File folders GLC 5241 #1–10, GLC 5241 #11–20, GLC 5241 #21–30, GLC 5241 #31–40 and GLC 5241—#41–51. Magie's letters are also filled with commentary about the logistics of their long-distance relationship and plenty of reminders that even in a pre-cell-phone era, there was ire about the annals of communication.

The steam age gave way J. K. Magie, "Ignorant Officials and Careless Voters," *Chicago Daily Tribune*, January 30, 1885.

When Lizzie was thirteen This detail is from a letter Lizzie Magie wrote that was enclosed in a copy of her poetry collection, *My Betrothed*. That book and this letter were accessed at the New York Public Library's Stephen A. Schwarzman Building, but have since gone missing. I know of no other publicly accessible copies of *My Betrothed*. David Sadowski deserves credit for photographing the book.

At the time, stenography was Leah Price, "Diary," *London Review of Books*, December 4, 2008. David Sadowski, author phone interview, May 5, 2012. Darren Sean Wershler-Henry, *The Iron Whim: A Fragmented History of Typewriting* (Ithaca, NY: Cornell University Press, 2005).

"I have often been called" "Rivals Mary M'Lane" *Washington Post*, October 13, 1906.

The Dead Letter clerks Lynn Heidelbaugh, "Dead Letter Office," National Postal Museum, May 1, 2006, available at http://arago.si.edu/index.asp?con= 1&cmd=1&mode=&tid=2032238. Marshall Cushing, *The Story of Our Postal Office* (Boston: A. M. Thayer, 1893). James H. Bruns, "Remembering the Dead," *EnRoute*, July–September 1992, available at http://www.postalmuseum .si.edu/research/articles-from-enroute/remembering-the-dead.html. Thank you to Evan Kalish for providing further context.

USPS Historian Office. "A Brief History of Women at Postal Service Headquarters." July 23, 2008. The *Washington Post* reported that Lizzie left the Dead Letter Office around 1903 because she "could not be a party to the government's manner of doing business." Her motives beyond that are unclear, but it is the same year she filed her Landlord's patent, so perhaps she wanted to pursue game design more thoroughly.

An 1869 article "The Chances for Women to Work," *New York Times*, February 18, 1869. Hat tip to the USPS historians for pointing out the clip and the context of women in the Dead Letter Office.

In the evening after work "Miss Lizzie Magie's Benefit," *Washington Post*, April 5, 1893. "Rivals Mary M'Lane," *Washington Post*. "Husbands and Wives Battle to Save 'Property' and 'Money' as the 'Mortgages' Eat Away Bankrolls and 'Fortunes' Dwindle," *Boston Sunday Post*, December 16, 1936. "Coming Events," *Washington Post*, December 10, 1905.

On January 3, 1893 Lizzie Magie 1893 patent, US425893A.

Two years after the death Lizzie Magie, "For the Benefit of the Poor," *Frank Leslie's Popular Monthly*, January 1895. An archive of *Frank Leslie's Popular Monthly* is available online, thanks to the generosity of a few university libraries: http://onlinebooks.library.upenn.edu/webbin/serial?id=flpmonth. The biblical passage is from Matthew 25:29, King James version. The term the "Matthew effect" is generally attributed to sociologist Robert Merton. Merton offered the example of how eminent researchers may get more credit than their lesser-known counterparts, even if their work mirrors each other's. For more, see Robert K. Merton, "The Matthew Effect in Science," *Science*, January 5, 1968, available at http://www.garfield.library.upenn.edu/merton/matthew1 .pdf.

About two years later Lizzie Magie, "The Theft of a Brain: The Story of a Hypnotized Novelist and a Cruel Deed," *Godey's*, May 1897.

She began speaking in public Many thanks to game historian Thomas Forsyth for pointing this out. And kudos to the Henry George Birthplace Archives and Museum for keeping it around. *Single Tax Review*, Autumn 1902.

Most women didn't do such things James Glen Stovall, *Seeing Suffrage: The Washington Suffrage Parade of 1913, Its Pictures, and Its Effects on the American Political Landscape* (Knoxville: University of Tennessee Press, 2013).

From its inception, the Landlord's Game Forsyth points out that it's unclear whether Lizzie's super-early versions of the game included both sets of rules, but it's likely that at least some early versions did, considering the early Ardenites and their fervent single tax views. Only a few copies of the rules from early games exist at all, and one could play by either set of rules on a board, so we're sadly left to mere speculation.

After years of tinkering "Rivals Mary M'Lane," *Washington Post*.

Soon thereafter This is a tricky one, based on the board of an Arden, Delaware, resident's board. While Lizzie patented her game in 1904 and published it on her own in 1906, it's possible that a handmade game made it to the single tax hub of Arden before her Economic Game Company board did. The idea of the game appears to have been around in this community before the game was mass-produced. No byline. *Single Tax Review*, Autumn 1902.

In one of history's coincidences Anne L. Macdonald. *Feminine Ingenuity: Women and Invention in America* (New York: Ballantine Books, 1992). J. E. Bedi. "Exploring the History of Women Inventors." The Smithsonian, available at http://invention.smithsonian.org/centerpieces/ilives/womeninventors.html.

3. A Utopia Called Arden

"You are welcome hither . . ." Greeting placard in Arden, Delaware. Author visit to the Arden Craft Shop Museum.

In the early 1900s Review of documents at the Delaware Historical Society.

Arden residents were among the first Mike Curtis, Georgist historian and teacher, author phone interview, October 5, 2012. Pat Aller, "The Georgist Philosophy in Culture and History," Henry George Institute, July 1999, http://www.henrygeorge.org/aller.htm.

Fels's dollars No byline. *Boston Evening Transcript*, November 20, 1915. "Single Tax in Andorra," Joseph and Mary Fels papers, Historical Society of Pennsylvania, Collection 1953, 1840–1966. My research assistant, Maureen Thompson, did a knockout job of investigating Fels and putting his role into context.

As games and sports flourished Arden Craft Shop Museum.

Poet Harry Kemp came to Arden William Brevda, *Harry Kemp, the Last Bohemian* (Cranbury, NJ: Associated University Presses, 1986). According to Delaware Historical Society documents, Kemp showed up in Arden with suitcases full of books, manuscripts, and a bundle of poems. Even though Kemp had a millionaire financier patron who bankrolled his creative work, Sinclair, seizing on the collectivist smell in Arden's air, paid all of Kemp's expenses. But that's not all Kemp took from Sinclair in Arden. Sinclair had confided to his friend that his marriage to his wife, Meta, was on the brink. Sexually unsatisfied, Meta had affairs, while Upton rejected radical sex theory. (Yet Sinclair biographers have noted that he had extramarital affairs of his own.) Kemp and Meta had a liaison in Arden, with Meta later in her memoirs calling the romantic interlude "pagan." Eventually, Meta left Arden for New York City with Kemp not far behind her. The Sinclairs divorced, and Meta later wrote to Sinclair in Arden that she and Kemp were trying to live as an example of "the rightness of free love." The story of how Sinclair's wife had left him in Arden was a national sensation, making the front pages of newspapers near and far from the once-quiet single tax haven: a love triangle between a famed socialist, a fiercely independent woman, and a renegade poet from Kansas. Arden became national news, the scene for one of the literary world's greatest sources of gossip.

Lizzie Magie also reached out Upton Sinclair, *The Cry for Justice* (self-published, 1915).

The Mother Earth space The Georgists and women's suffrage: *Georgist News*, Editor's Notes, November 28, 1999, http://www.georgist.com/all/GN2/GN2-G.htm. Aller, "The Georgist Philosophy."

Some of the property spaces Thomas Forsyth has a sensational website chronicling some of the earliest Landlord's Game boards. On a 1909 board played at Wharton (special thanks to Roy Heap and Becky Hoskins), we clearly see colors, but Forsyth pointed out that the lettering clearly links Heap's board to the Arden design, likely via Nearing's board. The Heap board was the earliest-known board to Ralph before he put the Lizzie Magie pieces together. A letter from Guy Nearing to a Mr. Rosenquist dated September 13, 1961, discusses his relationship with the Landlord's Game and is part of the Anti-Monopoly court documents. Thomas Forsyth, "Landlord's Game—1903: Arden Rules," 2006, http://landlordsgame.info/games/lg-1903/lg-1903_arden-rules.html.

4. George Parker and the Cardboard Empire

"A game . . . is like role playing" Maxine Brady, *The Monopoly Book: Strategy and Tactics of the World's Most Popular Game* (New York: David McKay, 1974).

During the second half Salem's history is explored wonderfully at the Peabody Essex Museum, a fantastic trove of the area's roots and evolution: http://www.pem.org/.

The ocean had captured Family tree: Philip Orbanes, *The Game Makers: The Story of Parker Brothers from Tiddledy Winks to Trivial Pursuit* (Boston: Harvard

Business Review Press, 2004). Orbanes said that the dates were provided to him by Randolph Barton and Channing Bacall Jr.

George Jr. enjoyed a relatively Ibid.

The U.S. economy was booming Michael Lind, *Land of Promise: An Economic History of the United States*, Kindle ed. (New York: HarperCollins, 2013).

Among the first widely selling Review of documents at Old Sturbridge Village, Sturbridge, Massachusetts. Jill Lepore, *The Mansion of Happiness: A History of Life and Death* (New York: Knopf, 2012).

He and his friends wanted Parker Brothers, *75 Years of Fun: The Story of Parker Brothers, Inc.* (Salem, MA: Parker Brothers, 1958).

In addition, the power of promotion In 1889, a judge overturned the patent decision, ruling in Edison's favor, but the history of those tinkering with light prior to Edison is lengthy. *The Wizard of Menlo Park* by Randall Stross is a good place to start (New York: Three Rivers Press, 2007).

It was against this backdrop Parker Brothers, *75 Years of Fun.*

The game reflected For more on booms and busts, see Carmen M. Reinhart and Kenneth Rogoff, *This Time Is Different: Eight Centuries of Financial Folly* (Princeton, NJ: Princeton University Press, 2011).

By adding the element of speculation Parker Brothers, *75 Years of Fun.*

George listened Ibid.

The newspaper industry The heyday owed in part to newspaper publisher Joseph Pulitzer, who, if this photograph is any indication, was a model of hipster style far ahead of his time: http://en.wikipedia.org/wiki/Joseph_Pulitzer.

Milton Bradley, the man Jill Lepore, "The Meaning of Life: What Milton Bradley Started," *New Yorker*, May 21, 2007, 38–43.

In 1860, Bradley created Milton Bradley 1866 patent, 53561.

Bradley's game was a huge hit James J. Shea Jr., *The Milton Bradley Story* (New York: Newcomen Society in North America, 1973). Shea's narrative is a copy of a speech he delivered at the "1972 Massachusetts Dinner" of the Newcomen Society in North America, held in Boston on November 2, 1972.

George Parker understood Ellen Wojahn, *The General Mills/Parker Brothers Merger*. Parker Brothers, *75 Years of Fun*. Philip Orbanes said that while Chivalry, the game George Parker claimed to be his own, was a "modest" seller, Parker kept it in the catalog for decades, and it was eventually successfully recast as Camelot in the 1930s.

A common problem "Fine New Games and Toys," *New York Times*, December 1, 1895. Far from the Parker Brothers game boomlet in New England, entrepreneur Fusajiro Yamauchi set up his own card game company in Kyoto, Japan, in 1889 and later gave it a name meaning "leave luck to heaven," or Nintendo.

"We may divide" Foster Rhea Dulles, *A History of Recreation: America Learns to Play* (New York: Appleton-Century-Crofts, 1965).

Activists argued Andrew McClary, *Toys with Nine Lives: A Social History of American Toys* (North Haven, CT: Shoestring Press, 1997).

Game makers wanted Inez McClintock and Marshall McClintock, *Toys in America* (Washington, D.C.: Public Affairs Press, 1961). The Smithsonian has some Parker Brothers catalogs from this era in its collection.

In the late 1880s Orbanes, *The Game Makers*, 25. Orbanes cites George Parker notes. If Hasbro acquired the archives of George Parker when they purchased the company, they declined to make those records available to me. Parker Brothers, *75 Years of Fun*.

Living in elegant homes Sally Parker's eventual wedding dress, for one: http://truthplusblog.com/2011/04/28/influential-images-peabody-essex-museums-2008-exhibit-wedded-bliss/.

Later that same year Advertisement, *Duluth News-Tribune*, May 29, 1902.

What started as buzz "Ping-Pong's the Fad Now: The Little Game of Indoor Tennis That Is All the Rage," *Kansas City Star*, January 9, 1902.

A champion player Arnold Parker, (no known relation to Parker Brothers) *Ping-Pong: The Game and How to Play It* (New York and London: G. P. Putnam's Sons, 1902). You can read Parker's tome for free here: http://babel.hathitrust.org/cgi/pt?id=loc.ark:/13960/t9087429k;view=1up;seq=9. If you do, bless your heart and feel free to write to me about your experience: marypilon@gmail.com. If it's the next *Moby-Dick*, I want to be in the loop.

Perhaps out of fear "Why You Mustn't Use the Word 'Ping-Pong,' " *Salt Lake Telegram*, May 31, 1902.

Eventually, in 1933 Jay Purves, *Table Tennis* (New York: A. S. Barnes, 1942). Orbanes, *The Game Makers*, 61–62.

But he didn't make it to the battlefront Flu epidemic: David E. Kyvig, *Daily Life in the United States, 1920–1940: How Americans Lived Through the Roaring Twenties and the Great Depression* (Chicago: Ivan R. Dee, 2002).

In the summer of 1921 "R. P. Parker Killed in Paris Plane's Fall," *New York Times*, September 9, 1921.

Halfway across the Atlantic Obituaries, *Boston Daily Globe*, September 21, 1921.

5. New Life for the Landlord's Game

"Every girl yearns" "Message to World: Girl's 'White Slave' Sale Brings Many Bids," *Washington Post*, October 14, 1906.

Finding it difficult "Rivals Mary M'Lane: Miss Magie, of Chicago, Lived Long in Washington . . .," the *Washington Post*, October 13, 1906.

Purchasing an advertisement "Thinks She Has Arrived," *Washington Post*, October 20, 1906.

She said that she didn't "Girl with Gray-Green Eyes Wants to Be Slave," *Muskogee Times-Democrat*, October 19, 1906.

The ad quickly "Miss Magie Explains," *Washington Post*, October 19, 1906.

"Money only has a relative value" "Message to World," *Washington Post*.

Despite the fact "A Mary M'Lain in the Limelight."*Waterloo Times-Tribune*, October 24, 1909.

"I'm thankful that I was taught" "Would Be Slave Girl Is Glad She Is Alive," *Kalamazoo Gazette*, October 17, 1909.

Many likened Lizzie Mary MacLane, *Tender Darkness: A Mary MacLane Anthology*, ed. Elisabeth Pruitt (Belmont, CA: Abernathy & Brown, 1993).

"I am not good," Mary MacLane, *I Await the Devil's Coming* (Brooklyn, NY: Melville House, 2013).

Lizzie found herself besieged "Miss Magie Explains," *Washington Post.* "Message to World," *Washington Post.*

If Lizzie's goal "Refused All Offers" *Loganville Daily Reporter*, October 24, 1906.

In 1909, Lizzie authored a paper It's unclear where the original essay was published, but it was reported on and quoted extensively. No byline. "Wail of a Woman." Grey River Argus, December 18, 1909.

A businessman St. Paul Globe, August 23, 1889. Hat tip to David Sadowski.

Lizzie's unusual marriage "Husbands and Wives Battle to Save 'Property' and 'Money' as the 'Mortgages' Eat Away Bankrolls and 'Fortunes' Dwindle," *Boston Sunday Post*, Februrary 16, 1936.

Georgism was not socialism Karl Marx to Friedrich Adolph Sorge, June 20, 1881. Available on Marxists.org. https://www.marxists.org/archive/marx/works/1881/letters/81_06_20.htm.

On April 28, 1923 Landlord's Game patent, No. 1,509,312, September 23, 1924.

Little did she know Alice Armstrong Mitchell, deposition, *Anti-Monopoly Inc. vs. General Mills Fun Group Inc.*, May 19, 1976.

At least one member Roger Angell, author phone interview, March 26, 2013.

6. Frat Boys and Quakers Change the Game

"I wasn't out to make a whole lot of money." Brooke Lerch, deposition, *Anti-Monopoly Inc. vs. General Mills Fun Group Inc.*, September 11, 1975.

The Landlord's Game may have begun Daniel Layman, deposition, *Anti-Monopoly Inc. vs. General Mills Fun Group Inc.*, January 17, 1975. Williams did not become coed until 1970, although some exchange programs existed that allowed some women to take courses. Image of the frat house, courtesy of the Library of Congress: http://www.loc.gov/pictures/item/det1994005551/PP/. How many times does someone get to write that sentence?

The Thun brothers Layman deposition.

Dubbing his game Finance Ibid.

The initial sales of Finance Brooke Lerch, deposition, *Anti-Monopoly Inc. vs. General Mills Fun Group Inc.*, September 11, 1975.

For half a year Wanamaker's, which today is a Macy's, with most of the original opulence preserved, was also where the iconic 1987 film *Mannequin* was filmed. Nothing's gonna stop us now.

Lerch showed up Pennsylvania Railroad advertisement, Atlantic City Historical Museum, visited October 12, 2012. Lerch deposition.

In the 1850s Library of Congress, Today in History: June 26, "On the Boardwalk," http://memory.loc.gov/ammem/today/jun26.html. Nelson Johnson, *Boardwalk Empire: The Birth, High Times, and Corruption of Atlantic City* (Medford, NJ: Medford, 2002). Exhibit, Atlantic City Historical Museum, visited October 12, 2012.

The Boardwalk was also home Richard Cahan, "A Court That Shaped America: Chicago's Federal District Court" (Evanston, IL.: Northwestern University Press, 2002). Carnival tangent: Somers and Ferris were engaged in a legal battle, which Ferris won, based in part on the claim that Ferris's wheel was significantly larger in design than Somers's roundabouts. Ferris's wheel was a sensation, and his name became glued to the invention, associated with jovial state fairs, vertigo, and first kisses. Somers's 1893 roundabout patent # 489238 was filed in 1891. His patent was issued just months before the Ferris wheel premiered at the Chicago World's Fair, but Somers had constructed several of his wheels in New Jersey and in New York's Coney Island. Somers sued Ferris, but the case was dismissed.

By the mid-1920s Johnson, *Boardwalk Empire*. Bryant Simon, *Boardwalk of Dreams: Atlantic City and the Fate of Urban America* (New York: Oxford University Press, 2004).

Enoch "Nucky" Johnson Atlantic City Convention Hall, National Historic Register of Places nomination form, U.S. Department of the Interior, http://pdfhost.focus.nps.gov/docs/NHLS/Text/87000814.pdf. Plaque, Ritz Condominiums, Atlantic City, visited October 12, 2012.

Hotels were the undisputed kings Atlantic City Historical Museum.

Among the many institutions Ruth Evelyn Hoskins, deposition, *Anti-Monopoly Inc. vs. General Mills Fun Group Inc.*, February 4, 1975.

Ruth Harvey created copies Dorothy Harvey Leonard, Game Researchers' Notes, no. 8, American Game Collectors Association, Bartlesville, OK, August 1990. Arden Craft Shop Museum and Swarthmore University, where Leonard donated all of her papers. The folks at Swarthmore were a great resource as I put together this leg of my research. Dorothy Leonard, deposition, *Anti-Monopoly Inc. vs. General Mills Fun Group Inc.*, February 4, 1975.

Jesse Raiford, a real estate agent Leonard deposition. Hoskins deposition.

To make ends meet Cyril Harvey, deposition, *Anti-Monopoly Inc. vs. General Mills Fun Group Inc.*, February 4, 1975.

Sometimes, their arguments Leonard deposition. Ruth Raiford, deposition, *Anti-Monopoly Inc. vs. General Mills Fun Group Inc.*, February 4, 1975.

The Raifords and the Todds U.S. Census, 1930, available on Ancestry. com.

At dinner, the couples conversed Charles E. Todd, deposition, *Anti-Monopoly Inc. vs. General Mills Fun Group Inc.*, February 6, 1975.

7. Charles Darrow's Secret

"How many men" Henry George, *Progress and Poverty.*

One night, the Darrows Charles E. Todd to John Droeger, November 8, 1974, Anspach archives. I've discussed the similarities and differences between the Todd board and the Darrow 1935 patent with several historians, including Jonathan Will. Author phone interview, September 27, 2012.

Over time, Darrow's questions Todd to Droeger, November 8, 1974. Charles E. Todd, deposition, *Anti-Monopoly Inc. vs. General Mills Fun Group Inc.*, February 6, 1975. In her deposition, Esther Darrow maintained that she only remembered playing monopoly with the Todds once.

Charles Darrow was unemployed Esther J. Darrow, deposition, *Anti-Monopoly Inc. vs. General Mills Fun Group Inc.*, April 23, 1975. She put William's birthday as June 15, 1928, and Richard's as 1932. U.S. Census for Philadelphia, dated 1900, available on Ancestry.com.

Thousands of landlords Lorena A. Hickok to Harry Hopkins, report, August 6, 1933. Accessible online (http://explorepahistory.com/odocument.php?docId= 1–4–1DF) or at the Franklin D. Roosevelt Presidential Library and Museum.

One day, the Darrows' youngest son Charles Darrow Jr., author interview, November 11, 2012. Scarlet fever symptoms: PubMed Health, U.S. National Library of Medicine, http://www.ncbi.nlm.nih.gov/pubmedhealth/PMH

0001969/. This is also consistent with the recollections of Mimi Simson (one of Franklin Alexander's daughters).

It was during this dark period Lyn Russek, author phone interview, February 6, 2011. Mimi Simson, author phone interview, February 1, 2011.

While he was publishing Anspach, *Monopolygate*. This was Anspach detective work, unearthed decades after the settlement between Rudy Copeland and Parker Brothers in 1936. David Sadowksi, author phone interview, May 5, 2012. Charles Darrow Jr., author interview, March 30, 2013.

Unclear whether Ralph Anspach discovered that the documents were missing during his Anti-Monopoly research, and sure enough, forty years later, I couldn't find them either. The specifics of what happened to them are unclear.

Darrow hired The use of Patterson and White as the printer comes up multiple times in the documents related to the Anti-Monopoly case, perhaps most notably in Esther Darrow's deposition.

On May 31, 1934 Manager, Milton Bradley Game Department, to Charles Darrow, May 31, 1934. The letter is currently in the possession of Charles Darrow Jr., Darrow's grandson, who was kind enough to share it with me.

8. Parker Brothers, from Depression to Boom

"The cry was raised against the great corporations." Speech of Franklin Delano Roosevelt, http://www.americanrhetoric.com/speeches/fdrcommonwealth.htm. Given at the Commonwealth Club in San Francisco, California. Sept 23, 1932.

On October 24, 1929 Morris Dickstein, *Dancing in the Dark: A Cultural History of the Great Depression* (New York: W. W. Norton, 2010).

Parker Brothers continued to pay dividends to its investors While board game executives anticipated a plunge in consumer spending on games, and their own company balance sheets may have been disastrous, it's worth pointing out this was a golden age for cinema, theater, and other fields of entertainment. And, of course, Monopoly was a blockbuster in 1935, a time when the U.S. economy was still dark. For more, see Morris Dickstein, *Dancing in the Dark*.

Across town James J. Shea Jr., *The Milton Bradley Story* (New York: Newcomen Society in North America, 1973).

In the fall of 1931 "Table Gossip," *Boston Globe*, September 27, 1931. George Auerbach, "Game Business No Child's Play," *New York Times*, December 7, 1958. Ellen Wojahn, *The General Mills/Parker Brothers Merger*.

The ability of average Americans The "Princes of Property" quote is attributed to Roosevelt in 1932, shortly before he would be sworn in as president of the United States. Speech, Commonwealth Club, San Francisco, September 23, 1932.

In 1933, George Parker Randolph Barton, author phone interview, November 13, 2012. Philip Orbanes, *The Game Makers: The Story of Parker Brothers from Tiddledy Winks to Trivial Pursuit* (Boston: Harvard Business Review Press, 2004).

In Philadelphia, far from Barton's office Benjamin Hunneman to Robert Barton, April 15, 1935, Anspach archives.

Traveling from Boston The letters between Barton and Darrow, which are part of the *Anti-Monopoly Inc. vs. General Mills Fun Group Inc.* documents, date this meeting to around March 1935.

One year later Associated Press, "Monopoly Celebrates Its 50th Anniversary," the *Day*, February 8, 1985. Hat tip to Stephen Pavlisko for pointing this one out to me.

As the Parker Brothers catalog Photocopies of the 1935–1936 pages of the Parker Brothers catalog are part of the discovery documents for *Anti-Monopoly Inc. vs. General Mills Fun Group Inc.* and are now part of the Anspach archives. "Monopoly Sales 1935–1974: Summary by Years Showing Sales of Monopoly Game Equipment," discovery documents, *Anti-Monopoly Inc. vs. General Mills Fun Group Inc.* The 1936 Parker Brothers catalog makes mention of Stock Exchange: Anspach archives. Stock Exchange rules: http://www.hasbro.com/common/instruct/StockExchangegame.pdf.

An outside artist, Dan Fox Philip Orbanes, "Meet Dan Fox," *Association of Game & Puzzle Collectors Quarterly* 10, no. 1 (June 4, 2013). Author phone interviews with Herb Fox and Elizabeth Fox-Wolfe, November 18, 2014.

Reports emerged Roy Bongartz, "Pass and Go and Retire," *Saturday Evening Post*, April 11, 1964, 26–27.

Some crazed players Also tapping into fan fervor and in a clever publicity move, in March 2014, Hasbro launched a campaign to have fans vote on their favorite "house rules," to be incorporated into a special edition of the game. Mary Pilon, "Can't Play by the Rules? It's Fine by Mr. Monopoly," *New York Times*, March 25, 2014. Meanwhile, some players have made the effort on their own, perhaps most notably with "Needlessly Complex Monopoly," a rule set devised by a group of recent college graduates to better reflect the post-financial-crisis sense of malaise. You can read the rules, which include things like joint ventures, insurance, and air rights, here: http://needlesslycomplexmonopoly .com/.

Parker Brothers wasn't the only one "Off the Record" column, publication unknown, Anspach archives. "Charles B. Darrow Dies at 78; Inventor of Game of Monopoly," *New York Times*, August 29, 1967. The *New York Times* wrote that Darrow's first royalty check was for seven thousand dollars in 1935 and that in the time between his invention of the game and his death, forty-five million sets had been sold.

One journalist after another Emma Dashevsky, "Another Germantown 'First,' 'Monopoly' Invented Here," *Germantown Bulletin*, February 13, 1936.

Before long, Parker Brothers "Play with a Purpose," Chicago Historical Society, available at http://chicagohistory.org/static_media/pdf/historylab/chm-historylabpc01.pdf. Researchers David Sadowski and Chris Williamson deserve full credit for piecing together the mystery of the metal tokens. Sadowski writes about the tokens, and other aspects of the game's history, extensively in his self-published book, *Passing Go*.

In a letter with the signature Robert B. M. Barton to Charles B. Darrow, Esq., part of the discovery documents for *Anti-Monopoly Inc. vs. General Mills Fun Group Inc.* and now part of the Anspach archives.

The Parker Brothers vice president Benjamin Hunneman to Robert Barton, as quoted in Robert Barton to Charles Darrow, April 15, 1935, discovery documents, *Anti-Monopoly Inc. vs. General Mills Fun Group Inc.*

Darrow never submitted Robert B. M. Barton, deposition, *Anti-Monopoly Inc. vs. General Mills Fun Group Inc.*, May 8, 1975.

Darrow had obtained Per Ralph, via e-mail and author interview, "It mattered not when copyright symbol was attached by Darrow, rather when he first published. Darrow tells Barton this was Aug 1933. He may have told the P&A office Oct 24th as this was filing date, most applications (copyright, trademark, patent) are retroactive enforceable to the filing date as this is the date of invention? Does statutory bar begin with date of invention or in copyright first publication? The symbol attached did not matter until 1978." This was a critical finding in Ralph's case. More on that later.

Rumors floated David W. Knapp to R. M. Barton, September 13, 1935. Discovery documents, *Anti-Monopoly Inc. vs. General Mills Fun Group Inc.*

R. M. Barton to David Knapp, September 17, 1935. Court documents, *Anti-Monopoly Inc. vs. General Mills Fun Group Inc.*

Next came Easy Money Vincent Martin, deposition, *Anti-Monopoly Inc. vs. General Mills Fun Group Inc.*, September 10, 1975.

Perhaps a bigger threat Inflation information is generously indexed online by Thomas Forsyth: http://landlordsgame.info/rules/infl-r.html.

Barton also visited Louis Thun, deposition, *Anti-Monopoly Inc. vs. General Mills Fun Group Inc.*, June 17, 1975.

George told Lizzie Barton deposition, May 8, 1975. Lizzie's 1904 patent by then had likely slipped into the public domain, meaning that Parker Brothers would only need to purchase the 1924 one. #1,509,312 Anspach archives. "And Now It's the Pastime of America's 'Rugged Individualists.'" *Washington Post*, January 28, 1936.

Two days after the ink Lizzie Magie to "Mr. Parker," November 8, 1935, Anspach archives.

Much to Lizzie Magie's dismay The three games are advertised in the 1939–1940 Parker Brothers catalog under the heading "Three Games by Elizabeth Magie Phillips (Famous Originator of Games)." Anspach archives. Perhaps this is as good of a place as any for a shout-out to the Norman Seldin song "Monopoly Woman": http://www.reverbnation.com/storminnormanseldin/song/8606682-monopoly-woman.

After the Landlord's Game's disappointing return For more on the patterns of women being silenced throughout history, see the work of Cambridge classics professor Mary Beard, namely her lecture, "Oh Do Shut Up Dear!" http://www.lrb.co.uk/v36/n06/mary-beard/the-public-voice-of-women.

The craze over Monopoly Victor Watson, *The Waddingtons Story: From the Early Days to Monopoly, the Maxwell Bids and into the Next Millennium* (London: Northern Heritage Publications, 2008).

9. Conflict, Intrigue, Revenge

"He had it handed to him on a silver platter" Eugene Raiford to Mr. Vince Leonard, January 2, 1964, discovery documents, *Anti-Monopoly Inc. vs. General Mills Fun Group Inc.*

Daniel Layman, the fraternity boy Dan Layman, deposition. *Time* changed its story on February 3, 1936, refuting the notion that Charles Darrow had created the game and acknowledging Lizzie.

Darrow's sale of the game Dorothy Harvey Leonard, Game Researchers' Notes, no. 8, American Game Collectors Association, Bartlesville, OK, August 1990. Arden Craft Shop Museum and Swarthmore University. Cyril Harvey, deposition, *Anti-Monopoly Inc. vs. General Mills Fun Group Inc.*, February 4, 1975.

One Tuesday night Eugene Raiford to Mr. Vince Leonard, January 2, 1964, discovery documents, *Anti-Monopoly Inc. vs. General Mills Fun Group Inc.*

Years later, when Jesse Dorothea Raiford, deposition, *Anti-Monopoly Inc. vs. General Mills Fun Group Inc.*, February 4, 1975.

Charles Todd didn't hear Charles E. Todd, deposition, *Anti-Monopoly Inc. vs. General Mills Fun Group Inc.*, February 6, 1975.

On the other side For more information about the indoctrination of youth by Hitler, see "Indoctrinating Youth," Holocaust Encyclopedia, United States Holocaust Memorial Museum, http://www.ushmm.org/wlc/en/article.php?ModuleId=10007820. For more information about the specific games, see BoardGameGeek.com.

In his letter, the agent Lloyd R. Shoemaker, *The Escape Factory: The Story of MIS-X, the Super-Secret U.S. Agency Behind World War II's Greatest Escapes* (New York: St. Martin's, 1990). Shoemaker's book includes a lot of detail on the POW escape mechanisms used by the Americans, and he makes several references to the use of Monopoly boards. Fact sheet, including a photograph of a cribbage board x-rayed, National Museum of the U.S. Air Force (aafha.org). Hat tip to Stephen Pavlisko, who has spent an incredibly long amount of time researching the POW-smuggling history and was nice enough to share his thoughts and paper trail with me. Alan Duke, "Table Tennis as an Escape Aid." Hat tip, Stephen Pavlisko. Also in Clayton Hutton, *Official Secret* (London: Max Parrish, 1960).

In America, military officers Shoemaker, *The Escape Factory.*

Milton Bradley turned James J. Shea Jr., *The Milton Bradley Story.*

Clank, clank, clank Letter to Mr. Watson, March 26, 1941. Also in Victor Watson, *The Waddingtons Story.*

The Germans were aware German flyer, via Stephen Pavlisko. Another choice quote: "The escape from prison camps is no longer a sport!"

It would be virtually impossible Researcher Mark Seaman at the Imperial War Museum in London "confirmed the escape kits were built into games and sports equipment smuggled into prison camps during World War II," according to an Associated Press story from January 16, 1985. It's worth noting that this also coincided with Waddingtons' fiftieth anniversary of publishing Monopoly, raising suspicion that the tale was more commercially motivated than historically accurate. "Asked whether anyone was able to escape using the aids hidden in recreational gear, Seaman replied, 'It's difficult to say.'" No byline. "Escape Devices Hidden Under Boards Smuggled into Camps: Monopoly Not a Game to WWII British POWs," *Los Angeles Times*, April 21, 1985.

The board games with their smuggled Associated Press, no byline. "Escape Devices Hidden Under Boards Smuggled into Camps: Monopoly Not a Game to WWII British POWs," *Los Angeles Times*, April 21, 1985.

With over one million "Monopoly Sales 1935–1974: Summary by Years Showing Sales of Monopoly Game Equipment," part of the discovery documents for *Anti-Monopoly Inc. vs. General Mills Fun Group Inc.* and now part of the Anspach archives.

As Parker Brothers ascended "Re-elected President of Toy Manufacturers," *New York Times*, September 21, 1940. "Elected to Presidency of Toy Manufacturers," *New York Times*, December 10, 1952.

With the introduction of television Paul M. Connell, Merrie Brucks, and Jesper H. Nielsen, "How Childhood Advertising Exposure Can Create Biased Product Evaluations That Persist into Adulthood," *The Journal of Consumer Research*, March 2014.

The Parker men Alexander R. Hammer, "Advertising: Yule Rush on for Parker Brothers," *New York Times*, June 7, 1959.

Monopoly was still the company's unofficial flagship game In the post Charles Darrow–Monopoly boom, Parker Brothers and rival firms were creating other perennial classics. In the 1950s, Selchow and Righter found success selling Scrabble, a word game credited to the unfortunately surnamed Alfred Mosher Butts. For more, see Stefan Fatsis, *Word Freak: Heartbreak, Triumph, Genius, and Obsession in the World of Competitive Scrabble Players* (New York: Penguin Books, 2002). In the late 1940s, Parker Brothers acquired Cluedo, a British murder mystery game that was supposedly invented by a musician to pass the tedious wartime hours. And at one point, there were issues trying to locate its credited inventor. See Robert McG. Thomas Jr. "Solved! Prof. Plum and Cohorts in the Clear." *New York Times*, December 1, 1996. http://www.nytimes.com/1996/12/01/world/solved-prof-plum-and-cohorts-in-the-clear.html. Around the same time, Candyland is said to have been developed in polio wards as a tool to raise spirits.

10. The Case for Anti-Monopoly

"I start out with the idea" John Droeger, author interview, November 7, 2011.

Ralph Anspach pushed "Scorecard," *Sports Illustrated*, August 16, 1976, 10.

"If anything, I'm pro-business . . ." Robert Duffy. "Game to Bust the Trusts," *St. Louis Post-Dispatch*, March 8, 1974. John Marshall. "Little Guy Who Beat Monopoly Is At It Again." *Seattle Post-Intelligencer*, Section B. November 8, 1988. John Droeger, author interview, November 7, 2011.

At twelve forty-five Ralph Anspach, deposition, *Anti-Monopoly Inc. vs. General Mills Fun Group Inc.*, March 22, 1974. Ralph Anspach, author phone interview, October 26, 2011.

Sometime later, Ralph sat Marvin Kaye, *A Toy Is Born* (New York: Stein and Day, 1973). Mark and William Anspach, author interview, New York City, November 2, 2011.

Startled and saddened John Droeger, author phone interview, October 27, 2011. Ralph Anspach, author interviews, 2009 to 2014. Charles Burress, "Joanna Droeger—S.F. Restaurateur Invented Mud Pie," *San Francisco Chronicle*, November 17, 2004.

Trademark lawyers use Marty Schwimmer (trademark attorney), author phone interview, May 21, 2012. For more on trademark law, Harvard Law School has a great summary here that's far more readable than most texts produced by aspiring lawyers: http://cyber.law.harvard.edu/metaschool/fisher/domain/tm.htm.

On the scorching morning Ralph Anspach, deposition, *Anti-Monopoly Inc. vs. General Mills Fun Group Inc.*, June 12, 1975.

Given the attitudes about women A fascinating digression could be made here on these mostly lost women physicists and mathematicians. NYU's Bobst Library has more information about the program, which was sponsored by the Chance-Vought Aviation Company.

It was good to know Ralph Anspach, author interview, February 19, 2013. John Droeger, author phone interview, October 27, 2011. Ralph Anspach, author phone interview, October 26, 2011.

Ralph's sons Ralph Anspach, author interview, February 19, 2013. Ruth Anspach, author interviews, New York City, November 4 and 10, 2011.

Much to Ralph's amazement Dan Layman, deposition, *Anti-Monopoly Inc. vs. General Mills Fun Group Inc.*, January 17, 1975.

Finally, Ralph and Droeger Alice Armstrong Mitchell, deposition, *Anti-Monopoly Inc. vs. General Mills Fun Group Inc.*, May 19, 1976. Just a reminder for those trying to keep the Quaker family trees straight: Joanna Raiford McKain is Ruth Raiford's niece, the daughter of Dorothea and the late Jesse Raiford. In 1933, Joanna was eight years old.

11. Anspach Connects the Dots

"All the ancient histories" Voltaire, "Jeannot et Colin," available in translation at http://www.gutenberg.org/cache/epub/4772/pg4772.html.

As the Anti-Monopoly trial Frederic Moritz, "'Monopoly' Game Monopolizing Market?," *Christian Science Monitor,* November 4, 1974.

Cyril's wife, Ruth Cyril Harvey, deposition, *Anti-Monopoly Inc. vs. General Mills Fun Group Inc.*, February 4, 1975. John Droeger, author phone interview, October 27, 2011. Ralph Anspach, author interview, February 20, 2012.

"Now tell me," Ralph Anspach, author interview, San Francisco, February 21, 2012.

Ralph asked Todd if Darrow Charles E. Todd, deposition, *Anti-Monopoly Inc. vs. General Mills Fun Group Inc.*, February 6, 1975. A deposition of his wife, Olive, in which she affirmed his claims, was taken the same day.

Meanwhile, Ruth Anspach's Ruth Anspach, author interviews, New York City, November 4 and 10, 2011.

Ralph's focus on the trial R. Ted Compton told Ralph that he had played the game in New York City in 1929 in Greenwich Village, among Yale and Columbia alumni and professors living there. It was a square oilcloth version, Compton said. From 1929 to 1932, Professor Sam Bass Warner of Harvard Law School brought the game into his office. The towns mentioned on that board were mostly Boston suburbs. R. Ted Compton to Ralph Anspach, September 11, 1975, Anspach archives. Play at Haverford College was confirmed by a letter from Howard Comfort. Howard Comfort to Ralph Anspach, July 6, 1977. Mentions of monopoly appear in that year's Haverford yearbook as well.

The board that Ralph saw Decades later, in 2014, one would surface in an eBay auction. Malcomb G. Holcombe purchased it and was kind enough to share some information with me leading both of us to conclude it long predates the Darrow board and fits with the folk game path.

After his rejection John Saltmarsh, *Scott Nearing: The Making of a Homesteader* (White River Junction, VT: Chelsea Green Publishing, 1998). Scott Nearing to Ralph Anspach, November 1974, Anspach archives.

One day while at his office William D. Boutwell to Ralph Anspach, October 26, 1974.

Ralph found an old photograph Patent assignment document, signed by Elizabeth Magie Phillips, November 6, 1935, discovery documents, *Anti-Monopoly Inc. vs. General Mills Fun Group Inc.* The lack of royalties was also reported in the *Washington Post. Washington Post*, January 28, 1936.

12. Barton Under Oath

"Because the game was completely worthless" Robert B. M. Barton, deposition, *Anti-Monopoly Inc. vs. General Mills Fun Group Inc.*, May 8, 1975.

At seventy-one years old Ibid.

"Now, sir," Ibid. The Strong National Museum of Play in Rochester, New York, acquired the *Playthings* archives.

On June 12, 1975 Ralph Anspach, deposition, *Anti-Monopoly Inc. vs. General Mills Fun Group Inc.*, June 12, 1975.

Charles Darrow never had Roy Bongartz, "Pass and Go and Retire," *Saturday Evening Post*, April 11, 1964, 26–27.

On a warm day Charles Darrow, SSN 188–36–8673, U.S. Social Security Death Index. This resource was made available to me by the Family Search Library in Salt Lake City and Ancestry.com. "Charles B. Darrow Dies at 78; Inventor of Game of Monopoly," *New York Times*, August 29, 1967. Darrow's grandson said it was a cerebral aneurysm, while the *New York Times* obituary says the cause of death was a heart attack.

Ralph flew east Esther J. Darrow, deposition, *Anti-Monopoly Inc. vs. General Mills Fun Group Inc.*, April 23, 1975.

Not everyone was eager William Anspach, author interview, November 2, 2011. Ruth Anspach, author interview, November 4, 2011.

Meanwhile, on a college campus Jeff Lehman, e-mail to author, June 13, 2013. Jay Walker, deposition audio file, *Anti-Monopoly Inc. vs. General Mills Fun Group Inc.*, date unknown.

Walker, Lehman, and their friends Jay Walker, author phone interview, June 20, 2013.

As word of the Ivy League Jeff Lehman, e-mail to author, June 13, 2013. Jim Bouton's book is considered a classic in the sports memoir genre and generated a flurry of controversy when it was published. Bouton confirmed the encounter via e-mail on July 16, 2014.

During Christmas vacation Jay Walker, author phone interview, June 20, 2013.

The two students Jay Walker and Jeff Lehman, *1000 Ways to Win Monopoly Games* (New York: Dell, 1975). Another thing that makes games go on forever: squatting in jail to avoid paying rent. Eric J. Friedman of Cornell University rightfully points out that if you're hanging out there to avoid paying rent, you've probably already lost. It's almost always worth paying to break free. And that assumption that a game can go on forever? Friedman and his colleagues found that "while many have cursed the length of Monopoly games, we have not found any detailed analyses of the game's length, nor any studies that compute the probability that the game goes on forever." Their abstract: "We estimate the probability that the game of Monopoly between two players playing very simple strategies never ends. Four different estimators, based respectively on straightforward simulation, a Brownian motion approximation, asymptotics for Markov chains, and importance sampling all yield an estimate of approximately twelve percent." Eric J. Friedman et al., "Estimating the Probability That the Game of Monopoly Never Ends," *Proceedings of the 2009 Winter Simulation Conference*, 380–391, available at http://www.informs-sim.org/wsc09papers/036.pdf.

*To **Walker** and his friends* Yes, most people play the game wrong. You can read more about the folly of house rules here: http://www.nytimes .com/2014/03/26/business/monopoly-fans-invited-to-rethink-rulebook. html?ref=business&_r=0. I know. I just changed your life.

On April 28, 1975 Janice C. Simpson, *Wall Street Journal*, April 28, 1975.

13. A Matter of Principle

"All for ourselves" Adam Smith, *The Wealth of Nations*. orig. 1776, Bantam Classics, reprint edition (New York: Bantam, 2003).

In June 1975 Ralph Anspach, diary entry, undated. Ralph Anspach, author phone interview. John Droeger, author phone interview.

Ralph asked Droeger Edward V. Pollack to Charles R. Garry and Benjamin Dreyfus, September 1, 1976, Anspach archives.

That turned out to be Joseph C. Goulden, *The Benchwarmers* (New York: Weybright and Talley, 1974). Goulden refers to Williams as a "bosom political ally of Governor Ronald Reagan who was clobbered when he ran for state attorney general." He adds, "Williams thinks prison authorities should have carte blanche to run their institutions pretty much as they wish" and criticizes how Williams handled cases involving violence at San Quentin prison.

"I started crying" William Anspach, author interview, New York City, November 2, 2011.

The phone rang Ralph names the whistle-blower in his files, and I researched his background. But because I was unable to get in touch with him and his notes weren't submitted as part of the court documents, I chose not to name him here.

First, lawyer Carl Person Carl Person, author interviews, 2009 to 2014.

Five days later "Toy Designer Kills Three Co-Workers, Then Himself," UPI, July 27, 1976, *Amarillo Globe*, via Google News Associated Press, "Toy Designer Kills Three, Himself, Notes Tell His Tale," Associated Press, July 28, 1976, *Ocala Star-Banner*, via Google News. A similar account ran in the *Chicago Tribune* the same day.

By November 1976 William R. Johnston and Roberta L. Rogers, *Reporters' Daily Transcript*, November 17, 1976, U.S. District Court in the Northern District of California, *Anti-Monopoly Inc. vs. General Mills Fun Group Inc.*, Anspach archives.

The attorneys launched Johnston and Rogers, *Reporters' Daily Transcript*. I have consolidated much of Dreyfus's and Daggett's comments for space.

14. The Burial

"It may be that all games are silly" Robert Lynd, *Solomon in All His Glory* (London: Grant Richards, 1922).

On July 5, 1977 Ralph Anspach, author interview, February 20, 2013. The Associated Press reported forty thousand games in its photo caption accompanying a shot of Russ Foster. Other accounts say that it was thirty-seven thousand games and parts to make three thousand more. Regardless, we're talking about a lot of Anti-Monopoly cardboard.

In a small, cluttered office Carl Person, author phone interviews, fall 2009 and October 27, 2011. Christian Thee, author phone interview, November 9, 2011. Jim Esposito, author phone interview, January 31, 2010.

Ralph had become aware Some of his thinking is outlined in Robert B. Chickering to Ralph Anspach, October 20, 1977, Anspach archives.

In January 1980 Ralph Vartabedian, "Inventor Passes Go, Collects Garbage," *Minneapolis Star*, January 23, 1980. "Return to 'Go,' Collect No Games," *Free Press*, January 24, 1980. "Monopoly Still Has One," *San Francisco Examiner*, July 12, 1980.

Edward Canapary Court documents, *Anti-Monopoly Inc. vs. General Mills Fun Group Inc.*, Anspach archives. "Anti-Monopoly Loses Again," *San Francisco Chronicle*, May 12, 1981. Opinion here: http://openjurist.org/684/f2d/1316/anti-monopoly-inc-v-general-mills-fun-group-inc. Anspach's timeline also dates this as August 1982. The *Wall Street Journal* reported on the ruling in a brief that ran on August 27, 1982.

Parker Brothers was also facing Richard Stearns (former president of Parker Brothers), author phone interview, May 10, 2012. Randolph Barton, author phone interview, October 27, 2011. Supposedly, the name Atari derives from a Japanese verb that means "to hit the target."

You are in the bowels of my endnotes. Bless you, you maniac. But one after my own heart. E-mail marypilon@gmail.com an anagram of your choice from the words in this book. Get a digital hug in response. It ain't two hundred dollars, but it has spirit.

Bushnell, perhaps even more This aphorism is known by some in the game world as "Bushnell's law." For further illustration of the principle, watch the stellar documentary *The King of Kong: A Fistful of Quarters*.

Others who joined Parker Brothers A note on the Crest quote in the *New York Times* story. It was somewhat misleading to tell the reader that the identification of the producer by name was the standard when actually the standard only required that the producer's name must be the primary significance of the mark rather than the product itself.

Parker Brothers hired Nathan Lewin to Hon. Alexander L. Stevas, January 27, 1983, court documents, Anspach archives. Carl Person to Hon. Alexander L. Stevas, January 31, 1983.

Peculiarly enough, Jeff Lehman Jeff Lehman, e-mail to author, June 13, 2013.

15. Redemption

"They monopolized Monopoly" Ralph Anspach, author interview, February 20, 2012.

Almost a decade to the day Reginald Smith, "'Anti-Monopoly' Wins Its Game," *San Francisco Chronicle*, February 23, 1983.

During the Reagan era Michael Pritchard, "Monopoly Creators Pass Go, Collect Credit," (undated), unknown New Jersey newspaper.

After years of decay Bryant Simon, *Boardwalk of Dreams: Atlantic City and the Fate of Urban America* (New York: Oxford University Press, 2004). "Atlantic City, New Jersey Boardwalk of Broken Dreams," *Time*, September 25, 1989.

In the year following Congressional testimony regarding the hearing can be found here: http://www.ipmall.info/hosted_resources/lipa/trademarks/S.%20 Hrg.%2098–901,%20The%20Trademark%20Clarification%20Act%20of% 201983,%20Subcomm.%20(Feb.%201,%201984).pdf. Carl Person, author phone interview, April 18, 2014. Paul Hemp, "A Lot Rides on a Good Name," *New York Times*, September 7, 1983.

It only makes sense Calvin Trillin, "Monopoly and History," U.S. Journal: Berkeley, CA, *New Yorker*, February 13, 1978. Calvin Trillin, author phone interview, March 22, 2013.

A 1985 version 1985 Monopoly rulebook, Parker Brothers, Anspach archives. Rich Uncle Pennybags as told to Philip Orbanes, *The Monopoly Companion* by Bob Adams (Adams Avon, MA: Media Corporation, 1999). Printout of Hasbro's official Monopoly page, March 20, 1997, Anspach archives.

His silence Ralph Anspach, author interview, October 2, 2009.

BIBLIOGRAPHY

Anspach, Ralph. *The Billion Dollar Monopoly Swindle*. Rev. ed. XLibris, 2011. (Later renamed *The Monopoly Detective*.)

Bell, Robert Charles. *Board and Table Games from Many Civilizations*. London: Oxford University Press, 1969.

Bordewich, Fergus M. *Washington: The Making of the American Capital*. New York: Amistad, 2008.

Darwin, Clarence D., as told to David Sadowski. *Passing Go: Early Monopoly 1933–37*. River Forest, IL: Folkopoly, 2009. Those interested in obtaining a copy can contact Sadowski at folkopolypress@gmail.com.

Dickstein, Morris. *Dancing in the Dark: A Cultural History of the Great Depression*. New York: W. W. Norton, 2010.

Fatsis, Stefan. *Word Freak: Heartbreak, Triumph, Genius, and Obsession in the World of Competitive Scrabble Players*. New York: Penguin Books, 2002.

George, Henry. *Progress and Poverty*. New York: Robert Schalkenbach Foundation, 2006. (Originally published in 1879). There are several ways to read *Progress* online for free: http://www.henrygeorge.org/pcontents.htm.

Johnson, Nelson. *Boardwalk Empire: The Birth, High Times, and Corruption of Atlantic City*. Medford, NJ: Plexus Publishing, 2002.

Kent, Steven L. *The Ultimate History of Video Games: From Pong to Pokémon and Beyond—The Story Behind the Craze That Touched Our Lives and Changed the World*. New York: Three Rivers Press, 2001.

Kyvig, David E. *Daily Life in the United States, 1920–1940: How Americans Lived Through the Roaring Twenties and the Great Depression*. Chicago: Ivan R. Dee, 2004.

Lind, Michael. *Land of Promise: An Economic History of the United States*. New York: HarperCollins, 2013.

Macdonald, Anne L. *Feminine Ingenuity: Women and Invention in America*. New York: Ballantine Books, 1994.

Orbanes, Philip E. *Monopoly: The World's Most Famous Game & How It Got That Way*. Cambridge, MA: Da Capo, 2006.

———. *The Game Makers: The Story of Parker Brothers from Tiddledy Winks to Trivial Pursuit*. Boston: Harvard Business School Publishing, 2004.

Parlett, David. *The Oxford History of Board Games*. New York: Oxford Press, 1999.

Simon, Bryant. *Boardwalk of Dreams: Atlantic City and the Fate of Urban America*. New York: Oxford University Press, 2004.

Stern, Sydney Ladensohn, and Ted Schoenhaus. *Toyland: The High-Stakes Game of the Toy Industry*. Chicago: Contemporary Books, 1990.

Van Meter, Jonathan. *The Last Good Time: Skinny D'Amato, the Notorious 500 Club & the Rise and Fall of Atlantic City*. New York: Crown, 2003.

Walker, Jay, and Jeff Lehman. *1000 Ways to Win Monopoly Games*. New York: Dell Publishing, 1975.

Walsh, Tim. *The Playmakers: Amazing Origins of Timeless Toys*. Sarasota, FL: Keys Publishing, 2004.

Watson, Victor. *The Waddingtons Story: From the Early Days to Monopoly, the Maxwell Bids and into the Next Millennium*. London: Northern Heritage, 2008.

Wojahn, Ellen. *The General Mills/Parker Brothers Merger: Playing by Different Rules*. Washington, D.C.: Beard Books, 2003.

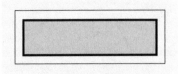

INDEX

Note: Italic page numbers refer to illustrations.

A NOTE
ON THE
AUTHOR

MARY PILON IS an award-winning reporter at the *New York Times*, where she currently covers sports. She previously worked as a staff reporter at the *Wall Street Journal*, where she wrote about various aspects of economics and the financial crisis. She has also worked at *Gawker*, *USA Today*, and *New York* magazine. She is an honors graduate of New York University and made *Forbes'* first-ever 30 Under 30 list for media. Her work has been featured in *The Best American Sports Writing* and has garnered Associated Press Sports Editors, Gerald Loeb, and Freedom Forum awards. A native Oregonian and fledgling marathoner, she lives in New York City, where she enjoys the occasional board game night. Visit her website at marypilon.com and find her on Twitter @marypilon.